*f***P**

WEBSTERISMS

A COLLECTION OF WORDS AND DEFINITIONS SET FORTH BY THE FOUNDING FATHER OF AMERICAN ENGLISH

INTENDED TO EXHIBIT

I. The origin, affinities, and primary signification of American English words
II. The peculiar personality and politics of Noah Webster,
and how they suffused his dictionary
III. The delightful discoveries, inventions, and mistakes of same

TO WHICH ARE PREFIXED

AN INTRODUCTORY ESSAY BY

JILL LEPORE

AN ESSAY "ON READING NOAH WEBSTER" BY

ARTHUR SCHULMAN

AND NOAH WEBSTER'S ORIGINAL PREFACE

FREE PRESS
NEW YORK   LONDON   TORONTO   SYDNEY

FREE PRESS
A Division of Simon & Schuster, Inc.
1230 Avenue of the Americas
New York, NY 10020

First Free Press hardcover edition October 2008

FREE PRESS and colophon are trademarks of Simon & Schuster, Inc.

For information about special discounts for bulk purchases,
please contact Simon & Schuster Special Sales at
1-800-456-6798 or business@simonandschuster.com

DESIGNED BY ERICH HOBBING

Manufactured in the United States of America

Library of Congress Cataloging-in-Publication Data
Websterisms: a collection of words and definitions set forth by the founding father
of American English / compiled by Arthur Schulman; with an introduction by Jill Lepore.
p.   cm.
1. Webster, Noah, 1758–1843. American dictionary of the English language.
2. English language—United States—Lexicography—History.
I. Schulman, Arthur.   II. Title.
PE1617.W7W43   2008
423.028   2007041155

ISBN-13: 978-1-4165-7701-0

Webster, *n.* The name of Noah *Webster,* the American lexicographer, used *absol.* to designate his Dictionary.
                                    —*The Oxford English Dictionary*

hell, *n.* The residence of the late Dr. Noah Webster, dictionary-maker.
                                    —Ambrose Bierce, *The Devil's Dictionary*

CONTENTS

TO THE READER:

Noah Webster's *American Dictionary of the English Language* was first published in 1828. It contained more than seventy thousand entries. This selection reproduces some fifteen hundred of them. It includes those we find most revealing, not to mention those we love best.

How should you read this book? If you want to know more about Webster the man, and how he came to write his dictionary, start with the historical essay, "A Nue Merrykin Dikshunary." If you want to hear from Webster himself on the same subject, read his Preface, but be assured that his definitions read better than his prose. If you want to get right to the meat of the matter, jump to the definitions themselves, but you'll regret it if you don't stop, first, at the compiler's guide, "On Reading Noah Webster," for an appetizer.

Whatever else you do, be sure to disagree with Noah Webster. Our language has changed since 1828. And, even if it hadn't, our language is ours, not his. As Webster liked to insist, "The man who undertakes to censure others for the use of certain words and to decide what is or is not correct in language seems to arrogate to himself a dictatorial authority, the legitimacy of which will always be denied."

Jill Lepore and Arthur Schulman
Cambridge, Massachusetts, and Charlottesville, Virginia
November 2007

A Nue Merrykin Dikshunary

Jill Lepore

On June 4, 1800, Noah Webster, a sometime schoolteacher, failed lawyer, and staggeringly successful spelling-book author, took out an ad in the back pages of a Connecticut newspaper, just above notices of a sailor's death, a shoe sale, and a farmer's reward for a stray cow. The sailor had drowned; the cheap shoes were "Ladies Morocco"; the cow was red with a white face. Webster, who was forty-two, had this to say: he was busy writing a "Dictionary of the American Language," and he wanted the world to know it.

"It is found that a work of this kind is absolutely necessary," Webster announced, "on account of considerable differences between the American and English language." The American people had declared independence and constituted their own government. Now they needed their own dictionary, a place to put all the new words they had coined—Americanisms like *lengthy*, a good word to describe both the dictionary and the amount of time it would take Webster to finish it. Seventy thousand entries and a quarter century later, he would write his last definition, much to the relief of his wife and seven children and, toward the end, the tumbles of grandchildren who stomped up and down the stairs while Dear Pa toiled away, *A* to *Z*, in a study whose walls had been packed with sand to keep out the noise of even their whispers ("RACKET, *n.* A confused, clattering noise. . . . We say, the children make a *racket*"), although, for those brave enough to open his study door, Webster stocked a desk drawer with raisins and peppermints.

1

Webster's epic, monumental *American Dictionary of the English Language* was published in 1828. It rivaled—and dwarfed—the Englishman Samuel Johnson's celebrated 1755 *Dictionary of the English Language:* Johnson listed some 43,000 words, Webster defined more than 70,000, and Webster, unlike Johnson, had written his dictionary himself, without so much as an amanuensis.

Webster's dictionary has this difference, too: when Americans think of Johnson's dictionary—if they think of it at all—they picture a fat, bewigged gentleman, with his decanter of port and his pot of ink. When they think of Webster's dictionary, they draw a blank on the man, but picture a book, kept near to hand, a modern edition, printed by any of a dozen American publishers. Webster's dictionary has earned him the kind of immortality reserved for only a handful of writers: embossed in gold on faux leather book spines, his name shimmers from shelves in every American library; dog-eared paperback *Webster's* have been lost and found under dormitory mattresses from Amherst to Berkeley; and chances are good that Webster lives on, unseen, on your hard drive, waiting for your need to know the meaning of GASTRILOQUIST.

To most Americans, Webster is a brand, not a man. That wasn't always the case, but, even before he died in New Haven in 1843, at the age of eighty-five, Webster's fame was strange. Outside his family, nearly everyone who knew him hated him; he was CRUSTY ("*a.* Peevish, snappish, morose; surly"). And strangers who thought they admired him usually didn't: they had mistaken him for another Webster, the fiery orator and Massachusetts senator. (If Noah Webster had written an ill-tempered autobiography, he might have titled it *I Am Not Daniel!*)

Websterisms aims to restore Noah Webster to his pivotal place in American letters, in American history, and in the founding of the United States. Samuel Johnson was a stylist, a wit, and a poet. Noah Webster was none of these things; nor did he try to be; in his 1828 dictionary, he used "Johnson's dignified style" as an example of things that are not IMITABLE. He was a different sort of man altogether: a pedant, a pedagogue, a politician. Johnson famously— and disingenuously—defined a lexicographer as a "harmless drudge." Webster may have been a drudge, but, if his critics are to be believed, he was far from harmless. And, for better or worse, he was the founding father of American English.

I.

In June of 1800, when Noah Webster announced his intention to compile a "Dictionary of the American Language," his proposal made national news. No news might have been better. Within a week, a Philadelphia newspaper editor called Webster's idea preposterous (it is "perfectly absurd to talk of the *American* language") and his motives mercenary ("the plain truth is that he means to *make money*").

To be fair, much the same scorn had greeted two even earlier American dictionaries, published just months before. A pair of Connecticut men, including the aptly-named-but-no-relation Samuel Johnson, Jr., offered a work promising "a number of words in vogue not included in any dictionary." Reviewers agreed that most of them didn't *belong* in any dictionary: *sans culottes* (no: French!), *tomahawk* (axe it: Indian!), and *lengthy* (good grief: what's next, *strengthy?*). "At best, useless," was one critic's three-word verdict on the first American dictionary. No better were notices of Massachusetts minister Caleb Alexander's *Columbian Dictionary*, containing "*Many NEW WORDS, peculiar to the United States.*" "A disgusting collection" of idiotic words "coined by presumptuous ignorance," wrote one reviewer, referring to Alexander's inclusion of Americanisms like *rateability* and *caucus*. His final ruling on the *Columbian Dictionary?* "A record of our imbecility."

For rancorous contempt in a literary review, it's hard to think of much worse than "at best, useless" and "a record of our imbecility," at least not without thumbing through a thesaurus for synonyms for *worthless* and *tripe*. But Webster's critics were pretty resourceful. Joseph Dennie, editor of the *Gazette of the United States,* began his reply to Webster's announcement by sneering, "If, as Mr. Webster asserts, it is true that many new words have already crept into the language of the United States, he would be much better employed in rooting out those anxious weeds, than in mingling them with the flowers." He then printed a pile of (fake) letters from readers, addressed to Webster, and atrociously spelled:

> Sur,
>   I find you are after meaking a nue Merrykin Dikshunary; your rite, Sir; for ofter lookin all over the anglish Books, you wont find a bit of SHILLALY big enuf to beat a dog wid.
>   Pat O'Dogerty

> As I find der ish no DONDER and BLIXSUM in de English Dikshonere I hope you put both in yours.
>   Hans Bubbleblower

> Massa Webser plese put sum HOMMANY and sum GOOD POSSUM fat and sum two tree good BANJOE in your new what-you-call-um Book for your fello Cytzen.
>   Cuffee

> Mr. Webster,
>   tother day as Jack Trotter and I were twigging an Old Codger with our Puns & Jokes. out came a develish keen thing from Jack—dang it, Thats a dagger says I.

> Jack says this is a new application of the word Dagger; if so, it is at your servis.
>   Dick Splashaway

Mistur Webstur

    please to let me know whether you buy words by the hundred or by the dozen, &c your price, I unclose your a certificat from my husband of my billyties

Martha O'Gabble

    I hereby certify that my wife martha has the best knack at coining new words of any I ever knew—& with the aid of a comforting drop she'll fill you two dictonerys in an hour if you please

Dermot O'Gabble

This kind of ranting—about the debasing influence of immigrants on American English—is so eerily, drearily familiar that it's easy to assume that editors like Dennie, mocking Pat, Hans, and Cuffee, drank from the same political well water as pundits who have more recently rallied against, say, bilingual education or Spanglish or Ebonics or the Frenchness of french fries. Or to imagine that early American literati who objected to the clunky *rateability* and the ill-gotten *lengthy* were just the kind of language purists who today scorn every *thru* and mistaken *hopefully* as just so many weeds in the garden of good English. It would make sense if Webster's critics were political and cultural conservatives. But they weren't, or at least they weren't only that. Webster's Nue Merrykin Dikshunary was conceived in the era in which modern political parties were born. He announced his plan during a presidential election year, the bitterly fought battle between the Republican, Thomas Jefferson and the Federalist, John Adams. His dictionary cannot be understood separate from that battle: in a year of polarizing political rhetoric, Webster's plan for an American dictionary had the very bad bipartisan luck of offending nearly everybody.

    The snootiest opposition came from members of Webster's own Federalist Party: well-heeled merchants and lawyers, doctors and scholars, who loved England, hated France, favored a strong central government run by the wealthiest and best-educated men, and despised all that was common. Webster himself was so ardent a conservative that even fellow Federalists called him "The Monarch." In 1800, with the power of Jefferson's Republican Party growing, Webster's assessment of man's capacity to govern himself was at its most pessimistic. In January of 1800, six months before he announced his plan to compile a dictionary, Webster elaborated on his political views in a series of lengthy public letters in which he held firm to conservative Federalist ideals. "Whatever may be thought of the position, I am persuaded from extensive reading and twenty years' observation that no truth is more certain than that a republican government can be rendered durable in no other way than by excluding from elections men who have so little property, education, or principle, that they are liable to yield their own opinions to the guidance of unprincipled leaders." In August, Republican editor William Duane replied in the Philadelphia newspaper the *Aurora*, "*Noah Webster* says that, in order to give republicanism a permanent existence, the poorer class of people should be excluded from elections . . . If excluding a portion of the people from elections constitute the only durable basis of republicanism, then we might truly say that republicanism may *mean any thing*."

As the months passed, and more and more Republicans were elected to legislative office, and Jefferson's elevation to the presidency seemed likely, Webster only became more committed to voting restrictions. In December of 1800, before Jefferson's victory was assured (an Electoral College tie between Jefferson and his running mate, Aaron Burr, would not be broken by the House of Representatives until February of 1801), the forty-three-year-old Webster wrote to Benjamin Rush with dismay, "It would be better for the people; they would be more free and more happy, if all were deprived of the right of suffrage until they were 45 years of age, and if no man was eligible to an important office until he is 50."

Despite his conservative political views, Webster was a radical when it came to his dictionary. He believed, extraordinarily for his time, that the mass of common people, not a few elites, form language and establish its rules. Their judgment, not the judgment of better-educated men, holds sway: "The lexicographer's business is solely to collect, arrange and define the words that usage presents to his hands. He has no right to proscribe words; he is to present them as they are." Again and again Webster insisted, "The man who undertakes to censure others for the use of certain words and to decide what is or is not correct in language seems to arrogate to himself a dictatorial authority, the legitimacy of which will always be denied."

Webster's ideas about language had not always been so entirely at odds with his political opinions. Born in October 1758, in West Hartford, Connecticut, he graduated from Yale in 1778. In 1783 he published his first book, a spelling book, an *American* spelling book, a *patriotic* spelling book, designed to celebrate—and to standardize—the distinctiveness of American writing and speaking. "A national language is a national tie," Webster insisted, "and what country wants it more than America?" Webster believed that the United States could only be truly independent if it could boast its own language. "Language, as well as government should be national," he wrote. "America should have her *own*, distinct from all the world." And he fully expected that one day the "American language" would be "as different from the future language of England, as the modern Dutch, Danish, and Swedish are from the German." His spelling book, which prescribed and nationalized pronunciation and orthography, was supposed to help things along, in the hope that no American schoolchild would ever again be so cowed by John Bull as to put a *u* in *honor* or a *k* in *publick*. His object was no less than "to diffuse an uniformity and purity of language in America, to destroy the provincial prejudices that originate in the trifling differences of dialect and produce reciprocal ridicule, to promote the interest of literature and the harmony of the United States." In its first two decades, Webster's *American Spelling Book* sold a million and a half copies. Its success spurred him on.

Webster next thought about taking more drastic steps to simplify American spelling, in the interest of nationalizing it. In 1786, while lecturing in Philadelphia, he met Benjamin Franklin. Some years before, Franklin had written *A Scheme for a New Alphabet and Reformed Mode of Spelling*, in which he proposed deleting the letters *c, w, y,* and *j* from the alphabet, and adding six new letters. (English spelling is notoriously idiosyncratic; Franklin wanted to fix it.) Webster had once considered such schemes preposterous, but Franklin's patronage was too tempting and, in an essay published in 1789, Webster announced his own plan for a reformed orthography, urging Americans to spell words the way they sounded. Writing just a year after the ratification of the Constitution, Webster insisted, "*NOW* is the time, and *this* is the country." Under his reform, reading and writing would be much easier and, even more important, American writers would pop out on the page, immediately distinguishable from British authors. To such a patriotic and practical change ("an object of VAST POLITICAL CONSEQUENCE"), Webster concluded, "There iz no alternativ."

But if Webster's 1783 *American Spelling Book* was a staggering success, his 1789 essay proposing a reform of American spelling was a disaster. A reviewer offered Webster two pieces of advice: "The first is, to reform *his own* language, before he attempts to correct that of *others;* the second, to learn to deliver his opinions with a less dictatorial air." A Bostonian mocked "No-ur Webstur eskwier junier" for advising Americans to spell words the way they sounded. What most critics bemoaned was Webster's alarming implication that *bad* spelling was good and that ill-educated Americans were the best spellers. As one Federalist critic put it, this bordered on insanity: "The perusal of this essay must strike every reflecting mind with a sense of the mildness of the municipal regulations of this land of *lib-*

erty, which permitted the writer to roam abroad, unrestrained by a strait waistcoat, and a keeper."

To Federalists, Webster's ideas about dictionaries were no less lunatic, which is to say, they were no less *republican.* As Joseph Dennie put it, the very idea of an "American language" was consistent only "with the character of a good republican." Jefferson himself had once written that dictionaries are no more than "the depositories of words already legitimated by usage." Webster sounded just like him. One Federalist critic, lampooning Webster's lexicographical republicanism, wrote, "To coin new words, or to use them in a new sense, is, incontrovertibly, one of the unalienable rights of freemen, and whoever disputes this right, is the friend of civil tyranny, and an enemy to liberty and equality."

Federalists could not abide Webster's proposed dictionary for more reasons, too. Their logic went something like this: Because any words new to the United States are either stupid or foreign, there is no such thing as the "American language"; there's just bad English. Webster's "embryo dictionary . . . must either be a dictionary of pure English words, and, in that case, superfluous, as we already possess the admirable lexicon of Johnson, or else must contain vulgar, provincial words, unauthorized by good writers and, in this case, must surely be the just object of ridicule and censure." "In what can a Columbian dictionary differ from an English one, but in barbarisms?" asked one Federalist newspaper editor, warning Webster: "if he will persist, in spite of common sense, to furnish us with a dictionary, which we do not want, in return for his generosity, I will furnish him with a title for it. Let, then, the projected volume of *foul* and *unclean* things, bear his own christian name, and be called NOAH'S ARK."

In this, Federalists agreed with the many English writers who were especially galled by Webster's claim that his proposed "Dictionary of the American Language" would surpass the work its title was meant to echo: Samuel Johnson's much-celebrated 1755 *Dictio-*

nary of the English Language. Besting Johnson had been attempted before, but never achieved. In 1797, Herbert Croft, an Englishman planning a dictionary to replace Johnson's, called his book an "English and American Dictionary," suggesting that he, for one, had no intention of ignoring Americanisms. "I shall look with impatience for the publication of your 'English and American dictionary,' " Jefferson wrote eagerly to Croft in 1798, but he ought not to have held his breath: Croft never completed his dictionary, and died in 1816 without publishing a page of it. Meanwhile, the mere announcement of the project raised hackles in England, where a correspondent in *Gentleman's Magazine* replied, "I would just ask how an English Dictionary can recommend itself in *America,* whence . . . , the English language is on the point of being discarded as the language of oppressors . . . ? If this be true, let us leave the inventors of this motley gibberish to make a Dictionary for themselves."

Croft proposed to welcome Americanisms into his dictionary, but most English compilers proposed to document them merely as a testament to the former colonists' folly. On hearing of Webster's plan, an Englishman named Jonathan Boucher set about compiling his own American dictionary or, really, an anti-American antidictionary, a list of words so useless and imbecilic that he could hardly believe that anyone, even uncouth Americans, had ever used them. For this, he had an explanation. Americans, he scoffed, were "addicted to innovation," no less in language than in everything else: "The United States of America, too proud, as it would seem, to acknowledge themselves indebted to this country, for their existence, their power, or their language, denying and revolting against the two first," are now making haste "to rid themselves of the last."

Boucher had a point. This was exactly what Webster intended. But with Boucher's criticism of Americans' addiction to innovation, Webster agreed. Too much innovation was heedless and rash and, worse, vaguely French. During the 1790s, especially during the bloodiest years of the French Revolution, American Federalists argued that France's revolution had gone too far, had experimented, had *innovated* too much, had not known when to stop. Federalists believed, urgently, that Americans must either stifle their impulse to innovate or risk their own Reign of Terror. Having ratified the U.S. Constitution and established an orderly government, the time had come for Americans to stop making the world anew, to leave off rethinking the social order, to forswear novelty. Wasn't the Bill of Rights enough already? Webster wholly shared this aversion to innovation. To the charge of "attempting to innovate, by changing the spelling of words," he pled not guilty, explaining that he was only returning words "to their original orthography": "I do *not* innovate, but *reject innovation.*"

This hardly stopped Federalists from labeling Webster an innovator. In 1800, Joseph Dennie, signing himself "An Enemy to Innovation," wrote about Webster's proposed dictionary, "These innovations in literature are precisely what Jacobinism is in Politics. They are both owing to the stupid vanity of the present day, which induces mankind to despise the well-tried principles of their Ancestors." It was just this kind of thing that led to anarchy. "If we once sanction the impertinence of individuals, who think themselves authorized to coin new words on every occasion," Dennie warned, "our language will soon become a confused jargon, which will require a new Dictionary every year."

It's not surprising that Webster's fellow Federalists wanted nothing to do with his dictionary. More difficult to explain is why his proposal was so fiercely attacked by Republicans, who billed themselves as champions of innovation. Led by Jefferson, Republicans believed that the American Revolution had not gone far enough, and blamed the Federalists for halting it. They embraced novelty, pointing to corrupt and decayed England as a place where, as Jefferson put it, "the dread of innovation and especially of any example set by France, has palsied the spirit of improvement." They supported the French Revolution, even as they decried the violence of Robespierre. And they admired the way France's revolution had revitalized the French language, spawning hundreds of new words—*les materialistes, les demagogues, Monsieur Veto, les sans culottes.* As Jefferson exulted, "What a language has the French become since the date of their revolution, by the free introduction of new words!"

Mocking Federalist criticism of his dictionary, Webster quipped, "An American Dictionary! Impossible! . . . Ridiculous! None but a blockhead would ever think of such a project! . . . I turn from the wretch with disgust and contempt! . . . New words! New ideas! What, Americans have *new* ideas! Why the man is mad!"

Republicans might have been sympathetic, but they weren't. They really *did* think Webster was mad. A "mortal and incurable lunatic," one Republican called him. And worse: a "pusillanimous, half-begotten, self-dubbed patriot," a writer of "nonsense pseudo political and pseudo philosophical," and, most memorably, a "dunghill cock of faction." Republicans didn't exactly object to Webster's dictionary, they objected to *him*. In the 1790s Webster had been an immensely prolific and partisan political pamphleteer and newspaper editor. He had cursed the French, derided Republicans, and supported every curb of liberty imposed by the Washington and Adams administrations, including the notorious 1798 Alien and Sedition Acts, under which Republican newspaper editors were jailed for calling John Adams's judgment into question. "Jacobinism must prevail," Webster warned, "unless more pains are taken to *keep public opinion correct.*"

As far as Noah Webster was concerned, Jacobinism did prevail. On March 4, 1801, Thomas Jefferson was inaugurated. Six months later, Webster sent the new president a letter—an unsparing and vicious critique of his administration—beginning, "I candidly acknowledge that I was one who regretted your elevation to the

Presidency of our empire." He then offered an exegesis of the president's inaugural address (on the ground that "surely every sentence of the philosophical Jefferson must carry with it *meaning*"). In his inaugural, Jefferson had declared, "Sometimes it is said that man can not be trusted with the government of himself. Can he, then, be trusted with the government of others? Or have we found angels in the form of kings to govern him? Let history answer this question." As for history, Webster had this answer: "If there ever was a government, which under the *name* of a republic or democracy, was generally guided by eminent wisdom, virtue and talents, it was a government of a mixed kind, in which an *aristocratic* branch existed independent of popular suffrage." After all, Webster asked, "what do men gain by elective governments, if fools and knaves have the same chance to obtain the highest offices, as honest men?"

Noah Webster lacked for tact. Jefferson, who considered Webster "a mere pedagogue, of very limited understanding," never replied to this outrageous letter. Webster added the slight to his list of grievances. The list was getting pretty long.

II.

The election that carried Thomas Jefferson to the White House sent Noah Webster to the statehouse. In 1800, Webster was elected to the Connecticut legislature. He served until 1807. As a legislator, he chiefly occupied himself with attempting to block bills eliminating the property qualification for voting—in the hope that no more fools and knaves like Jefferson would ever be elected again. He called men without property "porpoises" (by which he meant that they would swim in a school, and not think for themselves). He himself had earned the right to vote, he was keen to point out, by writing his spelling books. "I am a farmer's son and have collected all the small portion of property which I possess by untiring efforts and labors to promote the literary improvements of my fellow citizens." He would not stand for political decisions to be made for him by men who had no similar stake in the world. "If all men have an equal right of suffrage, those who have *little* and those who have *no* property, have the power of making regulations respecting the property of others," he reasons. "In truth, this principle of *equal suffrage* operates to produce extreme *inequality of rights,* a monstrous inversion of the natural order of society."

Despite Webster's best efforts, the United States grew more and more democratic, as more and more states lifted property restrictions on voting, and declaimed in favor of universal suffrage. "The men who have preached these doctrines have never defined what they mean by the *people,* or what they mean by *democracy,* nor how the *people* are to govern themselves," Webster complained. As he saw it, democracy is rule by the people and the people are, generally, insufferable idiots. In his 1828 dictionary, he put it this way:

PEOPLE, *n.* . . . 2. The vulgar, the mass of illiterate persons.
        The knowing artist may judge better than the *people.*   *Waller.*

One lone legislator, however ILL-NATURED (*a.* cross; crabbed), could scarcely slow the expansion of the franchise. As his home state grew more democratic, Webster insisted that he "wished to be forever delivered from the *democracy* of Connecticut." He would even be willing to make the great sacrifice of moving to Vermont, if that state could be "freed from our *democracy,*" adding, "as to the cold winters, I would, if necessary, become a troglodyte, and live in a cave."

Meanwhile, Webster's work as a member of the Connecticut legislature delayed his progress on his American dictionary. He had more distractions, too: revisions to his *American Spelling Book* and the births of his first son, William, in 1801, and of his fifth daughter, Eliza, two years later. By all evidence, Webster was a devoted husband

and father. On paper he is almost entirely without charm—not for nothing was he known as the "critick and coxcomb general of the United States"—except for his affectionate devotion to his wife, Rebecca Greenleaf, and their children, as when he once closed a letter abruptly by scrawling, "Becca has a crying child in her arms, and I must relieve her."

If Webster were ever going to finish his *magnum opus,* he'd need to find a better way to feed his family while he dedicated himself to his dictionary. In 1805, strapped for cash, he decided to publish a little dictionary, aimed at merchants, students, and travelers, a *Compendious Dictionary,* containing no etymologies or quotations and only pithy definitions. ("COMPENDIOUS, *a.* short, brief, concise, summary.") In 1806 he published this small volume ("DICTIONARY, *n.* a book of words explained in alphabetical order"), not much bigger than your average "Pocket Webster," but the granddaddy of every *Webster's* ever since. He hoped it would raise money and, at the same time, turn the tide of public opinion.

But reviews were brutal. "Believing that this Dictionary was intended by its author to promote his favorite project, *an American language,*" one critic wrote, "I cannot but hope that it will be excluded from all Colleges, schools and seminaries of learning; that it will be opposed by all that is correct in taste, and respectable in literature; by the acuteness of criticism, and the poignancy of ridicule." Often, reviewers attacked Webster's innovative spelling. One cobbled together an intentionally alarming "specimen of Webster's orthography," placing in italics words whose spelling he found in the *Compendious Dictionary:* "A *groop* of *Neger wimmen* black as *sut* were told to *soe* and hold their *tungs;* but *insted* of *soing* they left their *thred,* regardless of *threts,* and went to the *theater.*" Even Webster's supporters had their doubts about his spelling. "I ain't yet quite ripe for your *Orthography,*" his brother-in-law admitted. Other readers took issue with Webster's inclusion of particular words. John Quincy Adams, who admired Webster's doggedness, chided him for his "liberality of admission" in allowing in so many new words. But, on the whole, few people gave the dictionary much attention. One correspondent, who wrote to complain about words Webster had left out—*papoose, stall,* and *catbird*—confessed that he had written mostly "to convince you that one of your Readers, at least, has proceeded beyond the Preface."

Webster's severest critics marshaled the evidence of his hypocrisy. It took the editors of Boston's *Monthly Anthology* five tries and three years before they could find anyone willing to review Webster's *Compendious Dictionary* (Webster had written letters complaining of his treatment in the *Anthology* in the past). The editors' appraisal of him was best summed up by James Savage, a banker who, as secretary, reported of an *Anthology* meeting in August 1809, "The conversation of the evening was chiefly at the expense of Noah Webster, as long as the Secretary kept awake." When Savage himself finally accepted the task, he offered a monstrously long review spanning several issues in 1809 and 1810 ("the publick will never accuse us of neglecting him"). Savage had already made his views on Webster's work clear in a review, published in the *Anthology* in 1808, of Webster's *Philosophical and Practical Grammar* (1807), in which he concluded, "We scorn the notion of an American tongue, or of gaining our idiom from the mouths of the illiterate." In his review of the *Compendious Dictionary,* Savage attacked Webster without mercy, sparing not his "suspicions of the definitions of Johnson," his "ridiculous violations of grammar," nor his "hurtful innovations in orthography." "But the fault of most alarming enormity in this work," Savage concluded, "is the approbation given to the vulgarisms of some of our illiterate writers, and the unauthorized idioms of conversation." Those American vulgarisms included *congressional, presidential, departmental, crock, spry, tote, whop,* and the inevitable *lengthy.* Savage gleefully pointed out the hypocrisy of Webster's hating the common people while admiring their words. In Connecticut, Savage reported, in the midst of a people grave, stable and just, the foes to jacobins and disorder, no individual presents a bolder front against the demon of innovation than Mr. Webster. No contemptible epithet is in his estimation too severe for the common people. He characterizes them as "porpoises," the most senseless objects of creation. After making this comparison in a legislative body, Mr. W. could retire to his closet to write grammars and dictionaries, and declare in them that the common people alone are the lawful sovereigns over the realms of language; and that scholars and learned men ought to bend to their supremacy.

Webster, no fainter, battled back. "I am accused of introducing into my Dictionary *Americanisms and vulgarisms*," he wrote. But what is a lexicographer to do when the people of Connecticut use *fourfold* as a verb? "Is this *my* fault?" he asked. Moreover, English dictionaries, he pointed out, include only English words, and English usages, with the result that readers in England might well find themselves befuddled when reading prose written by an American, and Americans had little recourse to understanding their own lexicon. "What! must we have no Dictionary of our own language? Must we be condemned for ever to take such only as the English bestow upon us? Must we receive their definitions, whether right or wrong?"

He fought in vain. The first "Webster's" was a flop, a casualty of the checkered politics of the new nation. It failed because of who Webster was, a political conservative with liberal ideas about language, living in a democratizing nation. Only after what Noah Webster stood for no longer mattered, only after Americans had begun to forget who he was, would his dictionaries succeed.

III.

Meanwhile, Webster's domestic life darkened: in 1806, his second son, Henry Bradford, died within weeks of his birth. In April 1808, his wife, now forty-two, gave birth to her last child, a girl named Louisa, whose life would be blighted by severe mental and physical infirmities. Webster was at his lowest. That month, he found Jesus in his study: "a sudden impulse upon my mind arrested me, and subdued my will. I instantly fell on my knees and confessed my sins to God, implored his pardon, and made my vows to him that from that time I would live in entire obedience to his commands, and be devoted to his service." Webster's rebirth renewed his commitment to his work, and gave religion a more prominent place within his understanding of language.

When he first proposed his dictionary, in June of 1800, Webster had guessed it might take him five years, or eight, to finish it. Ten at the outside. But the work was much more painstaking than he had expected. Nevertheless, despite his slow pace and his dwindling resources, his ambition for the dictionary only grew bolder. "I am often asked, what progress I have made in the compilation of my proposed Dictionary; and when it will be completed," he wrote in 1809. "To these questions I am not able to give precise answers, as the field of inquiry enlarges with every step I take."

If he were ever to finish, he would need money to support his family. In 1807, he published a circular letter addressed "To the Friends of Literature," detailing his plans for the great dictionary, and seeking advanced subscriptions at ten dollars each. His brother-in-law Thomas Dawes tried valiantly to drum up funds, posting a copy of the circular at the Boston Athenaeum, but even he warned Webster, "I am really fearful that you will lose money by your intended great work, let it be ever so meritorious." In New York, Oliver Wolcott made an effort to determine "in what manner your plan would be received by the public" but told Webster to expect disappointment: "My experience of the world has satisfied me that it is in vain to reason with the greatest part of mankind, if they have to pay Ten Dollars, in consequence of being convinced." As Dawes reported from Boston, "Many men are loath to advance money for a book to be finished 12 years hence, when the author may be impaired or in his grave." From Albany, James Kent weighed in, "I am sorry to say that there is no Prospect of encouragement here," though the fault lay not with Webster but with a lack of interest in literature; "if *Samuel Johnson* was here on the spot, it would be the same thing."

Webster's dictionary had by now become a subject of such untiring mockery, at least in some quarters, that his critics even lampooned his circular letter. One spoof "Humbly recommended to Noah Webster, jun. esq. by Tom the Tinker, esq. Laureat" proposed a dictionary that would include such previously ignored words as *higgledy-piggledy* ("conglomeration and confusion"), *ding-dong* ("tintinnabulory chimes"), and *jemminy-cremminy* ("an emasculate obstentation").

Webster was left wounded and discouraged. "Were I a single man, I should probably leave my country, and seek patronage in a country where undertakings of this kind are never neglected, much less opposed," he complained. He wrote to John Jay that the time had come to think of moving farther than Vermont: "If I live to finish my proposed work, it is probable, I shall go to England to revise and publish it, and as my own country furnishes no patron, I may find one in Great Britain."

There was nothing left to do but set about collecting subscriptions in person, traveling from town to town, "soliciting patronage for his Dictionary," hawking his wares like an itinerant peddler. In September 1809, he found himself in Salem, north of Boston, where, as elsewhere, he met with little success. (Even after Webster had his circular letter printed and posted it on the doors of libraries all over the country, only seventeen men subscribed, of whom two never paid and two more demanded a refund.) One Salem man attributed Webster's failure to secure subscriptions to three factors: he lacked the support of Harvard faculty, he seemed "determined to run down Johnson," and he asked for ten dollars in *advance* from men whose "opinion of the man is not good enough to induce them, *hardly,* to become obligated to take his books *after* they are printed." Moreover, the good people of Salem were offended at Webster's "peddling his own production in person," rather than relying on a more discreet form of promotion, like publishing a sample of the proposed work. "But the great and capital defect," this observer concluded, "is the unbounded vanity of the man . . . which is so great as to excite ridicule."

Chief among Webster's Salem critics were John and Timothy Pickering. In the 1780s, the elder Pickering had admired young Noah Webster. In 1783, when his son John was six years old, Timothy Pickering had sent a copy of Webster's newly published spelling book to his wife, instructing her, "let John take it to his master . . . ; for I am determined to have him instructed upon this new, ingenious and at the same time easy plan." But by 1809, Timothy Pickering had no better than "a low idea of Mr. Webster." John Pickering's opinion was, if anything, lower still.

The younger Pickering was everything Noah Webster was not: cosmopolitan, sophisticated, rich. He had studied languages from a very young age, eventually learning French, Spanish, Portuguese, Italian, Turkish, Latin, and Greek. His philological research rivaled that of America's most eminent scholars; in 1806 he was elected Hancock Professor of Hebrew at Harvard, and in 1812 he was offered the chair of Greek literature (he turned down both offers). In 1806, he was among the five scholars the Anthology Society invited to review Webster's *Compendious Dictionary* (he refused). For most of his life, he earned a living as a lawyer. "Nothing is more pleasing to me than the study of languages," Pickering wrote in

1799, "but a person cannot devote all his life to that alone." As a young man, he traveled and worked in Paris, Amsterdam, and Lisbon. (Webster didn't travel abroad until 1824, at the age of sixty-seven.) In London from 1799 to 1801, where he served as a secretary to American minister Rufus King, Pickering became fascinated by Americanisms. Living among the English alerted him to peculiarities of the American idiom—which he came to despise. In the United States, Pickering maintained, "every writer takes the liberty to contaminate the language with the barbarous terms of his own tasteless invention." He began compiling a list of Americanisms—new words as well as new usages of old words—in an effort to stamp them out. Upon returning to the United States he continually added to the list, and in 1814 he delivered an address on "the present state of the English language in the United States" before the Cambridge-based American Academy of Arts and Sciences. (Webster's brother-in-law, Thomas Dawes, was in the audience. After Pickering concluded his lecture, Dawes rushed up to him and shouted, "There! that is what I have been trying to bring my brother Webster to agree to; but he won't do it.") Pickering's lecture, along with his word list, was published the following year as *Vocabulary, or Collection of Words and Phrases which have been supposed to be Peculiar to the United States.*

The "main design" of Pickering's *Vocabulary* was "to preserve our noble language in its purity." Pickering wanted American English to be *less* distinctive, not more. "Our countrymen may speak and write in a *dialect* of English, which will be generally understood in the *United States;* but if they are ambitious of having their works read by Englishmen as well as Americans, they must write in a language that Englishmen can read with facility and pleasure." Pickering's *Vocabulary* was a list of words that Americans should never use. Words that appeared in Webster's compendium Pickering maligned as vulgarisms; words that even Webster omitted were, by implication, even worse.

If Webster's *Compendious Dictionary* raised the hackles of literary
Cambridge and Boston, John Pickering's *Vocabulary* was greeted
with acclaim. Writing in the *North American Review,* Sidney Willard
acknowledged "with great pleasure" the "systematick labours of Mr.
Pickering." "We are bound to acknowledge our gratitude to Mr.
Pickering," Willard wrote, "and to welcome his appearance before
the publick, in so good a cause, as an event highly auspicious, and
one which bodes well to American learning."

Pickering nonetheless anticipated a negative reaction in some
quarters. Privately he wrote in July of 1816, "I expect to encounter
the displeasure of some of our American reformers, who think we
ought to throw off our native language as one of the badges of
English servitude, and establish a new tongue for ourselves. But I
have the satisfaction to know that the best scholars in our country
treat such a scheme with derision; they, on the contrary, are solicitous to retain the peculiar advantages we derive from a language
which is common to ourselves and the illustrious writers and ora-
tors of our mother country."

Cranky Noah Webster was one of those American reformers. In
December of 1817 Webster sent Pickering a long letter refuting the
Vocabulary, point by point. He soon had the letter published. Of the
word *crock,* which Webster had included in his dictionary ("an
earthen pot, pan, black of a pot") and which Pickering had derided,
Webster wrote, "shall its use among common people exclude it from
Dictionaries? If writers have not used it, they probably have had no
occasion for it. Elegant writers seldom have occasion for terms
that are peculiar to the humble occupations of life. Dryden and
Addison might have written ten times the number of volumes
which they actually wrote, and never have had occasion to mention
the *hub* or *tire* of a wheel, or the *snathe* of a scythe. And what then?
Are these, for that reason, to be denounced as illegitimate words or
not English?" Webster also once again championed the common
man as the ultimate arbiter of language. "To denounce the oldest

and some of the best words in a language as *barbarous,* because people of a particular class or in a particular place have lost the use of them, is as arrogant and uncivil as it is absurd."

Pickering, wise to the futility of an engagement, did not reply. And he took Webster's attack calmly, writing to his father in February of 1817, "W. wants to make an American language, and will of course feel hostile to those who take the opposite ground." But Sidney Willard defended Pickering on every point and insulted Webster, "our infallible guide in philology," for his unwillingness to accept criticism, even from his betters. "He seems every where to consider himself the great schoolmaster in his art, under whom there are no deserving pupils; and he goes about the forms feruling and filliping the dunces, and calling blockhead."

Willard was right. Webster could not stand to be corrected. He liked to call people blockheads. He had a knack for making enemies everywhere. He struggled, but much of his struggle was of his own making. His 1806 dictionary, like his proposal in 1800, was a debacle because he failed to secure the patronage of the people most likely to embrace his ideas: Republicans. Perhaps if Webster hadn't been so interested in calling Jefferson a fool and a knave, he might have found in the sage of Monticello a crucial supporter. "I am a friend to *neology,*" Thomas Jefferson wrote John Adams in 1820. "And give the word neologism to our language, as a root, and it should give us it's [sic] fellow substantives, neology, neologist, neologisation; it's adjectives neologous, neological, neologistical, it's verb neologise, and adverb neologically." Webster had included *neology, neological,* and even *neologist* in his *Compendious Dictionary,* years before. In 1806, Webster had sent Jefferson a copy, but the former president, the nabob of neology, probably never cracked its spine.

IV.

What saved Noah Webster's American dictionary was how long it would take him to finish it. Most of this delay was the result of his decision to investigate the origins of words. Even before he was born again, Webster had determined to study etymology. But after 1809, he brought to this work the zeal of a convert. He decided, in his dictionary, to offer proof that the Old Testament contained the literal truth: that all languages derive from a single, original pre-Babel language, the language of Eden. In search of this grail, he stopped working on definitions altogether, a detour he could ill afford. "I shall sell my house to get bread for my children," Webster wrote in 1811. The next year, he moved to Amherst, Massachusetts, where he could live more cheaply. (He was also happy to leave the vile democracy of Connecticut, though he had apparently decided against taking so bold a step as to move to the wilds of Vermont.)

In his new house, he installed a custom-made desk, "two foot wide, built in the form of a hollow circle," on which he placed dictionaries of twenty languages. Standing in the opening at the center of the table, Webster spent his days turning around in the circle, following the roots of words from one language to the next, his heart racing at the pursuit. (He liked to take his pulse: when he was working, it rose from 60 to 80 or 85 beats a minute.) For the ten years he lived in Amherst, Webster chased etymologies, round and round. By the time he finished his dictionary, he had also completed another manuscript, nearly half as long, a contorted treatise on etymology called *A Synopsis of Words in Twenty Languages*. It has never been published, and remains, largely unread, among Webster's papers at the New York Public Library.

In 1822, Webster and his family returned to New Haven. Two years later, he sailed to Europe on a research trip underwritten by a thousand-dollar loan from his daughter Harriet, who had married into a wealthy West Indian merchant family. Webster spent a year in France and England, continuing his studies at the world's best libraries. He was homesick. "I cannot endure most of the dishes of French Cookery," he wrote to his wife, though he did enjoy the *"very good* coffee" of Paris. Much that he met with abroad surprised him; dictionary entries that chronicle his adventures suggest a Connecticut Yankee in the Bibliothèque Nationale:

BATHING-TUB, *n.* A vessel for bathing, usually made either of wood or tin. In the Royal Library at Paris, I saw a bathing-tub of porphyry, of beautiful form and exquisite workmanship.

While in England, attempting to rally support for his project, Webster curried favor; he even went so far as to pledge that his dictionary would keep American English in *conformity* with British English: "The English language is the language of the United States; and it is desirable that as far as the people have the same things and the same ideas, the words to express them should remain the same. The diversities of languages among men may be considered as a curse."

In January of 1825, in a boardinghouse in Cambridge, England, Webster finally finished the dictionary. "When I had come to the last word," he later recalled, "I was seized with a trembling which made it somewhat difficult to hold my pen steady for writing." The manuscript his wife called "the babe which he had dandled twenty years and more" finally left his lap, to toddle off into history.

It took three years to set and proof the type. Webster boasted to James Madison that "types of the oriental languages" would come from Germany but "everything else about the work will be *American.*" The massive, two-volume *American Dictionary of the English Language* was printed in November of 1828. It had taken its compiler not five years, or ten, but twenty-eight.

By then, the Federalist Party was dead. So was almost everyone Webster had known in his youth, or even his middle age. Republicans from Virginia—Jefferson, Madison, and Monroe—had filled the White House for a quarter century. So far had republicanism prevailed that Andrew Jackson, who was not only a champion of the common man—a democrat—but also a notoriously bad speller (he spelled *government* with only one *n*), had just been elected president. With populism on the rise, no one now disputed the dictionary's republicanism, its embrace of lowly words like *crock*. And no one gave a fig about Webster's quaint Federalism. At seventy, Webster had outlived most of his enemies and aged into an anachronism, an elder statesman whose feebleness was mistaken for harmlessness.

It also helped that he had abandoned simplified spelling. He did spell *hore* without the *w*, and *goom* without the *r* (*whore* and *groom* he considered corruptions), and in his definition for SPELL ("*v.i.* To form words with the proper letters"), he offered this example of how to use the word in a sentence: "Our orthography is so irregular that most persons never learn to *spell*." But, except for dropping the *k* in words like *mimic* and the *u* in words like *favor*, he largely left spelling alone.

He had also quieted his nationalism: the proposed "Dictionary of the American Language" turned out to be *An American Dictionary of the English Language*. Webster would be an American Johnson, not the Johnson of an American language. Nevertheless, many of his entries display his fascination with fine, local distinctions:

> BUTTER-MILK, *n*. The milk that remains after the butter is separated from it. Johnson calls this *whey;* but whey is the thin part of the milk after the curd or cheese is separated. Butter-milk in America is not called *whey*.

And he enjoyed explaining words with reference to American people and places:

OPPOSITE, *a.* Standing or situated in front; facing; as an edifice *opposite* to the Exchange. Brooklyn lies *opposite* to New York, or on the *opposite* side of the river.

But he now doubted whether any Americanisms even existed. In the dictionary's Preface he wrote, "As to Americanisms, so called, I have not been able to find many words, in respectable use, which can be so denominated. These, I have admitted and, noted as peculiar to this country." These include words we still use, such as *lengthy, skunk, caucus,* and words that were already dying out in Webster's lifetime:

SHAVER, *n.* A boy or young man. This word is still in common use in New England. It must be numbered among our original words.

(About this, Webster was wrong. *Shaver* dates to the sixteenth century.) But, as to the rest, Webster wrote, "I have fully ascertained that most of the new words charged to the coinage of this country, were first used in England."

What most made Webster's dictionary American was his commitment to quoting American authors—especially Franklin, Washington, Madison, and Irving—to illustrate the meanings of words. Of these men, he wrote, "It is with pride and satisfaction that I can place them, as authorities." On proverbs suitable for guiding daily living, Webster loved best to quote Franklin:

DEBT, *n.* When you run in *debt* you give to another power over your liberty.

PANCAKE, *n.* Some folks think it will never be good times, till houses are tiled with *pancakes.*

GENTLEMAN, *n.* A plowman on his legs is higher than a *gentleman* on his knees.

HOPE, *n.* He that lives upon *hope,* will die fasting.

Webster was not a particularly avid reader of *belles lettres,* and he rarely quoted from American fiction. He never cited James Fenimore Cooper, for instance. But he did rely on Washington Irving, whose patriotic sentiments can be found throughout the dictionary:

PROMISE, *n.* My native country was full of youthful *promise.*

SCENERY, *n.* Never need an American look beyond his own country for the sublime and beautiful of natural *scenery.*

When an opportunity to make a political point presented itself, Webster relied on his favorite Federalist writers:

EXPERIMENT, *n.* A political experiment cannot be made in a laboratory, nor determined in a few hours.   *J. Adams.*

FACTION, *n.* By a *faction,* I understand a number of citizens, whether amounting to a majority or minority of the whole, who are united and actuated by some common impulse of passion, or of interest, adverse to the rights of other citizens, or to the permanent and aggregate interests of the community   .
                                    Federalist.   Madison.

FIDELITY, *n.* The best security for the *fidelity* of men, is to make interest coincide with duty.   *Federalist.   Hamilton.*

AMERICAN, *n.* The name *American* must always exalt the pride of patriotism.
                                    Washington.

Never once in his dictionary did Webster supply a quotation from Thomas Jefferson, arguably the most eloquent political writer of his age. It was a gross, and grossly partisan, omission.

Washington's place in the *American Dictionary* is so prominent that it could easily be argued that the two-volume set is a monument to the nation's first president. SURPASS is illustrated with this sentence: "Perhaps no man ever *surpassed* Washington in genuine patriotism and integrity of life." So, too, MODEL: "take Washington as a *model* of prudence, integrity and patriotism," "CELEBRATE, *v.t.* To honor or distinguish by ceremonies and marks of joy and respect; as, to *celebrate* the birthday of Washington," and FATHER, "Washington, as a defender and an affectionate and wise counselor, is called the *father* of his country."

But the dictionary is equally a celebration of the United States. Consider GAIN: "Any industrious person may *gain* a good living in America." "INESTIMABLE, *a.* . . . The privileges of American citizens, civil and religious, are *inestimable.*" At GUARANTY, Webster quoted from the Constitution: "The United States shall *guaranty* to every state in the Union a republican form of government." Often, the encomiums to Washington and to his nation intersect, as at CITIZEN: "If the *citizens* of the U. States should not be free and happy, the fault will be entirely their own. *Washington.*"

Webster also added plenty of his own political opinions ("PREPOSTEROUS, *a.* a republican government in the hands of females, is *preposterous*"), especially his views on slavery, which he expressed both in predictable places ("SLAVE-TRADE, *n.* The barbarous and wicked business of purchasing men and women, transporting them to a distant country, and selling them for slaves") and in unexpected entries, including FORMERLY, whose use he illustrated with the sentence, "We *formerly* imported slaves from Africa."

At twenty dollars a copy, the *American Dictionary of the English Language* didn't exactly fly off the shelves. But it was respected, and soon enough, revered. Webster's definitions could be spot-on: "DANDY, *n.* A male of the human species who dresses himself like a doll, and who carries his character on his back." Sir James Murray, first edi-

tor of the *Oxford English Dictionary*, called Webster "a born definer
of words." At definitions, Webster was arguably better than Johnson:
less literary, less witty, but more exact. Johnson defined *admiration*
as "wonder, the act of admiring or wondering"; to Webster it was
"wonder mingled with pleasing emotions, as approbation, esteem,
love, or veneration; a compound emotion excited by something
novel, rare, great, or excellent; applied to persons and their works.
It often includes a slight degree of surprise."

Webster's definitions could be erratic. He was, for instance,
more interested in animals than in musical instruments, and it
shows. He offered a minute description of

CAMEL, *n*. A large quadruped used in Asia and Africa for carrying burdens, and
for riders. As a genus, the camel belongs to the order of Pecora. The characteristics are; it has no horns; it has six fore teeth in the under jaw; the canine teeth
are wide set, three in the upper and two in the lower jaw; and there is a fissure
in the upper lip. The dromedary or Arabian camel has one bunch on the back,
four callous protuberances on the fore legs and two on the hind legs. The Bactrian
camel has two bunches on the back. The Llama of South America is a smaller animal, with a smooth back, small head, fine black eyes, and very long neck. The
Pacos or sheep of Chili has no bunch. Camels constitute the riches of an Arabian,
without which he could neither subsist, carry on trade nor travel over sandy
deserts. Their milk is his common food. By the camel's power of sustaining abstinence from drink, for many days, and of subsisting on a few coarse shrubs, he is
peculiarly fitted for the parched and barren lands of Asia and Africa.

Encycl.

yet a nearly useless definition of

FRENCH-HORN, *n*. A wind instrument of music made of metal.

The dictionary was scarcely criticized. The ridicule to which
Webster had once been exposed now only bolstered his claim to
greatness. In the *North American Review,* Yale scholar James Luce

Kingsley wrote, "The author, it is well known, met with much opposition at the commencement of his labors; and it is equally notorious, that as he proceeded in the accomplishment of his design, he
was seldom cheered with the voice of encouragement and approbation." That over the labor of so many years, one man, so unrewarded, so alone, had been so undeterred, formed no small part of
the dictionary's vaunted merit.

But what contributed most to the dictionary's success was its auspicious timing: it was published at the height of America's greatest
religious revival, the Second Great Awakening. Webster's own conversion, in 1809, came at the movement's beginning. Webster's dictionary was a Christian dictionary, almost a catechism. It wasn't only
the just-so, evangelical etymologies. Webster's faith shines through
on every page, even under the most unlikely bushels:

COLONY, *n.* . . . . The first settlers of New England were the best of Englishmen,
well educated, devout christians, and zealous lovers of liberty. There was never
a *colony* formed of better materials.   *Ames.*

INSTRUMENT, *n.* 2. . . . . The distribution of the Scriptures may be the *instrument* of a vastly extensive reformation in morals and religion.

DEROGATORY, *a.* . . . . Let us entertain no opinions *derogatory* to the honor of
God, or his moral government.

MERITORIOUS, *a.* . . . . We rely for salvation on the *meritorious* obedience and
sufferings of Christ.

LOVE, *n.* 1. The *love* of God is the first duty of man . . . *v.t.* 1. . . . . The christian
loves his Bible.

Born-again Americans applauded it; they loved it as they loved
their Bibles. Many still do: today you can buy a handsome facsimile

edition of Webster's 1828, published by the Foundation for American Christian Education, which plausibly reports that it contains
"the greatest number of Biblical definitions given in any secular volume." Webster's Federalist views on politics, his republican opinions
about language, his crustiness, the political turmoil that had swallowed up his 1806 dictionary—all these were forgotten. Webster
began writing for his country; he ended up writing for Christ.

V.

All dictionaries are copies, to one degree or another, and they
should be. Why tinker with a perfect definition? Webster liked to
profess his own incorruptibility: "It is a consolation to me that as far
as my recollection will aid me, I have never copied a sentence
from any other man's writings." But one-third of the definitions in
his 1828 dictionary he either copied from Johnson word for word,
or loosely borrowed, according to the literary scholar Joseph W.
Reed, Jr., who counted. In 1962, Reed compared the entries in Webster's letter L to those in the 1799 edition of Johnson's dictionary
that Webster kept on his circular desk. Of the 4,505 meanings
offered for the 2,024 words beginning with L in Webster's, 333 were
copied from Johnson, 987 were copied with only very slight alter-
ation, and 161 show definite influence. Given that nearly another
third of the L words in Webster's were not in Johnson's at all, Webster's debt to Johnson was enormous.

Again, why not? Give him this: Noah Webster knew a good definition when he saw one. What's striking is not that Webster borrowed from Johnson but that he denied it, and that he so
energetically prosecuted those who copied from his own work.
(His dictionary's definition of LITERARY PROPERTY, found under
PROPERTY, is particularly instructive on this account.) In 1826,
while his dictionary was still at the typesetter, Webster turned his

attention to the matter of copyright. "Every book I write is a fund for others, who copy what they want & publish it," he once complained, and not without cause. For decades, Webster had defended intellectual property, battling pirated editions of his spelling books, and traveling from state to state arguing for copyright reform. In later life, he liked to take credit for the copyright law passed by Congress in 1790. He certainly profited by it. By 1801, his American spelling book—his chief source of income throughout his life—had sold half a million copies; by 1829, it had sold twenty million. Even with copyright laws, most copies of the spelling book were sold in pirated editions. Without copyright protection, it would have earned Webster almost nothing.

In 1831, when the House of Representatives finally passed a law extending copyright protection to an author for twenty-eight years and to heirs for fourteen more, Webster was in the gallery, applauding, secure in the knowledge that his dictionary would provide a lasting legacy for his children and those tumbles of grandchildren. It did that, but it also condemned them to decades of bickering over his estate. His publishers bickered, too.

The battle went on long after Webster's death in 1843. In the 1850s and early 1860s, Charles and George Merriam, publishers of new editions of Webster's dictionary, accused Boston lexicographer Joseph E. Worcester of stealing from Webster for his *Universal and Critical Dictionary of the English Language*. In "The War of the Dictionaries," the *Atlantic Monthly* took Worcester's side; Congress defended Webster. After the publication in 1864 of the extraordinarily impressive *Webster's Unabridged,* Webster's prevailed. (No one today calls a dictionary a "Worcester.")

That success soon became the problem. By the end of the nineteenth century, dozens of publishers were printing dictionaries they called "Webster's," whether they borrowed Webster's definitions or not. As far as the G. & C. Merriam Company was con-

cerned, it was stealing the name, not the definitions, that constituted the crime. When Merriam sued, one court ruled, "The contention that the complainants have any special property in
'Webster's Dictionary' is all nonsense." Over a century of litigation
followed, in which the courts have repeatedly ruled that Merriam
has no exclusive right to Webster's name. In 1982, the company simply added his name to its own, and became "Merriam-Webster's."
(In 1991 it trademarked the phrase, *Not just Webster. Merriam-
Webster.*™)

After G. & C. Merriam published *Webster's New International Dictionary* in 1909, a second edition followed in 1934 and, in 1961, a
third. Each was greeted by renewed debate about who, or whether
anyone, should decide what should be in it. In a 1962 issue of the
New Yorker, Dwight Macdonald complained that *Webster's Third* had
debased the language "in the name of democracy." Macdonald
was especially galled that the editorial staff of *Webster's Third* called
for a show of hands to decide whether a word ought to be listed as
slang or *colloq.* or not marked out at all. He despised both the
method and its premise. "If nine-tenths of the citizens of the
United States, including a recent President, were to use *inviduous,*
the one-tenth who clung to *invidious* would still be right, and they
would be doing a favor to the majority if they continued to maintain
the point." (In a Rex Stout novel published the same year, Nero
Wolfe, the fat detective, enacted Macdonald's outrage; he ripped
out the pages of *Webster's Third,* one by one, and threw them into the
fire of his West Thirty-fifth Street brownstone. "Do you use 'infer'
and 'imply' interchangeably?" Wolfe asks a guest. "This book says
you may. Pfui.")

Noah Webster would have found this debate disheartening at
best. He might have called Macdonald's argument FLAWY ("*a.*
full of flaws or cracks; broken; defective; faulty"). He could never
have had an editorial staff; he didn't get along with anyone but his
wife. He considered the American people a bunch of blockheads,

who ought not to be allowed to vote for political office. But he did think they ought to have the last word about their native tongue. "Languages are not formed by philosophers," he wrote in 1798, "but by ignorant barbarians; and as nations advance in knowledge, new words and new combinations of words are added to their language to express the new ideas which they may acquire."

There iz no alternativ.

Preface to the 1828 Dictionary

Noah Webster

In the year 1783, just at the close of the revolution, I published an elementary book for facilitating the acquisition of our vernacular tongue, and for correcting a vicious pronunciation, which prevailed extensively among the common people of this country. Soon after the publication of that work, I believe in the following year, that learned and respectable scholar, the Rev. Dr. Goodrich of Durham, one of the trustees of Yale College, suggested to me, the propriety and expediency of my compiling a dictionary, which should complete a system for the instruction of the citizens of this country in the language. At that time, I could not indulge the thought, much less the hope, of undertaking such a work; as I was neither qualified by research, nor had I the means of support, during the execution of the work, had I been disposed to undertake it. For many years therefore, though I considered such a work as very desirable, yet it appeared to me impracticable; as I was under the necessity of devoting my time to other occupations for obtaining subsistence.

About twenty seven years ago, I began to think of attempting the compilation of a Dictionary. I was induced to this undertaking, not more by the suggestion of friends, than by my own experience of the want of such a work, while reading modern books of science. In this pursuit, I found almost insuperable difficulties, from the want of a dictionary, for explaining many new words, which recent discoveries in the physical sciences had introduced into use. To remedy this defect in part, I published my Compendious

Dictionary in 1806; and soon after made preparations for undertaking a larger work.

My original design did not extend to an investigation of the origin and progress of our language; much less of other languages. I limited my views to the correcting of certain errors in the best English Dictionaries, and to the supplying of words in which they are deficient. But after writing through two letters of the alphabet, I determined to change my plan. I found myself embarrassed, at every step, for want of a knowledge of the origin of words, which Johnson, Bailey, Junius, Skinner and some other authors do not afford the means of obtaining. Then laying aside my manuscripts, and all books treating of language, except lexicons and dictionaries, I endeavored, by a diligent comparison of words, having the same or cognate radical letters, in about twenty languages, to obtain a more correct knowledge of the primary sense of original words, of the affinities between the English and many other languages, and thus to enable myself to trace words to their source.

I had not pursued this course more than three or four years, before I discovered that I had to unlearn a great deal that I had spent years in learning, and that it was necessary for me to go back to the first rudiments of a branch of erudition, which I had before cultivated, as I had supposed, with success.

I spent ten years in this comparison of radical words, and in forming a synopsis of the principal words in twenty languages, arranged in classes, under their primary elements or letters. The result has been to open what are to me new views of language, and to unfold what appear to be the genuine principles on which these languages are constructed.

After completing this synopsis, I proceeded to correct what I had written of the Dictionary, and to complete the remaining part of the work. But before I had finished it, I determined on a voyage to Europe, with the view of obtaining some books and some assistance which I wanted; of learning the real state of the pronunciation of our language in England, as well as the general state of philology in that country; and of attempting to bring about some agreement or coincidence of opinions, in regard to unsettled points in pronunciation and grammatical construction. In some of these objects I failed; in others, my designs were answered.

It is not only important, but, in a degree necessary, that the people of this country, should have an *American Dictionary* of the English Language; for, although the body of the language is the same as in England, and it is desirable to perpetuate that sameness, yet some differences must exist. Language is the expression of ideas; and if the people of one country cannot preserve an identity of ideas, they cannot retain an identity of language. Now an identity of ideas depends materially upon a sameness of things or objects with which the people of the two countries are conversant. But in no two portions of the earth, remote from each other, can such identity be found. Even physical objects must be different. But the principal differences between the people of this country and of all others, arise from different forms of government, different laws, institutions and customs. Thus the practice of hawking and hunting, the institution of heraldry, and the feudal system of England originated terms which formed, and some of which now form, a necessary part of the language of that country; but, in the United States, many of these terms are no part of our present language,—and they cannot be, for the things which they express do not exist in this country. They can be known to us only as obsolete or as foreign words. On the other hand, the institutions in this country which are new and peculiar, give rise to new terms or to new applications of old terms, unknown to the people of England; which cannot be explained by them and which will not be inserted in their dictionaries, unless copied from ours. Thus the terms, *land-office; land-warrant; location of land; consociation* of churches; *regent* of a university; *intendant* of a city; *plantation, selectmen, senate, congress, court, assembly, escheat,* &c. are either words not belonging to the language of England, or they are applied to things in this country which do not exist in that. No person in this country will be satisfied with the English definitions of the words *congress, senate* and *assembly, court,* &c. for although these are words used in England, yet they are applied in this country to express ideas which they do not express in that country. With our present constitutions of government, *escheat* can never have its feudal sense in the United States.

But this is not all. In many cases, the nature of our governments, and of our civil institutions, requires an appropriate language in the definition of words, even when the words express the same thing, as in England. Thus the English Dictionaries inform us that a *Justice* is one deputed by the *King* to do right by way of judgment—he is a *Lord* by his office—Justices of the peace are appointed by the *King's commission*—language which is inaccurate in respect to this officer in the United States. So *constitutionally* is defined by Todd or Chalmers, *legally,* but in this country the distinction between *constitution* and *law* requires a different definition. In the United States, a *plantation* is a very different thing from what it is in England. The word *marshal,* in this country, has one important application unknown in England or in Europe.

A great number of words in our language require to be defined in a phraseology accommodated to the condition and institutions of the people in these states, and the people of England must look to an American Dictionary for a correct understanding of such terms.

The necessity therefore of a Dictionary suited to the people of the United States is obvious; and I should suppose that this fact being admitted, there could be no difference of opinion as to the *time,* when such a work ought to be substituted for English Dictionaries.

There are many other considerations of a public nature, which serve to justify this attempt to furnish an American Work which shall be a guide to the youth of the United States. Most of these are too obvious to require illustration.

One consideration however, which is dictated by my own feelings, but which I trust will meet with approbation in correspondent feelings in my fellow citizens, ought not to be passed in silence. It is this. "The chief glory of a nation," says Dr. Johnson, "arises from its authors." With this opinion deeply impressed on my mind, I have the same ambition which actuated that great man when he expressed a wish to give celebrity to Bacon, to Hooker, to Milton and to Boyle.

I do not indeed expect to add celebrity to the names of *Franklin, Washington, Adams, Jay, Madison, Marshall, Ramsay, Dwight, Smith, Trumbull, Hamilton, Belknap, Ames, Mason, Kent, Hare, Silliman, Cleaveland, Walsh, Irving,* and many other Americans distinguished by their writings or by their science; but it is with pride and satisfaction, that I can place them, as authorities, on the same page with those of *Boyle, Hooker, Milton, Dryden, Addison, Ray, Milner, Cowper, Davy, Thomson* and *Jameson.*

A life devoted to reading and to an investigation of the origin and principles of our vernacular language, and especially a particular examination of the best English writers, with a view to a comparison of their style and phraseology, with those of the best American writers, and with our colloquial usage, enables me to affirm with confidence, that the genuine English idiom is as well preserved by the unmixed English of this country, as it is by the best *English* writers. Examples to prove this fact will be found in the Introduction to this work. It is true, that many of our writers have neglected to cultivate taste, and the embellishments of style; but even these have written the language in its genuine *idiom.* In this respect, Franklin and Washington, whose language is their hereditary mother tongue, unsophisticated by modern grammar, present as pure models of genuine English, as Addison or Swift. But I may go farther, and affirm, with truth, that our country has produced some of the best models of composition. The style of President Smith; of the authors of the Federalist; of Mr. Ames; of Dr. Mason; of Mr. Harper; of Chancellor Kent; [the prose] of Mr. Barlow; of the legal decisions of the Supreme Court of the United States; of the reports of legal decisions in some of the particular states; and many other writings; in purity, in elegance and in technical precision, is equaled only by that of the best British authors, and surpassed by that of no English composi- tions of a similar kind.

The United States commenced their existence under circum- stances wholly novel and unexampled in the history of nations. They commenced with civilization, with learning, with science, with constitutions of free government, and with that best gift of God to man, the christian religion. Their population is now equal to that of England; in arts and sciences, our citizens are very little behind the most enlightened people on earth; in some respects, they have no superiors; and our language, within two centuries, will be spoken by more people in this country, than any other language on earth, except the Chinese, in Asia, and even that may not be an exception.

It has been my aim in this work, now offered to my fellow citi- zens, to ascertain the true principles of the language, in its orthog- raphy and structure; to purify it from some palpable errors, and reduce the number of its anomalies, thus giving it more regularity and consistency in its forms, both of words and sentences; and in this manner, to furnish a standard of our vernacular tongue, which we shall not be ashamed to bequeath to *three hundred millions of peo- ple,* who are destined to occupy, and I hope, to adorn the vast terri- tory within our jurisdiction.

If the language can be improved in regularity, so as to be more easily acquired by our own citizens, and by foreigners, and thus be rendered a more useful instrument for the propagation of science, arts, civilization and christianity; if it can be rescued from the mis- chievous influence of sciolists and that dabbling spirit of innovation which is perpetually disturbing its settled usages and filling it with anomalies; if, in short, our vernacular language can be redeemed from corruptions, and our philology and literature from degradation; it would be a source of great satisfaction to me to be one among the instruments of promoting these valuable objects. If this object cannot be effected, and my wishes and hopes are to be frustrated, my labor will be lost, and this work must sink into oblivion.

This Dictionary, like all others of the kind, must be left, in some degree, imperfect; for what individual is competent to trace to their source, and define in all their various applications, popular, scientific and technical, *sixty* or *seventy thousand* words! It satisfies my mind that I have done all that my health, my talents and my pecuniary means would enable me to accomplish. I present it to my fellow citizens, not with frigid indifference, but with my ardent wishes for their improvement and their happiness; and for the continued increase of the wealth, the learning, the moral and religious elevation of character, and the glory of my country.

To that great and benevolent Being, who, during the preparation of this work, has sustained a feeble constitution, amidst obstacles and toils, disappointments, infirmities and depression; who has twice borne me and my manuscripts in safety across the Atlantic, and given me strength and resolution to bring the work to a close, I would present the tribute of my most grateful acknowledgments. And if the talent which he entrusted to my care, has not been put to the most profitable use in his service, I hope it has not been "kept laid up in a napkin," and that any misapplication of it may be graciously forgiven.

New Haven, 1828. N. Webster.

On Reading Noah Webster

Arthur Schulman

WEBSTER VS. JOHNSON

Before Noah Webster came along, the best dictionary in the English-speaking world was Samuel Johnson's, which first appeared in 1755. As he concludes the long Introduction to his 1828 work, Webster acknowledges Johnson's greatness but finds nine "principal faults" in his dictionary. Among these are the omission of some common words, and especially of many scientific ones; inadequate distinctions among words that are "nearly synonymous"; and "mistakes in etymology." (He also thought that Johnson was mistaken in using so many illustrative quotations, particularly for everyday words, but most readers have found that to be one of Johnson's glories.) Fearing that Johnson's opinions, "when wrong, have a weight of authority that renders them extremely mischievous," Webster set out in his own work to undo that mischief.

Webster advanced lexicography by his attention to new words, to old words with new meanings, and by his nuanced synonymies. Yet in his entries he takes issue with Johnson less often than you would expect. Only rarely does he catch Johnson in an outright error, as at BUTTER-MILK, or accuse him of one, as in FAIN. More often he finds a Johnsonian definition incomplete or merely reflecting usage differences in England and America (see LIKELY). He picks two bones with Johnson at MENIAL, and thinks Johnson's use of FLAUNT is "unfounded."

What Luther did for Christianity, Webster proposed to do for philology: lead a "reformation." Still, he was forced to acknowledge that "a considerable part of Johnson's Dictionary is . . . well executed; and when his definitions are correct and his arrangement judicious, it seems to be expedient to follow him. It would be mere affectation or folly to alter what cannot be improved." Webster reproduced many of Johnson's definitions verbatim; but he would also transpose words and phrases, presumably to avoid seeing himself as a mere copyist.

An American Dictionary of the English Language contained thousands of words that Johnson missed or never dreamt of. (The ninth edition of Johnson, the one that Webster owned and knew, had 58,000 entries; the 1828 Webster's had 70,000). To the A's alone Webster added ABDALS, ACUPUNCTURE, AERONAUT, ALBINOS, ANDROID, ARCHIPELAGO, and ASTEROID, as well as proper nouns (Johnson deliberately ignored them) such as ABELIANS, ALLEGHANY, AMERICAN, and APALACHIAN.

Of the fifteen hundred entries in our selection, about a quarter do not appear in Johnson at all. Nearly all the rest deserve inclusion because of a distinctive Websterian elaboration. No one would claim Webster was a great stylist or wit—he himself tells us that "the dignified style of Johnson is scarcely IMITABLE"—but he could turn a nice phrase, clarify meanings, and display his own prejudices. Often he is unintentionally funny. And then there are his encyclopedic entries, his exploration of the roots of language, his quarrels with Johnson, and much more. Our selection highlights Webster's wit, wisdom, piety, patriotism, and prudery. The reader will find moralistic exemplars (expected ones like MARRIAGE, PUNISHMENT, SEDUCER, VICE, and WAR, and more surprising ones like EDUCATION, INDEBTED, LOTTERY, and SUBJECTION); encyclopedic entries (for animals such as BADGER and KANGAROO, and for many plants and minerals besides); words new to the language, mostly from science and technology, like CRANIOSCOPY,

LITHOGRAPHY, POLYNESIA, and URANIUM; words striking Webster as barbarous, such as YOLK (for YELK); entries revealing his ignorance, or at least his oddly selective knowledge (for example, BRAMIN, CARAVAN, CARTESIAN, FAKIR, and GIPSEY); entries displaying curious etymologies, in which Webster often finds cognates that would elude linguists who followed him; and many entries, often nuanced, of great style and grace (including ADMIRATION, CLEVER, and DANDY). Webster deliberately avoided the inclusion of certain words (not just ones offensive to polite society) and missed others through inadvertence or ignorance. Thus while he includes definitions for ATOMIC THEORY, COTTON GIN, PIANOFORTE, TELEGRAPH, VACCINATION, and WROUGHT IRON, there are no entries for *fountain pen, digitalis, semaphore,* and *torpedo* (the weapon), and he had not yet heard of the *grizzly bear.*

WEBSTER THE DEFINER

Webster was sensitive to the often subtle differences in meaning among words and tried to clarify these differences through examples of their use. (Today's synonymies owe a great deal to him). He compares DRAW with *pull;* OBTAIN with *acquire;* ANIMOSITY with *enmity* and *malice;* BANTER with RIDICULE and *derision;* JEALOUSY with *envy;* HOPE, *wish,* DESIRE, and EXPECTATION; and PUNISHMENT, *chastisement, correction,* and *revenge.* He contrasts the ways in which the English and the Americans use words like CLEVER and FULSOME, and he takes the time to expand on the nature of ELEGANCE and on things that might ENCROACH. He points out that words like MUTINY have lost some of their recent meanings and that others, especially many of the Americanisms he is eager to define, have taken on new ones.

The practice of ACCUBATION, Webster tells us, was not known

"until luxury had corrupted manners." We BAIT a hook in order to "lure fish, fowls and other animals into human power." A DANDY is "a male of the human species, who dresses himself like a doll, and who carries his character on his back." "HOIST" is what milkmaids say to cows "when they wish them to lift and set back the right leg." "When your friend falls asleep at church, give him a JOG." A WALKING-STAFF is "carried in the hand for support or amusement in walking." HOLY WARS "were carried on by most unholy means."

Webster's self-referential intrusions—there are quite a few of them—are not subtle. He remembers his favorite daughter under EMBALM; recounts a sojourn in Europe at ARRIVE, STAY, LEAVE, MAIN, STALL, SWIM, VOLUME, BATHING-TUB, and CIRCUMFORANEOUS; he tells us WHEN he saw Lafayette, that he was a WITNESS to the ratification of the Constitution, and that he once saw a COMET, a stellar TRANSIT, and the *Aurora Borealis;* he describes his DIET; and he comments on the weather (UNSEA-SONABLE and REMARKABLE). He initials several entries so that we won't mistake his authorship—ANNO DOMINI is signed off with a *W.*—and it is hard to believe that some of the illustrative quotes marked *Anon.* were not penned by Webster himself.

He foresees a great future for his country and its language: "within two hundred years," he predicts, "the English TONGUE "will probably be spoken by two or three hundred millions of people in North America." Quite right.

WEBSTER AT THE PULPIT

Webster's moralism is pervasive and inescapable. Minisermons are everywhere, as Webster instructs us to follow God's laws, to defer to authority, to know one's place, to fulfill one's duties and obligations. We are told that MARRIAGE "was instituted by God himself"; that it is "an unnatural parent" who is CARELESS about her children; that to FREQUENT "a dram-shop, an ale house, or a gaming table, is in the road to poverty, disgrace, and ruin." The study of JURISPRUDENCE, "next to that of theology, is the most important and useful to men."

He tells us, frequently and with passion, what he doesn't like about his world: slavery, dueling, seduction, gambling, drunkenness, pauperism, bad manners, irreligiosity. He ridicules fashion and deplores Jacobinism. He interjects his antipathies at every opportunity: for slavery at CHEAP, FORMERLY, and SCOURGE, not merely at FREEDOM; for dueling at BRAVERY, CONTEMPTIBLE, and FORFEIT; for drunkenness at PEST.

WEBSTER THE CRITIC

Webster was no abolitionist, at least not when he was compiling his dictionary, but he was appalled by slavery and took every opportunity to say so. He was concerned with growing PAUPERISM; went on at length about LIBERTY (natural, civil, political, and religious, with special concern for "liberty of the press"); and believed firmly in private PROPERTY, the right to which he felt was a biblical dispensation. He saw no reason why literary property should be less valued than real estate, and was an early crusader for COPYRIGHT protection. He opposed SUMPTUARY laws. He finds a place in his definitions for his American heroes: Washington appears, for example, at FATHER, MODEL, and SURPASS. In foreign affairs he notes that while the United States was officially NEUTER during the French Revolution, its citizens were hardly indifferent to what was going on there. Webster himself condemned the JACOBINs, worrying that the American republic might be undermined by those sympathetic to their cause. On matters of POLICY, Webster found both good and bad in English trade decisions; as for France, it was its POLICY "to preclude females from the throne." He hoped that the Greeks would prevail in their REVOLUTION against the Turks.

WEBSTER THE PATRIOT

Webster defends, in his Preface, his inclusion of Americanisms: words that his young country had created a need for. "Thus the terms, land-office; land-warrant; location of land; consociation of churches; regent of a university; intendant of a city; plantation, selectmen, senate, congress, court, assembly, escheat, &c. are either words not belonging to the language of England, or they are applied to things in this country which do not exist in that." Webster's argument seems unassailable, even if today's readers are more likely to be impressed by the staying power of Americanisms like CAUCUS, LEVEE, and PALAVER.

Webster also defends in his Preface his choice of Americans as sources illustrating usage. "I do not expect to add celebrity to the names of Franklin, Washington, Adams, Jay, Madison, Marshall, Ramsay, Dwight, Smith, Trumbull, Hamilton, Belknap, Ames, Mason, Kent, Hare, Silliman, Cleaveland, Walsh, Irving, and many other Americans distinguished by their writings or by their science; but it is with pride and satisfaction, that I can place them, as authorities, on the same page as those of Boyle, Hooker, Milton, Dryden, Addison, Ray, Milner, Cowper, Davy, Thomson and Jameson." (Jefferson is conspicuously absent from Webster's hall of fame.) Webster goes on to single out Americans noted for their style. Aside from Hamilton, Jay, and Madison—the *Federalist* authors— none of his favorites is a household name today: Samuel Stanhope Smith (1751–1819), president of Princeton from 1795 to 1812; John Mitchell Mason (1770–1829), a theologian and pulpit orator; Robert Goodloe Harper (1765–1825), the senator who suggested Liberia and Monrovia for the colony in Africa and its capital; James

Kent (1763–1847), a jurist who from 1814 was chancellor of the New York Court of Chancery; Fisher Ames (1758–1808), a Hamilton supporter who distrusted Jefferson's democratic tendencies; and Joel Barlow (1754–1812), a Yale classmate of Webster's—both a diplomat and a poet, but Webster praises him only for his prose.

As chauvinistic as Webster was, however, he was unable to cite American sources, much less quote from them, in more than a tiny percentage of his entries. Our selection includes some of Webster's best American quotes: mainly from Franklin for DEBT, GENTLEMAN, HOPE, LAZINESS, MAD, MAINTAIN, PANCAKE, PRIDE, PURCHASE, SLOTH, TAX, TEMPERATE, TIME, TO-MORROW, and TROT; from John Adams for DISABUSE, ERUDITION, EXPERIMENT, and GOVERNMENT; from Washington for AMERICAN, ANTIPATHY, CITIZEN, MELIORATING, RELIGION, TEST, and UNPARALLELED; from Irving for CASCADE, CLASSICAL, DARK, EXPECTATION, MONOTONY, PROMISE, and SCENERY; and from the *Federalist* (Hamilton, Jay, or Madison) for DISEASE, EXECUTIVE, FACTION, FIDELITY, GOOD, HEMLOCK, PURVIEW, and WILL.

Webster injects American place-names into his definitions wherever he can; most of these, but not all, are from locales familiar to him. Thus Hudson turns up not only at BAY but at HIGHLAND, STRAND, and WALNUT; Niagara at CATARACT and FALL; Hartford at DUMB and OAK; Boston at FIRE, LATITUDE, LONGITUDE, NECK, PEACH, POLICE, SCENERY, and WHARF; Philadelphia at ELM; Springfield at LABORATORY; Windsor at FERRY; Nantucket at MAIN; Bunker Hill at MONUMENT; Amherst at STAR-SHOOT; Northampton at VIEW; Charleston, South Carolina, at RETIRE; and Carolina at SESAME. He finds reason or excuse to refer to Plymouth at COMMEMORATION; Maryland at AMBER; New York at EMPORIUM, EVACUATE, LOT, and METROPOLIS; Mississippi at FLOOD and SAWYER; Connecticut at GARDEN and MEAD; Kaatskill at MOUNTAIN; Brook-

lyn at OPPOSITE; Massachusetts at PAGE; the Erie Canal at
UNDERTAKING; New England at QUILTING, SAUCE, SIGN-
POST, SPELL, and UNSEASONABLE; Lake Superior at VOYAGE;
New Hampshire at RIOT; Georgia at PLANTATION; and Ohio at
WEST. In addition to all of these are hundreds of Americanisms,
most of them terms used by New Englanders; some, like SOZZLE,
seem to have passed out of the language, while others, like SPANK,
are still very much with us.

WEBSTER'S WORLD

Webster tried to describe the everyday American world as he
encountered it. It was newly lit by GASLIGHT; white oak and white
pine were its most important TIMBER; common TRANSPORTA-
TION was by carriages or sleds; STRANGERs showed up at college
commencements; a moderate bill for college tuition and board
was twenty-five dollars per QUARTER; and "money at interest
[could] GAIN five, six or seven percent." Good horses were
SCARCE. Boys everywhere were seen to WHITTLE. To escape
from everyday fare, a Websterian epicure might dine on canvas-
back duck as a LUXURY.

ETYMOLOGY RUN AMOK

Webster came to believe, with Bishop Ussher, that the world was
young. Even before he was born again he had published, as an
appendix to his *Compendious Dictionary*, a table of important dates
in human history, beginning with the creation in 4004 B.C. and the
birth of Cain in 4003. Webster was convinced that Adam must
have been using an ur-language when he named the animals, so
that it was the historical lexicographer's task to figure out how all

modern languages descended from that original one. Though he rarely traces clear lines of descent—indeed, he claims in his Introduction that all he is doing is unearthing affinities—he revels in his discoveries of similarities of words from almost unimaginably different languages. (To give examples of this, his dictionary required the reproduction of Ethiopic, Persian, Arabic, Hebrew, and Cyrillic scripts.)

Webster loved to speculate on the meaning of the primitive roots of modern words. Sometimes he admits to being flummoxed about a word's origin, but as a rule he does not shrink from a guess, even when the evidence to support it is meager. His etymologies are often plausible, and usually they are correct, but scholars in his own time—a great age for the study of linguistic evolution, a field that predated the study of biological evolution—let alone those in our own, could not take very seriously his forays into the history of English. Our selection of Webster's entries with fanciful etymologies includes DRAGON, FOREST, GINSENG (from the Chinese and the Iroquois), HERRING, MOTHER, MUD, SHILLY-SHALLY (from the Russian), TOTE, WALK, and YANKEE. He is right about the derivation of ARRIVE, and is often rightly critical of others' etymologies. He faulted Johnson for his etymologies; he was determined to do much better. To his credit, all major dictionaries that followed his were obliged to deal in a serious way with the history of the words they chose to define.

WEBSTER THE CRUSADER

Webster understood that language changes over time. New words are needed to deal with new realities, while others become obsolete or come to be used in different ways. A dictionary, Webster thought, should reflect the language as it is actually used, not as it ought to be used. Yet the moralistic Webster, the man whose definitions are

forever urging us to obey and to defer, cannot avoid being a pre-
scriptivist. Certain spellings and pronunciations and usages drive
him crazy, and he tells us that we are wrong to use them. According
to Webster, words we shouldn't use include ABORIGINES, AMA-
ZON (for the river), AUTOMATA (as the plural), BIRD (for fowl),
DIGAMMA (we should call a letter by its sound, not its shape), and
JEOPARDIZE (for jeopard). We should pronounce DEAF to rhyme
with *leaf,* not pronounce the *g* in RECOGNIZE, and to spell *horde* as
HORD, *whore* as HORE, *island* as IELAND, *reindeer* as RANEDEER,
thumb as THUM, *whippoorwill* as WHIPPOWIL, and *yolk* as YELK.
Many words in everyday use should not be used in "elegant" speech
or writing, including CRUSTY, DODGE, and STINGY.

Webster was not oblivious to the fact that he had often changed
his mind. His views on religion and the state were transformed as
he looked with alarm at deists like Jefferson who, he believed,
were undermining Christian education. He was an early champion of the American experiment, but became increasingly pes-
simistic about its prospects. Once a radical spelling reformer, he
gave up the crusade, but still allowed some of his forlorn hopes
(see HALLELUIAH, for example) to creep into his great dictionary. (He himself had spelled it with a *j* in the *Compendious.*) And he
argues that DIPHTHONG should not be pronounced as if it were
spelled *dipthong,* even though he had spelled it and pronounced it
that way in the *Compendious.* His definitions are almost never tenta-
tive, and it seems never to occur to him that he might be wrong.
According to David Micklethwait, "no matter how often he had
changed his opinion, he was always unshakeably convinced that he
was right." He is always positive or, as Ambrose Bierce would later
cynically put it, "mistaken at the top of [his] voice."

WEBSTER THE GEOGRAPHER

Webster was unsystematic, to say the least, in choosing place-names. He leaves out the islands of *Malta, Cyprus, Sicily, Sardinia,* and *Elba,* as well as adjectival forms like *Cuban* and *Cretan,* but finds room for island groups like the KURILIAN, the ALEUTIAN, POLYNESIA ("a new term in geography"), and the BALEARIC (probably included only so that he could say that *Balearis* may be from the Greek "to throw, because the inhabitants were good slingers"). Geographical adjectives that he had included in his *Compendious Dictionary* (among them *Siamese, Tibetan, Venetian, Hungarian, Tunisian,* and *Ethiopian*) he now leaves out, making room for ABYSSINIAN, PROVENCIAL (pertaining to Provence), and many others.

WEBSTER THE SCIENTIST

Webster conceded that Johnson "was certainly one of the brightest luminaries of English literature" and that "whenever correctness depended on his own mind . . . he seldom made a mistake." But though "Johnson was SECOND to none in intellectual powers, [he] was second to many in research and erudition." And Johnson, despite his many quotes from Newton, cared much more about literature than science. "Technical precision of terms," Webster says, "is to be learnt only by a knowledge of the sciences to which they belong; and with some of the sciences, [Johnson] had very little or no acquaintance." He was determined that a similar criticism could not be made of his *American Dictionary of the English Language.*

Webster tried mightily to make his dictionary up-to-date about science and technology; his entries on rocks and minerals, many of them recently discovered, could be compulsive in their detail and esoteric in their descriptive vocabulary. If they had been found in

New England, Webster would tell us so: see, for example, GIBBSITE and SILLIMANITE. "Chimistry," mineralogy, and astronomy were fields of endless fascination for Webster; physics and physiology, less so. He gives us encyclopedic entries for ACID, ELECTRICITY, FERMENTATION, HEAT, and MOTION; for HYDROGEN, OXYGEN, SUGAR, and TIN; for MOOSE, PENGUIN, SALAMANDER, and SALMON. As for mathematics, Webster lacked either the ability to explain its terms or the understanding—perhaps even the curiosity—to do so. See, for example, his definitions of HARMONICAL MEAN, HEPTAGONAL NUMBERS, PERMUTATION, and RABDOLOGY, which are impenetrable, and of CIRCLE, which is redundant. At the same time he felt obliged to list all ten NUMERALs; to provide examples of EVEN numbers (beginning, oddly, with "4"); to show us how to compute an AVERAGE and a CUBE; and to illustrate BINARY ARITHMETIC by listing the first ten positive integers in binary form. Webster was probably mystified about how the ABACUS and SLIDING-RULE worked, as he was for nonmathematical devices like the MAGIC LANTERN. As a saving grace, he does pretty well with LOGARITHM (though much of his entry derives from Johnson), and has an entry for ROUND NUMBER, a phrase that has inexplicably vanished from nearly all modern dictionaries besides the OED.

Webster's decision to include such exotica as ABAGUN, AXAYACAT, BOM, LANGTERALOO, SCAPAISM, and SEROON, none of them in Johnson, can be hard to fathom. SEROON is there because Webster never met a weight or measure he didn't like, but other terms, like HETEROSCIAN, just may have struck his fancy as he leafed through the references at his elbow.

WEBSTER'S SOURCES

Despite his stated aim of making his dictionary American in orien-
tation, Webster was obliged to fall back upon English sources,
most of them used by Samuel Johnson before him, for the lion's
share of his attributions. His favorites are Addison and Dryden,
whose style he admires (see STANDARD), but Locke, Pope,
Bacon, and Shakespeare make many appearances as well.

Sir William Blackstone (1723–80), the eminent jurist, is Webster's authority on the law, an engrossing subject for him; Blackstone is named as the source for scores of entries, many of them
encyclopedic. Johnson, of course, is frequently cited and com-
mented on, at times critically, even if most of Webster's borrowings
from Johnson go unacknowledged. Johnson's dictionary was
always at hand as Webster made his own compilation, as were Dob-
son's Philadelphia reprint of the third edition of the *Encyclopædia
Britannica,* his major source (*"Encyc."*) next to Johnson; Bailey's
and Ash's dictionaries; Martyn's *The Language of Botany;* Nicholson's *Dictionary of Practical and Theoretical Chemistry;* Quincy's *Lexicon Physico-Medicum;* and Kirwan's *Elements of Mineralogy.* "*Cyc."*
denotes Abraham Rees's heroic *Cyclopædia* (1802–20, thirty-nine
volumes of text issued in installments); Webster used Rees in preference to *Britannica* beginning late in the S's, so much so that 98
percent of such encyclopedic citations under T were to *Cyc.* Other
commonly used sources include Falconer's *Dictionary of the Marine*
(*"Mar. Dict."*), or another work based upon it, and a *Dict. of Nat.
Hist.* Webster sometimes refers to "*Journ. of Science.,"* suggesting
that he had consulted that journal himself, when in fact he owed
his definition to a citation in Ure's *Dictionary of Chemistry.*

GOING TO PRESS

As Webster worked feverishly to complete his dictionary, he knew that Napoleon had died and that Missouri had become a state (1821); that the Monroe Doctrine had been promulgated (1823); that Faraday, Herschel, and Volta were doing important scientific work; and that the Erie Canal had been completed (he celebrated this UNDERTAKING, at the same time casting doubt on the search for a Northwest Passage). He seems to have been unaware of the work of such mathematicians as Laplace, Gauss, and Babbage, and of the educational reforms of Pestalozzi (perhaps surprising, given Webster's own significant contributions in this realm). He never refers to artists or composers of any era, including his own (Beethoven died in 1827, Goya in 1828). In 1828, when his dictionary came out, Jackson defeated J. Q. Adams for the presidency, sounding the death knell for federalism; Washington Irving published his *History of the Life and Voyages of Christopher Columbus;* and construction began on the Baltimore & Ohio Railroad, or B&O, the first American railroad built for the transportation of passengers and freight.

REDISCOVERING WEBSTER

The themes we have found in Webster do not exhaust the ones an attentive browser may discover. What Webster tells us about his language, his world, and himself is often fascinating, even when it is wrongheaded. He sometimes contradicts himself; he spells a word in different ways, even in the same entry; and his punctuation can be idiosyncratic. He has favorite words and turns of phrase. He tells us what he thinks are beautiful, and marvels at certain curiosities of nature. He is proud of how far we have come from the beliefs and practices not only of our "rude ancestors" but from the "pretended sciences" of recent memory. He reminds us, over and over again, of our "duties." And he heaps scorn on the "barbarous," the "clownish," the "absurd," the "mischievous," the "detestable," and the "wicked." His dictionary is a treasure trove; explore it and see what you can find.

The Dictionary

TO THE READER:

We present the entries in alphabetical order. None of Webster's syllabic-stress marks have been retained, nor have (with few exceptions) his indications of pronunciation. We include only selected etymologies, either alone or preceding the definition in square brackets [ ]. (Occasionally Webster injects an etymological comment in the definition itself.) Webster's entries usually provide meanings for all of the senses in which he believed a word might be used; we seldom include more than one or two of these. Except where ellipsis points, . . . , indicate that some of Webster's words have been left out, however, the definitions we do include are as originally printed. The reader will find inconsistencies, mostly of spelling and punctuation, in the entries we include here, but we have chosen not to "correct" Webster even when the temptation was great to do so.

A–Z

Webster's entries for the letters of the alphabet deal with the manner of their articulation, their pronunciation, and to varying extents with the history, as Webster understood it, of their shape and sound. All modern dictionaries have followed Webster in this practice. We provide the first three paragraphs of the entry for A, the longest, and offer brief excerpts from Webster's entries for other letters. Each of these may be found, boxed, at the foot of the first page of entries that begin with that letter.

A

☞ A is the first letter of the Alphabet in most of the known languages of the earth; in the Ethiopic however it is the *thirteenth*, and in the Runic the *tenth*. It is naturally the first letter, because it represents the first vocal sound naturally formed by the human organs: being the sound uttered with a mere opening of the mouth without constraint, and without any effort to alter the natural position or configuration of the lips. Hence this letter is found in many words first uttered by infants; which words are the names of the objects with which infants are first concerned, as the breast, and the parents. Hence in Hebrew אם *am,* is mother, and אב *ab,* is father. In Chaldee and Syriac *abba* is father; in Arabic, *aba;* in Ethiopic, *abi;* in Malayan and Bengalese, *bappa;* in Welsh, *tad,* whence we retain *daddy;* in Old Greek and in Gothic, *atta;* in Irish, *aithair;* in Cantabrian, *aita;* in Lapponic, *atki;* in Abyssinian, *abba;* in Amharic, *aba;* in Shilhic and Melindane, African dialects, *baba;* and *papa* is found in many nations. Hence the Latin *mamma,* the breast, which is, in popular use, the name of mother; in Swedish, *amma,* is a nurse. This list might be greatly extended; but these examples prove *A* to be the first natural vocal sound, and entitled to the first place in alphabets. The Hebrew name of this letter, *aleph,* signifies an *ox* or a *leader.*

A has in English, three sounds; the long or slender, as in *place, fate;* the broad, as in *wall, fall,* which is shortened in *salt, what;* and the open, as in *father, glass,* which is shortened in *rather, fancy.* Its primitive sound was probably *aw. A* is also an abbreviation of the Saxon *an* or *ane, one,* used before words beginning with an articulation; as *a* table, instead of *an* table. This is a modern change; for in Saxon *an* was used before articulations, as well as vowels, as *an tid,* a time, *an gear,* a year.

This letter serves as a prefix to many English words, as in *asleep; awake; afoot; aground; agoing.* In some cases, this is a contraction of the Teutonic *ge,* as in *asleep, aware,* from the Saxon *geslapan,* to sleep; *gewarian,* to beware; the Dutch *gewaar.* Sometimes it is a corruption of the Saxon *on,* as *again* from *ongean, awake* from *onwacian,* to watch or wake. Before contractions, it may be a participle of the Celtic *ag,* the sign of the participle of the present tense; as, *ag-radh,* saying; *a saying, a going.* Or this may be a contraction of *on,* or what is equally probable, it may have proceeded from a mere accidental sound produced by negligent utterance. In some words, *a* may be a contraction of *at, of, in, to,* or *an.* In some words of Greek original, *a* is privative, giving to them a negative sense, as in *anonymous,* from **α** and **ονομα** name.

ABACUS. Henry Knighton was a fourteenth-century Augustinian canon whose four-volume chronicle told the history of England from 959 to 1366.

ABACUS, *n.* 2. An instrument to facilitate operations in arithmetic; on this are drawn lines; a counter on the lowest line, is *one;* on the next, *ten;* on the third, a *hundred,* &c. On the spaces, counters denote half the number of the line above. Other schemes are called by the same name. The name is also given to a table of numbers cast up, as an *abacus* of addition; and by analogy, to the art of numbering, as in Knighton's Chronicon. *Encyc.*

ABACUS PYTHAGORICUS, *n.* The multiplication table, invented by Pythagoras.

ABAGUN, *n.* The name of a fowl in Ethiopia, remarkable for its beauty and for a sort of horn, growing on its head. The word signifies stately Abbot.
Crabbe.

ABANDON, *v.t.* 1. To forsake entirely; as to *abandon* a hopeless enterprise.
Wo to that generation by which the testimony of God shall be *abandoned.*
Dr. Mason.

ABBEY-LUBBER, *n.* A name given to monks, in contempt for their idleness.

ABDALS, *n.* The name of certain fanatics in Persia, who, in excess of zeal, sometimes run into the streets, and attempt to kill all they meet who are of a different religion; and if they are slain for their madness, they think it meritorious to die, and by the vulgar are deemed martyrs. *Encyc.*

ABELIANS, ABELONIANS or ABELITES, in Church history, a sect in Africa which arose in the reign of Arcadius; they married, but lived in continence, after the manner, as they pretended, of Abel, and attempted to maintain the sect by adopting the children of others. *Encyc.*

ABET, *v.t.* 1. To encourage by aid or countenance, but now used chiefly in a bad sense. "To *abet* an opinion," in the sense of *support,* is used by Bishop Cumberland, but this use is hardly allowable.

ABHORRENT, *a.* 2. Contrary, odious, inconsistent with, expressive of extreme opposition, as, "Slander is *abhorrent* to all ideas of justice." In this sense, it should always be followed by *to*—abhorrent *from* is not agreeable to the English idiom.

ABOLITION, *n.* The act of abolishing; or the state of being abolished; an annulling; abrogation; utter destruction; as the abolition of laws, decrees, ordinances, rites, customs, debts, &c.

The application of this word to persons and things, is now unusual or obsolete. To abolish persons, canals and senses, the language of good writers formerly, is no longer legitimate.

ABOMINATION, *n.* 3. Hence, defilement, pollution, in a physical sense, or evil doctrines and practices, which are moral defilements, idols and idolatry, are called *abominations.* The Jews were an *abomination* to the Egyptians; and the sacred animals of the Egyptians were an *abomination* to the Jews.

ABORIGINAL, *n.* An original, or primitive inhabitant. The first settlers in a country are called *aboriginals;* as the Celts in Europe, and Indians in America.   *President Smith.*

ABORIGINES, *n. plu.* Aboriginals—but not an English word. It may be well to let it pass into disuse. [See *Aboriginal.*]

ABOVE, *prep.* 10. In a book or writing, it denotes *before* or in a former place, as what has been said *above;* supra. This mode of speaking originated in the ancient manner of writing, on a strip of parchment, beginning at one end and proceeding to the other. The beginning was the *upper* end.

ABSENT, *a.* 3. In *familiar language,* not at home; as, the master of the house is *absent.* In other words, he does not wish to be disturbed by company.

ABSTRACTION, *n.* 2. . . . Abstraction is the ground-work of classification, by which things are arranged in orders, genera, and species. We separate in idea the qualities of certain objects which are of the same kind, from others which are different in each, and arrange the objects having the same properties in a class, or collected body.

ABSURD, *a.* Opposed to manifest truth; inconsistent with reason, or the plain dictates of common sense. An *absurd* man acts contrary to the clear dictates of reason or sound judgment. An *absurd* proposition contradicts obvious truth. An *absurd* practice or opinion is repugnant to the reason or common apprehension of men. It is *absurd* to say six and six make ten, or that plants will take root in stone.

ACCLAMATION, *n.* A shout of applause, uttered by a multitude. Anciently, acclamation was a form of words, uttered with vehemence, somewhat resembling a song, sometimes accompanied with applauses which were given by the hands. Acclamations were ecclesiastical, nuptial, senatorial, synodical, theatrical, &c; they were musical and rhythmical; and bestowed for joy, respect, and even reproach, and often accompanied with words, repeated, five, twenty, and even sixty and eighty times. In the later stages of Rome, acclamations were performed by a chorus of music instructed for the purpose.

In modern times, acclamations are expressed by huzzas; by clapping of hands; and often by repeating *vivat rex, vivat respublica,* long live the king or republic, or other words expressive of joy and good wishes.

ACCUBATION, *n.* A lying or reclining on a couch, as the ancients at their meals. The manner was to recline on low beds or couches with the head resting on a pillow or on the elbow. Two or three men lay on one bed, the feet of one extended behind the back of another. This practice was not permitted among soldiers, children, and servants; nor was it known, until luxury had corrupted manners. *Encyc.*

ACEPHALOUS. ☞ For other dissipated fictions, see, e.g., ALCHIMY and ALKAHEST.

ACEPHALOUS, *a.* Without a head, headless. . . . applied to the Blemmyes, a pretended nation of Africa, and to other tribes in the East, whom ancient naturalists represented as having no head; their eyes and mouth being placed in other parts. Modern discoveries have dissipated these fictions.

ACID, *n.* In *chimistry,* acids are a class of substances, so denominated from their taste, or the sensation of sourness which they produce on the tongue. But the name is now given to several substances, which have not this characteristic in an eminent degree. The properties, by which they are distinguished, are these:
1. When taken into the mouth, they occasion the taste of sourness. They are corrosive, unless diluted with water; and some of them are caustic.
2. They change certain vegetable blue colors to red, and restore blue colors which have been turned green, or red colors which have been turned blue by an alkali.
3. Most of them unite with water in all proportions, with a condensation of volume and evolution of heat; and many of them have so strong an attraction for water, as not to appear in the solid state.
4. They have a stronger affinity for alkalies, than they have for any other substance; and in combining with them, most of them produce effervescence.
5. They unite with earths, alkalies and metallic oxyds, forming interesting compounds, usually called salts.
6. With few exceptions, they are volatilized or decomposed by a moder-

ate heat. The old chimists divided acids into animal, vegetable, and mineral—a division now deemed inaccurate.

Lavoisier. Thomas. Nicholson. Aikin.

Acoustic vessels, in *ancient theaters,* were brazen tubes or vessels, shaped like a bell, used to propel the voice of the actors, so as to render them audible to a great distance; in some theaters at the distance of 400 feet. *Encyc.*

ACUPUNCTURE, *n.* Among the Chinese, a surgical operation, performed by pricking the part affected with a needle, as in head-aches and lethargies.

Encyc.

ADMIRATION, *n.* Wonder mingled with pleasing emotions, as approbation, esteem, love or veneration; a compound emotion excited by something novel, rare, great, or excellent; applied to persons and their works. It often includes a slight degree of surprise. Thus, we view the solar system with *admiration.*

Very near to *admiration* is the wish to admire. *Anon.*

ADULTERATION, *n.* . . . . The *adulteration* of liquors, of drugs, and even of bread and beer, is common, but a scandalous crime.

ADULTERY, *n.* 1. Violation of the marriage bed; a crime, or a civil injury, which introduces, or may introduce, into a family, a spurious offspring.

By the *laws of Connecticut,* the sexual intercourse of any man, with a married woman, is the *crime* of adultery in both: such intercourse of a married man, with an unmarried woman, is fornication in both, and adultery of the man, within the meaning of the law respecting divorce; but not a felonious adultery in either, or the crime of adultery at common law, or by statute. This latter offense is, in England, proceeded with only in the ecclesiastical courts.

AERONAUT, *n.* One who sails or floats in the air; an aerial navigator; *applied to persons who ascend in air balloons.* *Burke.*

AIR, *n.* 1. The fluid which we breathe. Air is inodorous, invisible, insipid, colorless, elastic, possessed of gravity, easily moved, rarefied, and condensed.

Atmospheric air is a compound fluid, consisting of oxygen gas, and nitrogen or azote; the proportion of each is stated by chimists differently; some experiments making the oxygen a twenty-eighth part of a hundred; others, not more than a twenty-third, or something less. The latter is probably the true proportion.

Oxygen gas is called vital air. The body of air surrounding the earth is called the *atmosphere.* The specific gravity of air is to that of water, nearly as

1 to 828. Air is necessary to life; being inhaled into the lungs, the oxygenous part is separated from the azotic, and it is supposed to furnish the body with heat and animation. It is the medium of sounds and necessary to combustion.

AIR-JACKET, *n.* A leather jacket, to which are fastened bags or bladders filled with air, to render persons buoyant in swimming. *Encyc.*

ALBINOS, *n.* A name signifying white men, given by the Portuguese to the white negroes of Africa. The color of this race appears like that of persons affected with leprosy; and the negroes look upon them as monsters. *Encyc.*

ALCHIMY, *n.* 1. The more sublime and difficult parts of chemistry, and chiefly such as relate to the transmutation of metals into gold, the finding a universal remedy for diseases, and an alkahest or universal solvent, and other things now treated as ridiculous. This pretended science was much cultivated in the sixteenth and seventeenth centuries, but is now held in contempt.

ALCO, *n.* A quadruped of America, nearly resembling a dog, but mute and melancholy; and this circumstance seems to have given rise to the fable that dogs, transported to America, become mute. The animal was used for food by the native Americans, and the first Spanish settlers; but it is said to be now extinct. It is known also by the name of Techichi. *Clavigero.*

ALECTRYOMANCY, *n.* An ancient practice of foretelling events by means of a cock. The twenty four letters were laid on the ground, and a grain of corn on each; a cock was then permitted to pick up the grains, and the letters under the grains selected, being formed into words, were supposed to foretell the event desired. *Encyc.*

ALEUTIAN, or ALEUTIC, *a.* Designating certain isles in the Pacific ocean, eastward of Kamtschatka, extending northeastward towards America. The word is formed from *aleut,* which, in Russian, is a bald rock.
Tooke. Pinkerton.

ALKAHEST, *n.* A universal dissolvent; a menstruum capable of dissolving every body, which Paracelsus and Van Helmont pretended they possessed. This pretense no longer imposes on the credulity of any man.

ALKORAN, *n.* The book which contains the Mohammedan doctrines of faith and practice. It was written by Mohammed, in the dialect of the Koreish, which is the purest Arabic; but the Arabian language has suffered such changes, since it was written, that the language of the Alkoran is not now intelligible to the Arabians themselves, without being learnt like other dead languages. *Niebuhr. Encyc.*

ALCO. A creole Jesuit priest born in Veracruz, Francesco X. Clavigero (1731–87) celebrates indigenous culture in *The History of Mexico,* an encyclopedic work published in English translation in 1787. Jefferson and Franklin owned copies, and Webster must have enjoyed extracting from the *History* at least a dozen such exotica as ALCO and AXAYACAT. ☞

ALEUTIAN. ☞ Modern dictionaries say ALEUTIAN derives from a Russian word, but avoid Webster's specificity.

J. HORNE TOOKE

☞   J. Horne Tooke (1736–1812) promoted parliamentary reform in England and support for the American colonists, "but stopped short of advocating democracy" (*Encyclopædia Britannica*). But it was in philology, not just in politics, that Webster saw him as a kindred spirit. Indeed, Webster's *Dissertation on the English Language* (1789) incorporated ideas that Horne Tooke had advanced in his *Diversions of Purley* (first appearing in 1786), an early attempt at scientific language study. (Anthony Burgess, in *A Mouthful of Air*, calls *Purley* "a dangerous book that went in for philosophical conjecture about the origin of words and was quite capable of deriving 'hash' from the Persian *ash*, meaning stew.") Webster acknowledges a small debt to Horne Tooke in the Introduction to the *American Dictionary*, but insists he has "made no use of his writings, in this work" (he does not, Burgess would be glad to know, derive *hash* from the Persian). According to Horace E. Scudder, Webster's first biographer in 1881 (and not always a sympathetic one), Horne Tooke "was the man who opened Webster's eyes [to comparative philology], and him he followed so long as he followed anybody. But Tooke was a guesser, and Webster, with all his deficiencies, had always a reliance upon system and method. He made guesses also, but he thought they were scientific analyses, and he came to the edge of real discoveries without knowing it." Webster may have ignored Horne Tooke as he compiled his dictionary, but he names him as a source for a number of entries. Unaccountably, these have nothing to do with either politics or philology (see, e.g., CAVIAR and NOMAD).   ☜

ALLEGHANY, *n*. The chief ridge of the great chains of mountains which run from N. East to S. West through the middle and southern states of North America; but, more appropriately, the main or unbroken ridge, which casts all the waters on one side to the east, and on the other side to the west. This ridge runs from Pennsylvania to Georgia, and chains extend through the U. States.

This name is given also to the river Ohio, above its confluence with the Monongahela; but improperly, as the Indian name of the river to its source is Ohio.

ALLIGATOR, *n*. The American crocodile. The animal is of the lizard genus, having a long naked body, four feet, with five toes on the fore feet, and four on the hind, armed with claws, and a serrated tail. The mouth is very large, and furnished with sharp teeth; the skin is brown, tough, and, on the sides, covered with tubercles. The largest of these animals grow to the length of seventeen or eighteen feet. They live in and about the rivers in warm climates, eat fish, and sometimes catch hogs, on the shore, or dogs which are swimming. In winter, they burrow in the earth, which they enter under water and work upwards, lying torpid till spring. The female lays a great number of eggs, which are deposited in the sand, and left to be hatched by the heat of the sun.   *Encyc.*

ALMANACK, *n.* A small book or table, containing a calendar of days, weeks and months, with the times of the rising of the sun and moon, changes of the moon, eclipses, hours of full tide, stated festivals of churches, stated terms of courts, observations on the weather, &c. for the year ensuing. This calendar is sometimes published on one side of a single sheet, and called a *sheet-almanack.*
   The Baltic nations formerly engraved their calendars on pieces of wood, on swords, helves of axes, and various other utensils, and especially on walking sticks. Many of these are preserved in the cabinets of the curious. They are called by different nations *rimstocks, primstaries, runstocks, run-staffs, clogs,* &c.   *Junius.   Encyc.   Tooke's Russia.*

ALTERNATION, *n.* 2. The different changes or alterations of orders, in numbers. Thus, if it is required to know how many changes can be rung on six bells, multiply the numbers 1, 2, 3, 4, 5, 6, continually into one another, and the last product is the number required. This is called *permutation.*

AMAZON, *n.* [. . . History informs us, that the Amazons cut off their right breast, that it might not incommode them in shooting and hurling the javelin. This is doubtless a fable.]
   1. The Amazons are said by historians, to have been a race of female warriors, who founded an empire on the river Thermodon, in Asia Minor, on the coast of the Euxine. They are said to have excluded men from their society; and by their warlike enterprises, to have conquered and alarmed surrounding nations. Some writers treat these accounts as fables.   *Herodian.   Justin.*
   3. The name has been given to some American females, on the banks of the largest river in the world, who joined their husbands in attacking the Spaniards that first visited the country. This trivial occurrence gave the name Amazon to that river, whose real name is Maranon. *Garcilasso,* p. 606.

AMBER, *n.* A hard semi-pellucid substance, tasteless and without smell, except when pounded or heated, when it emits a fragrant odor. It is found in alluvial soils, or on the sea shore, in many places; particularly on the shores of the Baltic, in Europe, and at Cape Sable, in Maryland, in the U. States.

The ancient opinion of its vegetable origin seems now to be established, and it is believed or known to be a fossil resin. . . . It is highly electrical, and is the basis of a varnish.   *Journ. of Science.   Encyc.   Chambers.*

AMERICA, *n.* [from Amerigo Vespucci, a Florentine, who pretended to have first discovered the western continent.] One of the great continents, first discovered by Sebastian Cabot, June 11, O. S. 1498, and by Columbus, or Christoval Colon, Aug. 1, the same year. It extends from the eightieth degree of North, to the fifty-fourth degree of South Latitude; and from the thirty-fifth to the one hundred and fifty-sixth degree of Longitude West of Greenwich, being about nine thousand miles in length. Its breadth at Darien is narrowed to about forty-five miles, but at the northern extremity is nearly four thousand miles. From Darien to the *North,* the continent is called *North America,* and to the *South,* it is called *South America.*

AMERICAN, *n.* A native of America; originally applied to the aboriginals, or copper-colored races, found here by the Europeans; but now applied to the descendants of Europeans born in America.

The name *American* must always exalt the pride of patriotism.*Washington.*

AMUSE, *v.t.* 1. To entertain the mind agreeably; to occupy or detain attention with agreeable objects, whether by singing, conversation, or a show of curiosities. Dr. Johnson remarks, that *amuse* implies something less lively than *divert,* and less important than *please.* Hence it is often said, we are *amused* with trifles.

ANACONDA, *n.* A name given in Ceylon to a large snake, a species of Boa, which is said to devour travelers. Its flesh is excellent food.   *Encyc.*

ANDROID, *n.* A machine, in the human form, which, by certain springs, performs some of the natural motions of a living man. One of these machines, invented by M. Vaucanson, appeared in Paris in 1738, representing a flute player.   *Encyc.*

ANGER, *n.* 1. A violent passion of the mind excited by a real or supposed injury; usually accompanied with a propensity to take vengeance, or obtain satisfaction from the offending party. This passion however varies in degrees of violence, and in ingenious minds, may be attended only with a desire to reprove or chide the offender.

Anger is also excited by an injury offered to a relation, friend or party to which one is attached; and some degrees of it may be excited by cruelty, injustice or oppression offered to those with whom one has no immediate connection, or even to the community of which one is a member. Nor is it unusual to see something of this passion roused by gross absurdities in oth-

ANDROID. Jacques de Vaucanson (1709–82) was a French engineer who built his first automaton, the life-size "Flute Player," in 1737. The next year he created "The Digesting Duck," a masterpiece with four hundred moving parts. In 1745 he invented the first automated loom, preparing the ground for Jacquard's revolutionary work more than half a century later.

ers, especially in controversy or discussion. Anger may be inflamed till it rises to rage and a temporary delirium.

ANIMAL, *n.* An organized body, endowed with life and the power of voluntary motion; a living, sensitive, locomotive body; as, man is an intelligent *animal.* Animals are essentially distinguished from plants by the property of *sensation.* The contractile property of some plants, as the mimosa, has the appearance of the effect of *sensation,* but it may be merely the effect of *irritability.*

The distinction here made between animals and vegetables, may not be philosophically accurate; for we cannot perhaps ascertain the precise limit between the two kinds of beings, but this is sufficiently correct for common practical purposes.

ANIMOSITY, *n.* Violent hatred accompanied with active opposition; active enmity. *Animosity* differs from *enmity* which may be secret and inactive; and it expresses a less criminal passion than *malice.* *Animosity* seeks to gain a cause or destroy an enemy or rival, from hatred or private interest; *malice* seeks revenge for the sake of giving pain.

ANNO DOMINI. In the year of our Lord, noting the time from our Savior's incarnation; as, *Anno Domini,* or *A.D.* 1800.

This was written *Anno Domini,* 1809, and revised A.D. 1825 and 1827. *W.*

ANTELOPE, *n.* In *zoology,* the gazelle; a genus of ruminant quadrupeds, intermediate between the deer and goat. Their horns are solid and permanent, straight or curved; in some species annulated; in others, surrounded by a spiral; and in others, smooth. They resemble the deer in the lightness and elegance of their forms, and in their agility. They inhabit open plains or mountains, and some species in herds of two or three thousand. Their eyes are large, black, and of exquisite beauty and vivacity; and are therefore a favorite image with the eastern poets.   *Encyc.   Cyc.*

ANTIPATHY, *n.* 2. In *ethics,* antipathy is hatred, aversion or repugnancy; *hatred* to persons; *aversion* to persons or things; *repugnancy* to actions. Of these *hatred* is most voluntary. *Aversion,* and *antipathy,* in its true sense, depend more on the constitution; *repugnancy* may depend on reason or education.   *Encyc.*

Inveterate *antipathies* against particular nations, and passionate attachments to others, are to be avoided.   *Washington.*

APALACHIAN, *a.* Pertaining to the Apalaches, a tribe of Indians, in the western part of Georgia. Hence the word is applied to the mountains in or near their country, which are in fact the southern extremity of the Alleghanean ridges.

A

APPETITE, n.1. The natural desire of pleasure or good; the desire of gratification, either of the body or of the mind. *Appetites* are passions directed to general objects, as the *appetite* for fame, glory or riches; in distinction from passions directed to some particular objects, which retain their proper name, as the *passion* of love, envy or gratitude. *Passion* does not exist without an object; natural *appetites* exist first, and are then directed to objects. *Encyc.*
    4. The thing desired.
        Power being the natural *appetite* of princes. *Swift.*
    Appetites are *natural* or *artificial*. Hunger and thirst are *natural* appetites; the appetites for olives, tobacco, snuff, &c. are *artificial*.
    In old authors, appetite is followed by *to*, but regularly it should be followed by *for* before the object, as an appetite *for* pleasure.

APPLAUSE, n. A shout of approbation; approbation and praise, expressed by clapping the hands, acclamation or huzzas; approbation expressed. In antiquity, *applause* differed from *acclamation; applause* was expressed by the hands, and *acclamation* by the voice. There were three species of applause, the *bombus*, a confused din made by the hands or mouth; the *imbrices* and *testae*, made by beating a sort of sounding vessels in the theaters. Persons were appointed for the purpose of applauding, and masters were employed to teach the art. The applauders were divided into choruses, and placed opposite to each other, like the choristers in a cathedral. *Encyc.*

APPRENTICESHIP, n. The term for which an apprentice is bound to serve his master. This term in England is by statute seven years. In Paris, the term is five years; after which, the person, before he is qualified to exercise the trade as a master, must serve five years as a journeyman; during which term, he is called the *companion* of his master, and the term is called his *companionship*. *Encyc.*

ARCHIPELAGO, n. In *a general sense*, a sea interspersed with many isles; but particularly the sea which separates Europe from Asia, otherwise called the Egean Sea. It contains the Grecian isles, called Cyclades and Sporades.

ARK, n. 4. A large boat used on American rivers, to transport produce to market.

ARMADA, n. A fleet of armed ships; a squadron. The term is usually applied to the Spanish fleet, called the *Invincible Armada*, consisting of 130 ships, intended to act against England in the reign of Queen Elizabeth, A. D. 1588.

ARMADILLO, n. quadruped peculiar to America, called also *tatoo*, and in zoology, the *dasypus*. This animal has neither fore-teeth, nor dog-teeth; it is covered with a hard, bony shell, divided into movable belts, except on the forehead, shoulders and haunches, where it is not movable. The belts are connected by a membrane, which enables the animal to roll itself up like a hedge hog. These animals burrow in the earth, where they lie during the day time, seldom going abroad except at night. They are of different sizes; the largest 3 feet in length, without the tail. They subsist chiefly on fruits and roots; sometimes on insects and flesh. When attacked, they roll themselves into a ball, presenting their armor on all sides to any assailant; but they are inoffensive, and their flesh is esteemed good food. *Encyc.*

ARRIVE, *v.i.* [. . . Fr. *rive*, the shore or sloping bank of a river . . .] 1. Literally, to come to the shore, or bank. Hence to come to or reach in progress by water, followed by *at*. We *arrived* at Havre de Grace, July 10, 1824.—*N. W.*

ARTICULATE, *a.* Formed by jointing or articulation of the organs of speech; *applied to sound.* An *articulate* sound is made by closing and opening the organs of speech. The junction or closing of the organs forms a joint or articulation, as in the syllables *ab, ad, ap;* in passing from one articulation to another, the organs are, or may be opened, and a vowel is uttered, as in *attune;* and the different articulations, with the intervening vocal sounds, form what is called *articulate sounds;* sounds distinct, separate, and modified by articulation or jointing. This articulation constitutes the prominent difference between the human voice and that of brutes. Brutes open the mouth and make vocal sounds, but have, either not at all, or very imperfectly, the power of articulation.

ASK. The royal ☞ pedigree of today's "substandard" pronunciation. "Calmuc" (today spelled "Kalmuck") is a Ural-Altaic language.

ASK, *v.t.* [. . . In former times, the English word was pronounced *ax*, as in the royal style of assenting to bills in Parliament. "Be it as it is *axed*." In Calmuc, *asoc* signifies to inquire. The sense is to urge or press.]

ASK, *v.i.* This verb can hardly be considered as strictly intransitive, for some person or object is always understood. *Ask* is not equivalent to demand, claim, and require, at least, in modern usage; much less, is it equivalent to *beg* and *beseech*. The first three words, demand, claim, require, imply a right or supposed right in the person asking, to the thing requested; and *beseech* implies more urgency, than *ask*. *Ask* and *request* imply no right, but suppose the thing desired to be a favor. The French *demander* is correctly rendered by *ask,* rather than by *demand.*

ASS, *n.* 1. A quadruped of the equine genus. This animal has long slouching ears, a short mane, and a tail covered with long hairs at the end. He is usually of an ash color, with a black bar across the shoulders. The tame or domestic ass is patient to stupidity, and carries a heavy burden. He is slow, but very sure footed, and for this reason very useful on rough steep hills.
  2. A dull, heavy, stupid fellow; a dolt.

ASTEROID, *n.* A name given by Herschel to the newly discovered planets between the orbits of Mars and Jupiter.

The *atomic theory*, in chimistry, or the doctrine of *definite proportions*, teaches that all chimical combinations take place between the ultimate particles or *atoms* of bodies, and that these unite either atom with atom, or in proportions expressed by some simple multiple of the number of atoms.

Dalton.

ATTAINDER, *n.* 1. Literally a staining, corruption, or rendering impure; a corruption of blood. Hence,

2. The judgment of death, or sentence of a competent tribunal upon a person convicted of treason or felony, which judgment *attaints*, taints or corrupts his blood, so that he can no longer inherit lands. The consequences of this judgment are, forfeiture of lands, tenements and hereditaments, loss of reputation, and disqualification to be a witness in any court of law. A statute of Parliament attainting a criminal, is called an *act of attainder. Note.* By the constitution of the United States, no crime works an attainder.

Aurora Borealis, or *lumen boreale;* northern twilight. This species of light usually appears in streams, ascending towards the zenith from a dusky line a few degrees above the horizon. Sometimes it assumes a wavy appearance, as in America, in March 1782, when it overspread the whole hemisphere. Sometimes it appears in detached places; at other times, it almost covers the hemisphere. As the streams of light have a tremulous motion, they are called, in the Shetland isles, merry dancers. They assume all shapes, and a variety of colors, from a pale red or yellow to a deep red or blood color; and in the northern latitudes, serve to illuminate the earth and cheer the gloom of long winter nights. This light is sometimes near the earth. It is said to have been seen between the spectator and a distant mountain.

AUTOMATIC, AUTOMATICAL, *a.* Belonging to an automaton; having the power of moving itself; mechanical. *Johnson. Stewart.*

2. Not voluntary; not depending on the will. Dr. Hartley has demonstrated that all our motions are originally *automatic*, and generally produced by the action of tangible things on the muscular fiber.

AUTOMATON, *n.* [. . . The Greek plural, *automata*, is sometimes used; but the regular English plural, *automatons*, is preferable.] A self-moving machine, or one which moves by invisible springs.

AVERAGE, *n.* 2. From the practice of contributing to bear losses, in proportion to each man's property, this word has obtained the present popular sense, which is, that of a mean proportion, medial sum or quantity, made out

AUTOMATIC. David Hartley (1705–57) was an influential British associationist, but his speculative notions about the sources of automaticity could hardly be viewed as demonstrations.

of unequal sums or quantities. Thus, if A loses 5 dollars, B 9 and C 16, the sum is 30, and the average, 10.

AXAYACAT, *n.* A fly in Mexico, whose eggs, deposited on rushes and flags, in large quantities, are sold and used as a sort of caviare, called ahuauhtli. This was a dish among the Mexicans, as it now is among the Spaniards.

Clavigero.

B

BABE, *n.* [. . . Syr. *babosa,* a little child. It is remarkable that this Syriac and Arabic word for an infant, is retained by the natives of America, who call an infant *pappoos* . . . papa, a word taken from the first attempts of children to pronounce the name of a parent.]

BABYROUSSA, *n.* In zoology, the Indian hog, a native of Celebes, and of Buero, but not found on the continent of Asia or of Africa. This quadruped belongs to the genus *Sus,* in the class *Mammalia,* and order *Bellua.* From the outside of the upper jaw, spring two teeth twelve inches long, bending like horns, and almost touching the forehead. Along the back are some weak bristles, and on the rest of the body only a sort of wool. These animals live in herds, feed on herbage, are sometimes tamed, and their flesh is well tasted. When pursued hard, they rush into the sea, swim or dive and pass from isle to isle. In the forest, they rest their heads by hooking their upper tusks on a bough. *Encyc.*

BADGER, *n.* A quadruped of the genus *Ursus,* of a clumsy make, with short, thick legs, and long claws on the fore feet. It inhabits the north of Europe and Asia, burrows, is indolent and sleepy, feeds by night on vegetables, and is very fat. Its skin is used for pistol furniture; its flesh makes good bacon, and its hair is used for brushes to soften the shades in painting. *Encyc.*

BAIT, *v.t.* To put meat on a hook or line, or in an inclosure, or among snares, to allure fish, fowls and other animals into human power.

BALEARIC, *a.* [from *Balearis,* the denomination given to Majorca and Minorca. Qu. from Gr. βαλλω, to throw, because the inhabitants were good

☞ BABYROUSSA. According to the Saint Louis Zoo, this animal (whose Malaysian name means hog-deer) "sets the standard for bizarre." It is no longer considered a member of *Sus,* a genus of pigs; its current scientific name is *Babyrousa babyrussa,* and it is the only member of its new genus. The Indonesian island of Celebes is today known as Sulawesi; Webster's Buero is Buru, one of the Spice Islands, which are now called the Moluccas.

☞ B. In the Ethiopic, it is the ninth letter, and its shape is that of a hut. Perhaps from this or other like figure, it received its Hebrew name, *beth,* a house. ☜

---

slingers.] Pertaining to the isles of Majorca and Minorca, in the Mediterranean sea.

BALL, *n.* An entertainment of dancing; originally and peculiarly, at the invitation and expense of an individual; but the word is used in America, for a dance at the expense of the attendants.

BALLISTICS, *n.* The science or art of throwing missive weapons, by the use of an engine. The ballista was a machine resembling a cross-bow.
Encyc.   Math. Dict.   Ash.

BALLOON, *n.* 4. In *fireworks,* a ball of pasteboard, or kind of bomb, stuffed with combustibles, to be played off, when fired, either in the air, or in water, which, bursting like a bomb, exhibits sparks of fire like stars.
Johnson.   Encyc.
5. A game, somewhat resembling tennis, played in an open field, with a large ball of leather, inflated with wind.   *Encyc.*

BALLOT, *n.* 1. A ball used in voting. Ballots are of different colors; those of one color give an affirmative; those of another, a negative. They are privately put into a box or urn. 2. A ticket or written vote, being given in lieu of a ballot, is now called by the same name. 3. The act of voting by balls or tickets.

BANTER, *v.t.* To play upon in words and in good humor; to rally; to joke, or jest with. *Banter* hardly amounts to ridicule, much less to derision. It consists in being pleasant and witty with the actions of another, and raising a humorous laugh at his expense, often attended with some degree of sarcasm.

BARBARIAN, *n.* 2. A cruel, savage, brutal man; one destitute of pity or humanity.   *Philips.*
3. A foreigner. The Greeks and Romans denominated most foreign nations barbarians and many of these were less civilized than themselves, or unacquainted with their language, laws and manners. But with them the word was less reproachful than with us.

BARBECUE, *n.* In the *West Indies,* a hog roasted whole. It is, with us, used for an ox or perhaps any other animal dressed in like manner.

BARGE, *n.* 1. A pleasure boat; a vessel or boat of state, furnished with elegant apartments, canopies and cushions, equipped with a band of rowers, and decorated with flags and streamers; used by officers and magistrates.
Encyc.
2. A flat-bottomed vessel of burthen, for loading and unloading ships.
Mar. Dict.

BARN, *n.* A covered building for securing grain, hay, flax, and other productions of the earth. In *the northern states of America*, the farmers generally use
barns for stabling their horses and cattle; so that among them, a barn is both
a cornhouse or grange, and a stable.

BARREL, *n.* 1. A vessel or cask, of more length than breadth, round and
bulging in the middle, made of staves and heading, and bound with hoops.
    2. The quantity which a barrel contains. In America, the contents of a bar-
rel are regulated by statutes. In Connecticut, the barrel for liquors must contain
31 gallons, each gallon to contain 231 cubic inches. In New-York, a barrel of
flour by statute must contain either 196 lb. or 228 lb. nett weight. The barrel of
beef and pork in New-York and Connecticut, is 200 lbs. In general, the contents
of barrels, as defined by statute in this country, must be from 28 to 31 gallons.

BARREN, *n.* In the *States west of the Alleghany,* a word used to denote a
tract of land, rising a few feet above the level of a plain, and producing trees
and grass. The soil of these *barrens* is not *barren,* as the name imports, but
often very fertile. It is usually alluvial, to a depth sometimes of several feet.
                                                    Atwater, Journ. of Science.
    2. Any unproductive tract of land; as the pine *barrens* of South Carolina.
                                                    Drayton.

BASSET, *n.* A game at cards, said to have been invented at Venice, by a
nobleman, who was banished for the invention. The game being introduced
into France by the Venetian embassador, Justiniani, in 1674, it was prohibited by severe edicts.   *Encyc.*

BAT, *n.* A race of quadrupeds, technically called *Vespertilio,* of the order *pri-
mates,* in Linne's system. The fore feet have the toes connected by a membrane, expanded into a kind of wings, by means of which the animals fly. The
species are numerous. Of these, the vampire or Ternate bat inhabits Africa
and the Oriental Isles. These animals fly in flocks from isle to isle, obscuring
the sun by their numbers. Their wings when extended measure five or six
feet. They live on fruits; but are said sometimes to draw blood from persons
when asleep. The bats of the northern latitudes are small; they are viviparous
and suckle their young. Their skin resembles that of a mouse. They enter
houses in pleasant summer evenings, feed upon moths, flies, flesh, and oily
substances, and are torpid during the winter.   *Encyc.*

BATHING-TUB, *n.* A vessel for bathing, usually made either of wood or tin.
In the Royal Library at Paris, I saw a bathing-tub of porphyry, of beautiful
form and exquisite workmanship.

BAWDRY, *n.* The abominable practice of procuring women for the gratification of lust.

BASSET.   Probably
included only because
its inventor was ban-
ished and the game
was prohibited.

BATHING-TUB. James
Orchard Halliwell's *Dic-
tionary of Archaic and
Provincial Words* (1847)
explains that this was "a
kind of bath, formerly
used by persons afflicted
with a certain disease."
Thomas Wright's *Dictio-
nary of Obsolete and
Provincial English* (1857)
is less coy: "a bath for-
merly administered to
people affected with the
venereal disease."

BAY, *n.* An arm of the sea, extending into the land, not of any definite form, but smaller than a gulf, and larger than a creek. The name however is not used with much precision, and is often applied to large tracts of water, around which the land forms a curve, as Hudson's *Bay.* Nor is the name restricted to tracts of water with a narrow entrance, but used for any recess or inlet between capes or head lands, as the *bay* of Biscay.

BAY, *n.* A state of expectation, watching or looking for; as, to keep a man *at bay.* So a stag *at bay* is when he turns his head against the dogs. Whence *abeyance,* in law, or a state of expectancy.

BAZAR, *n.* Among the Turks and Persians, an exchange, market-place, or place where goods are exposed to sale. Some bazars are open, others are covered with lofty ceilings or domes, pierced to give light. The bazar at Tauris will contain 30,000 men. *Encyc.*

BEAVER, *n.* An amphibious quadruped, of the genus Castor. It has short ears, a blunt nose, small fore feet, large hind feet, with a flat ovate tail. It is remarkable for its ingenuity in constructing its lodges or habitations, and from this animal is obtained the castor of the shops, which is taken from cods or bags in the groin. Its fur, which is mostly of a chesnut brown, is the material of the best hats.

BEECH, *n.* [. . . In Saxon *bec* and *boc* is a book. It is probable that *beech* is properly the name of bark, and this being used, by our rude ancestors, as the material for writing, the word came to signify a book.] A tree arranged by Linne under the genus *fagus,* with the chesnut. The beech grows to a large size, with branches forming a beautiful head, with thick foliage. The bark is smooth and of a silvery cast. The mast or nuts are the food of swine, and of certain wild animals, and yield a good oil for lamps. When eaten by man, they are said to occasion giddiness and headach. *Encyc.*

BELLES-LETTRES, *n. plu. bel' letter,* or anglicised, *bell-letters.* Polite literature; a word of very vague signification. It includes poetry and oratory; but authors are not agreed to what particular branches of learning the term should be restricted. *Encyc.*

BESTIALITY, *n.* 2. Unnatural connection with a beast.

BEVERAGE, *n.* Drink; liquor for drinking. It is generally used of a mixed liquor. Nectar is called the *beverage* of the gods.
In the middle ages, *beverage, beveragium,* or *biberagium* was money for drink given to an artificer or other person over and above his hire or wages. The practice has existed, to a certain extent, in America, within my memory, and I know not but it still exists in some parts of this country. A person who

B

had a new garment, was called on to *pay beverage*, that is, to treat with liquor. Hence,
    2. A treat on wearing a new suit of clothes, or on receiving a suit from the tailor; also a treat on first coming into prison; a garnish.

BEWITCH, *v.i.* To fascinate; to gain an ascendancy over by charms or incantation; an operation which was formerly supposed to injure the person bewitched, so that he lost his flesh, or behaved in a strange unaccountable manner; ignorant people being inclined to ascribe to evil spirits what they could not account for.

BIBLE, *n.* THE BOOK, by way of eminence; the sacred volume, in which are contained the revelations of God, the principles of Christian faith, and the rules of practice. It consists of two parts, called the Old and New Testaments.
    The *Bible* should be the standard of language as well as of faith.   *Anon.*

BIBLIOMANIA, *n.* Book-madness; a rage for possessing rare and curious books.

Binary arithmetic, the invention of Leibnitz is that in which two figures only, 0 and 1, are used, in lieu of ten; the cypher multiplying every thing by two, as in common arithmetic by 10. Thus, 1 is one; 10 is two; 11 is three; 100 is four; 101 is five; 110 is six; 111, is seven; 1000 is eight; 1001 is nine; 1010 is ten. It is said this species of arithmetic has been used by the Chinese for 4000 years, being left in enigma by Fohi.   *Encyc.*

BIRD, *n.* [Sax. *bird,* or *bridd,* a chicken; from the root of *bear,* or W. *bridaw,* to break forth.] 1. Properly, a chicken, the young of fowls, and hence a small fowl. 2. In *modern use,* any fowl or flying animal.
    It is remarkable that a nation should lay aside the use of the proper generic name of flying animals, *fowl,* Sax. *fugel,* D. *vogel,* the flyer, and substitute the name of the young of those animals, as the generic term. The fact is precisely what it would be to make *lamb,* the generic name of sheep, or *colt,* that of the equine genus.

BIRDCALL, *n.* A little stick, cleft at one end, in which is put a leaf of some plant for imitating the cry of birds. A laurel leaf counterfeits the voice of lapwings; a leek, that of nightingales; &c.   *Encyc.*

BIRDSNEST, *n.* 3. In *cookery,* the nest of a small swallow, of China, and the neighboring countries, delicately tasted, and mixed with soups. This nest is found in the rocks; it is of a hemispherical figure, of the size of a goose egg, and in substance resembles isinglass. In the East, these nests are esteemed a great luxury, and sell at a very high price.   *Encyc.*

Binary arithmetic. Leibniz, in his *Remarks on Chinese Rites and Religion* (1708), tells us that "Fohi, the most ancient prince and philosopher of the Chinese, had understood the origin of things from unity and nothing, i.e. his mysterious figures reveal something of an analogy to Creation, containing the binary arithmetic (and yet hinting at greater things) that I rediscovered after so many thousands of years." The Jesuits identified Fohi with the biblical Noah, while Sir William Jones, the first to realize that Sanskrit and Greek must have had a common ancestor, believed he was the same person as the Buddha.

WEBSTER'S BIRDS

☞ Webster did not know much about American birds. He could probably recognize the BLUE-BIRD, but he placed it with the family of wagtails and pipits (the Motacillidae)—it was removed from that genus in 1769—and separately, indentified it as a species of WARBLER. He records, in a diary entry in 1804, the spring arrival of the first martins, and defines the bird in his dictionary. But most common American birds, like the cardinal, the chickadee, and the blue jay, completely escape his notice. His confused entry for RED-BIRD claims that the term is used not only for both tanagers (the scarlet and the summer, given only by their Latin names) but for the Baltimore oriole, which is not red at all. The titmouse is found only under TIT, in an entry copied from Johnson; Webster seems more interested in the senses in which the word was used "in contempt." He includes BIRD-CALL and QUAIL-PIPE, more secure with these luring devices than with birds themselves. The SCREECH-OWL's cry is not really ominous, he tells us, no more so than the nightingale's. Long before Webster's time Americans realized that their birds were not the same as the English ones, and urged their poets to replace the skylark with the mockingbird. Webster knows that the English and American ROBIN are quite different birds, but most of the European species he defines, not to mention the exotic ones like ABAGUN, cannot be found in America. ☙

BISON, *n.* A quadruped of the bovine genus, usually but improperly called the buffalo. The proper buffalo is a distinct species, peculiar to the warmer climates of the Eastern Continent. The bison is a wild animal, with short, black, rounded horns, with a great interval between their bases. On the shoulders is a large hunch, consisting of a fleshy substance. The head and hunch are covered with a long undulated fleece, of a rust-color, divided into locks. In winter, the whole body is covered in this manner; but in summer, the hind part of the body is naked, and wrinkled. The tail is about a foot long, naked, except a tuft of hairs at the end. The fore parts of the body are very thick and strong; the hind parts are slender and weak. These animals inhabit the interior parts of North America, and some of the mountainous parts of Europe and Asia. *Pennant.*

Pennant alledges that the bison of America is the same species of animal as the bison and aurochs of Europe, the *bonasus* of Aristotle, the *urus* of Cesar, the *bos ferus* or wild ox of Strabo, the *bison* of Pliny, and the *biston* of Oppian.

Cuvier has not separated the bison of America from that of Europe. He considers their identity as doubtful. The former has the legs and tail shorter, and the hairs of its head and neck longer than in the latter.

Regne Anim.

BLACK-WORK, *n.* Iron wrought by black-smiths; so called in distinction from that wrought by white-smiths. *Encyc.*

BLANDILOQUENCE, *n.* Fair, mild, flattering speech.

BLEAK, *a.* 2. Open; vacant; exposed to a free current of air; as a *bleak* hill or shore. This is the true sense of the word; hence cold and cheerless. A *bleak* wind is not so named merely from its coldness, but from its blowing without interruption, on a wide waste; at least this is the sense in America. So in Addison. "Her desolation presents us with nothing but *bleak* and barren prospects."

BLINK, *n.* Blink of ice, is the dazzling whiteness about the horizon, occasioned by the reflection of light from fields of ice at sea.

BLUE-BIRD, *n.* A small bird, a species of Motacilla, very common in the U. States. The upper part of the body is blue, and the throat and breast, of a dirty red. It makes its nest in the hole of a tree.

BOB, *n.* Any little round thing, that plays loosely at the end of a string, cord, or movable machine; a little ornament or pendant that hangs so as to play loosely. *Dryden.*

Our common people apply the word to a knot of worms, on a string, used in fishing for eels.

BOG, *n.* 1. A quagmire covered with grass or other plants. It is defined by *marsh*, and *morass*, but differs from a marsh, as a part from the whole. Wet grounds are *bogs*, which are the softest and too soft to bear a man; *marshes* or fens, which are less soft, but very wet; and *swamps*, which are soft spongy land, upon the surface, but sustain man and beast, and are often mowed.

2. A little elevated spot or clump of earth, in marshes and swamps, filled with roots and grass. [*This is a common use of the word in New-England.*]

BOGGLE, *v.t.* To embarrass with difficulties; *a popular or vulgar use of the word in the United States.*

BOM, *n.* A large serpent found in America, of a harmless nature, and remarkable for uttering a sound like *bom.* *Dict. of Nat. Hist.*

BOMB, *n.* 2. A large shell of cast iron, round and hollow, with a vent to receive a fusee, which is made of wood. This being filled with gunpowder and

BOM. Webster is probably referring to the *aboma,* "one of several large South American serpents of the genus *Constrictor*" (*Webster's New International Dictionary,* 2nd edition). According to the *Oxford English Dictionary,* the BOM is "a huge nonpoisonous snake swallowing deer," scarcely the "harmless" creature defined by Webster.

the fusee driven into the vent, the fusee is set on fire and the bomb is thrown from a mortar, in such a direction as to fall into a fort, city or enemy's camp, when it bursts with great violence and often with terrible effect. The inventor of bombs is not known; they came into common use about the year 1634.

Encyc.

BOMBAST, *n.* Originally a stuff of soft loose texture, used to swell garments. Hence, high sounding words; an inflated style; fustian; a serious attempt, by strained description, to raise a low or familiar subject beyond its rank, which, instead of being sublime, never fails to be ridiculous. *Encyc.*

BONNY-CLABBER, *n.* A word used in Ireland for sour buttermilk.

Johnson.

It is used, in America, for any milk that is turned or become thick in the process of souring, and applied only to that part which is thick.

BONZE, *n.* An Indian priest; a name used in China, Tunkin and the neighboring countries. In China, the Bonzes are the priests of the Fohists, or sect of Fohi. They are distinguished from the laity by their dress. In Japan, they are gentlemen of family. In Tunkin, every pagoda has at least two bonzes belonging to it, and some have thirty or forty. In China, the number of bonzes is estimated at fifty thousand, and they are represented as idle dissolute men.

Encyc.

BOROUGH, *n.* In Connecticut, this word, *borough,* is used for a town or a part of a town, or a village, incorporated with certain privileges, distinct from those of other towns and of cities; as the *Borough* of Bridgeport.

BOTTOM, *n.* 4. A low ground; a dale; a valley; *applied in the U. States to the flat lands adjoining rivers, &c. It is so used in some parts of England.*

Mitford.

BOUNDARY, *n.* A limit; a bound. *Johnson.*

This word is thus used as synonymous with bound. But the real sense is, a visible mark designating a limit. *Bound* is the limit itself or furthest point of extension, and may be an imaginary line; but *boundary* is the thing which ascertains the limit; *terminus,* not *finis.* Thus by a statute of Connecticut, it is enacted that the inhabitants of every town shall procure its *bounds* to be set out by such marks and *boundaries* as may be a plain direction for the future; which marks and *boundaries* shall be a great heap of stones or a ditch of six feet long, &c. This distinction is observed also in the statute of Massachusetts. But the two words are, in ordinary use, confounded.

BOURGEOIS, *n.* [It appears to be a French word, but I know not the reason of its application to types.] A small kind of printing types, in size between long primer and brevier. The type on which the main body of this work is printed.

B

BRAIN, *n.* 1. That soft whitish mass, or viscus, inclosed in the cranium or skull, in which the nerves and spinal marrow terminate, and which is supposed to be the seat of the soul or intelligent principle in man. It is divided above into a right and left hemisphere, and below into six lobes. It is composed of a *cortical* substance, which is external, and a *medullary,* which is internal. From the brain proceed nine pair of nerves, which are distributed principally to the head and neck.   *Hooper.   Encyc.*

BRAMIN, BRAHMIN, *n.* A priest among the Hindoos and other nations of India. There are several orders of Bramins, many of whom are very corrupt in their morals; others live sequestered from the world devoted to superstition and indolence. They are the only persons who understand the Sanscrit, or ancient language of the country, in which their sacred books are written; and to them are European nations indebted for their knowledge of the language. They worship Brama, the supposed creator of the world, but have many subordinate deities.

BRANDY, *n.* An ardent spirit distilled from wine. The same name is now given to spirit distilled from other liquors, and in the U. States particularly to that which is distilled from cyder and peaches.

BRANK, *n.* 1. Buckwheat, a species of polygonum; a grain cultivated mostly for beasts and poultry; but in the U. States, the flour is much used for making breakfast cakes.
2. In some parts of England and Scotland, a *scolding-bridle,* an instrument for correcting scolding women. It consists of a headpiece, which incloses the head of the offender, and of a sharp iron which enters the mouth and restrains the tongue.   *Plott. Encyc.*

BRAVERY, *n.* Courage; heroism; undaunted spirit; intrepidity; gallantry; fearlessness of danger; often united with generosity or dignity of mind which despises meanness and cruelty, and disdains to take advantage of a vanquished enemy.
The duellist, in proving his *bravery,* shows that he thinks it suspected.
Anon.

BRAZIL, BRAZIL-WOOD, *n.* [Port. *braza,* a live coal, or glowing fire. This name was given to the wood for its color, and it is said that King Emanuel of Portugal gave this name to the country in America on account of its producing this wood. It was first named Santa Cruz, by its discoverer, Pedro Alvares Cabral. *Lindley's Narrative of a voyage to Brazil. Med. Rep.* Hex. 2. vol. 3. 200.]

BRAZIL. The country was indeed named for the wood, and Webster may be right about the etymology as well.

BRIDECAKE, *n.* The cake which is made for the guests at a wedding; called, in the U. States, *wedding cake.*

BRIDEGOOM, *n.* [. . . Dan. *brudgom;* a compound of *bride,* and *gum, guma,* a man, which, by our ancestors, was pronounced *goom.* This word, by a mispronouncing of the last syllable, has been corrupted into *bridegroom,* which signifies a *bride's hostler;* groom being a Persian word, signifying a man who has the care of horses. Such a gross corruption or blunder ought not to remain a reproach to philology.] A man newly married; or a man about to be married. The passage of Shakspeare cited by Johnson proves that the last definition is just.
As are those dulcet sounds in break of day,
That creep into the dreaming *bridegroom's* ear,
And summon him to marriage.

BROOK, *n.* A small natural stream of water, or a current flowing from a spring or fountain less than a river. In some parts of America, *run* is used in a like sense; but *run* is also applied to larger streams than *brook.*

BROTH, *n.* 2. In *America,* the word is often applied to foaming water, and especially to a mixture of snow and water in the highways which is called *snow-broth.*

BRUTE, *n.* A beast; any animal destitute of reason, and of course the word comprehends all animals except *man,* but is applied mostly to the larger beasts.
2. A brutal person; a savage in heart or manners; a low bred, unfeeling man.

BUCANEER, BUCANIER, *n.* [Fr. *boucaner,* to broil fish or flesh, to hunt oxen for their skins.] Primarily, a bucaneer is said to be one who dries and smokes flesh or fish after the manner of the Indians. The name was first given to the French settlers in Haiti or Hispaniola, whose business was to hunt wild cattle and swine. It was afterwards applied to the piratical adventurers, English and French, who combined to make depredations on the Spaniards in America. *Encyc.*

BUFFALO, *n.* The Bubalus, a species of the bovine genus, originally from India, but now found in most of the warmer countries of the Eastern Continent. It is larger and less docile than the common ox, and is fond of marshy places and rivers. The name is also applied to wild oxen in general, and particularly to the Bison of North America. *Cyc. Cuvier.*

BUG, *n.* In *common language,* the name of a vast multitude of insects, which infest houses and plants. In *zoology,* this word is applied to the insects arranged under the genus *Cimex*, of which several hundred species are described. Bugs belong to the order of hemipters. They are furnished with a rostrum or beak, with antennae longer than the thorax, and the wings are folded together crosswise. The back is flat, the throat margined, and the feet are formed for running. Some species have no wings. The house-bug, or bed-bug, is a troublesome and disgusting insect.   *Encyc.*

BUGGERY, *n.* The unnatural and detestable crime of carnal intercourse of man or woman with a beast; or of human beings unnaturally with each other. Sodomy.   *Encyc.*

BULL-FIGHT, *n.* A combat with a bull; an amusement among the Spaniards and Portuguese. A horseman, called a *toreador* or *picador* attacks a bull in a circus or inclosed arena, in presence of multitudes of spectators, irritating him with a spear, till the bull rushes upon the horseman, and perhaps dismounts the rider. After the bull has been tormented a long time, the horseman leaves him, and some persons on foot attack him and plunge darts into his neck; and at a signal given by the president, the barbarous sport is ended by the dagger of a *matador*.   *Encyc.*

BURGESS, *n.* 1. An inhabitant of a borough, or walled town; or one who possesses a tenement therein; a citizen or freeman of a borough.   *Blackstone.*
4. Before the revolution, the representatives in the popular branch of the legislature of Virginia, were called *burgesses*, as the *House of Burgesses*. It is now called the *House of Delegates*.

BURGLARY, *n.* The act or crime of nocturnal house breaking, with an intent to commit a felony. To constitute this crime, the act must be committed in the night, or when there is not day-light enough to discern a man's face. It must be in a mansion house, or in an adjoining building which is a part or parcel of the mansion. There must be an actual breaking and an entry; but an opening made by the offender, as by taking out a pane of glass, or lifting a window, raising a latch, picking a lock, or removing any fastening, amounts to a breaking; and a putting in of the hand, after such breaking, is an entry. The act must also be done with an intent to commit felony.   *Blackstone.*

To bury the hatchet, in the striking metaphorical language of American Indians, is to lay aside the instruments of war, forget injuries, and make peace.

BUTTER-MILK, *n.* The milk that remains after the butter is separated from it. Johnson calls this *whey*; but whey is the thin part of the milk after the curd or cheese is separated. Butter-milk in America is not called *whey*.

BULL-FIGHT. Also barbarous, in Webster's view, are COCK-FIGHTs, SCAPAISM, and the SLAVE-TRADE. He does not use the epithet to describe *bear-baiting* or *dogfight*.

C

CABAL, *n.* 1. A number of persons united in some close design; usually to promote their private views in church or state by intrigue. A junto. It is sometimes synonymous with *faction,* but a *cabal* usually consists of fewer men than a party, and the word generally implies close union and secret intrigues. This name was given to the ministry of Charles II., Clifford, Ashley, Buckingham, Arlington, and Lauderdale, the initials of whose names compose the word.

CABOOSE, *n.* 1. The cook-room or kitchen of a ship. In smaller vessels, it is an inclosed fire-place, hearth or stove for cooking, on the main deck. In a ship of war, the cook room is called a galley.   *Mar. Dict.*
  2. A box that covers the chimney in a ship.   *Encyc.*

CADMEAN, CADMIAN, *a.* Relating to Cadmus, a reputed prince of Thebes, who introduced into Greece, the sixteen simple letters of the alphabet . . . These are called Cadmean letters.   *Bryant.*
  This personage may be a fabulous being, or if such a person ever existed, he may have been named from his knowledge of letters, for in the ancient Persian, *kadeem* signified language; Ir. *cuadham,* to tell or relate; *ceadach,* talkative; *ceadal,* a story. Or he may have been named from his eminence or antiquity, **קדם** *kadam,* to precede; Arabic, to excel; whence the sense of priority and antiquity; or his name may denote a man from the East.

CALICO, *n.* In the United States, calico is printed cotton cloth, having not more than two colors. I have never heard this name given to the unprinted

---

☞ C. In the old Etruscan, it was written Ɔ, with the corners rounded, but not inverted; in Arcadian, C, as is now written. [Compiler's note: Webster defines ARCADIAN as "pertaining to Arcadia, a mountainous district in the heart of the Peloponnesus."] ☜

CADMEAN. William Thornton (1759–1828), promoter of a universal alphabet and aptly described, along with Webster, as a man of "flawed earnestness," paid homage to his Greek predecessor in *Cadmus: Or, a Treatise on the Elements of Written Language* (1793). Thornton's alphabet of thirty characters was intended to represent the sounds of English; he expected fifty or so to serve for all known spoken languages. In this goal Thornton anticipated the International Phonetic Alphabet, even if he underestimated the number of phonemes that would need to be symbolized (more than one hundred, not counting the suprasegmentals, as of 2007). Thornton, a self-taught architect, designed the U.S. Capitol; he also worked with John Fitch on the steamboat.

cloth. Calico was originally imported from India, but is now manufactured in Europe and the United States.

CALUMET, *n.* Among the *aboriginals of America,* a pipe, used for smoking tobacco, whose bowl is usually of soft red marble, and the tube a long reed, ornamented with feathers. The calumet is used as a symbol or instrument of peace and war. To accept the calumet, is to agree to the terms of peace, and to refuse it, is to reject them. The calumet of peace is used to seal or ratify contracts and alliances, to receive strangers kindly, and to travel with safety. The calumet of war, differently made, is used to proclaim war.

CAMEL, *n.* 1. A large quadruped used in Asia and Africa for carrying burdens, and for riders. As a genus, the camel belongs to the order of Pecora. The characteristics are; it has no horns; it has six fore teeth in the under jaw; the canine teeth are wide set, three in the upper and two in the lower jaw; and there is a fissure in the upper lip. The dromedary or Arabian camel has one bunch on the back, four callous protuberances on the fore legs and two on the hind legs. The Bactrian camel has two bunches on the back. The Llama of South America is a smaller animal, with a smooth back, small head, fine black eyes, and very long neck. The Pacos or sheep of Chili has no bunch. Camels constitute the riches of an Arabian, without which he could neither subsist, carry on trade nor travel over sandy desarts. Their milk is his common food. By the camel's power of sustaining abstinence from drink, for many days, and of subsisting on a few coarse shrubs, he is peculiarly fitted for the parched and barren lands of Asia and Africa.
2. In Holland, Camel, [or Kameel, as Coxe writes it,] is a machine for lifting ships, and bearing them over the Pampus, at the mouth of the river Y, or over other bars. It is also used in other places, and particularly at the dock in Petersburg, to bear vessels over a bar to Cronstadt. *Coxe. Encyc.*

Camera obscura, or dark chamber, in optics, an apparatus representing an artificial eye, in which the images of external objects, received through a double convex glass, are exhibited distinctly, and in their native colors, on a white matter, placed within the machine, in the focus of the glass.

CANOE, *n.* 1. A boat used by rude nations, formed of the body or trunk of a tree, excavated, by cutting or burning, into a suitable shape. Similar boats are now used by civilized men, for fishing and other purposes. It is impelled by a paddle, instead of an oar.
2. A boat made of bark or skins, used by savages.

CARAVAN, *n.* A company of travellers, pilgrims or merchants, marching or proceeding in a body over the deserts of Arabia, or other region infested with robbers.

CARELESS, *a.* Having no care; heedless; negligent; unthinking; inattentive; regardless; unmindful; followed by *of* or *about;* as a *careless* mother; a mother *careless of* or *about* her children, is an unnatural parent.

CARICATURE, *n.* A figure or description in which beauties are concealed and blemishes exaggerated, but still bearing a resemblance to the object.
Encyc.

CARICATURE, *v.t.* To make or draw a caricature; to represent as more ugly than the life.   *Lyttleton.*

CARNIVAL, CARNAVAL, *n.* The feast or season of rejoicing, before Lent, observed, in Catholic countries, with great solemnity, by feasts, balls, operas, concerts, &c.   *Encyc.*

CAROB, *n.* The carob-tree, *Ceratonia siliqua,* a native of Spain, Italy, and the Levant. It is an evergreen, growing in hedges, and producing long, flat, brown-colored pods, filled with a mealy, succulent pulp, of a sweetish taste. In times of scarcity, these pods are eaten by poor people, but they are apt to cause griping and lax bowels.   *Miller. Encyc.*

CARPENTER, *n.* An artificer who works in timber; a framer and builder of houses, and of ships. Those who build houses are called *house-carpenters,* and those who build ships are called *ship-carpenters.*
In New England, a distinction is often made between the man who frames, and the man who executes the interior wood-work of a house. The framer is the *carpenter,* and the finisher is called a *joiner.* This distinction is noticed by Johnson, and seems to be a genuine English distinction. But in some other parts of America, as in New-York, the term *carpenter* includes both the framer and the joiner; and in truth both branches of business are often performed by the same person. The word is never applied, as in Italy and Spain, to a coach-maker.

CARRIER, *n.* 3. A pigeon that conveys letters from place to place, the letters being tied to the neck.

CART, *n.* A carriage with two wheels, fitted to be drawn by one horse, or by a yoke of oxen, and used in husbandry or commercial cities for carrying heavy commodities. In Great Britain, carts are usually drawn by horses. In America, horse-carts are used mostly in cities, and ox-carts in the country.

CARTESIAN, *a.* Pertaining to the philosopher Des Cartes, or to his philosophy, which taught the doctrine of vortexes round the sun and planets.

CARTESIAN. Descartes' "doctrine of vortices" had been discredited for two hundred years. Still, Webster describes it under VORTEX. Other Cartesian entries are at PINEAL, the gland he supposed was the seat of the soul, and at EGOIST, a believer in "cogito ergo sum." Webster ignores Descartes' lasting contributions.

CASTANET, *n.* An instrument of music formed of small concave shells of ivory or hard wood, shaped like spoons, placed together, fastened to the thumb and beat with the middle finger. This instrument is used by the Spaniards, Moors and Bohemians, as an accompaniment to their dances, sarabands and guitars.   *Span. Dict.   Encyc.*

CASTRATE, *v.t.* 1. To geld; to deprive of the testicles; to emasculate.
2. To take away or retrench, as the obscene parts of a writing.
3. To take out a leaf or sheet from a book, and render it imperfect.

CASUAL, *a.* 3. Taking place, or beginning to exist without an efficient intelligent cause, and without design.
      Atheists assert that the existence of things is *casual.*   *Dwight.*

CATARACT, *n.* 1. A great fall of water over a precipice; as that of Niagara, of the Rhine, Danube and Nile. It is a cascade upon a great scale.
      The tremendous *cataracts* of America thundering in their solitudes. *Irving.*

CATCHUP, CATSUP, *n.* A liquor extracted from mushrooms, used as a sauce.

CATEGORY, *n.* In *logic,* a series or order of all the predicates or attributes contained under a genus. The school philosophers distributed all the objects of our thoughts and ideas into genera or classes. Aristotle made ten categories, viz. substance, quantity, quality, relation, action, passion, time, place, situation and habit.   *Encyc.*

CAT-GUT, *n.* The intestines of sheep or lambs, dried and twisted together, used as strings for violins and other instruments, and for other purposes. Great quantities are imported from Lyons and Italy.

CATTLE, *n.* 2. In the United States, cattle, in common usage, signifies only beasts of the bovine genus, oxen, bulls, cows and their young. In the laws respecting domestic beasts, horses, sheep, asses, mules and swine are distinguished from *cattle,* or neat cattle. Thus the law in Connecticut, requiring "that all the owners of any cattle, sheep or swine, shall ear-mark or brand *all their cattle,* sheep and swine," does not extend to horses. Yet it is probable that a law, giving damages for a trespass committed by *cattle* breaking into an inclosure, would be adjudged to include horses.

CAUCUS, *n.* A word used in America to denote a meeting of citizens to agree upon candidates to be proposed for election to offices, or to concert measures for supporting a party. The origin of the word is not ascertained.

CAUSE, *n.* 5. That which a party or nation pursues; or rather pursuit, prosecution of an object. We say, Bible Societies are engaged in a noble *cause.*

Hence the word *cause* is used to denote that which a person or thing favors; that to which the efforts of an intelligent being are directed; as, to promote religion is to advance the cause of God. So we say, the *cause* of truth or of justice. In all its applications, *cause* retains something of its original meaning, struggle, impelling force, contest, effort to obtain or to effect something.

CAVIAR, *n.* The roes of certain large fish, prepared and salted. The best is made from the roes of the sterlet, sturgeon, sevruga, and beluga, caught in the lakes or rivers of Russia. The roes are put into a bag with a strong brine, and pressed by wringing, and then dried and put in casks, or into cisterns, perforated at bottom, where they are pressed by heavy weights. The poorest sort is trodden with the feet.   *Tooke.*

CELEBRATE, *v.t.* 3. To honor or distinguish by ceremonies and marks of joy and respect; as, to *celebrate* the birthday of Washington; to *celebrate* a marriage.

CENSOR, *n.* 2. One who is empowered to examine all manuscripts and books, before they are committed to the press, and to see that they contain nothing heretical or immoral.   *Encyc.*

CENSUS, *n.* In ancient Rome, an authentic declaration made before the censors, by the citizens, of their names and places of abode. This declaration was registered, and contained an enumeration of all their lands and estates, their quantity and quality, with the wives, children, domestics, tenants, and slaves of each citizen. Hence the word signifies this enumeration or register, a man's whole substance, and the tax imposed according to each man's property.
    2. In the *United States of America*, an enumeration of the inhabitants of all the States, taken by order of the Congress, to furnish the rule of apportioning the representation among the States, and the number of representatives to which each State is entitled in the Congress; also, an enumeration of the inhabitants of a State, taken by order of its legislature.

Master of ceremonies, an officer who superintends the reception of embassadors. A person who regulates the forms to be observed by the company or attendants on a public occasion.

CERES, *n.* In *mythology*, the inventor or goddess of corn, or rather the name of corn deified.
    2. The name of a planet discovered by M. Piozzi, at Palermo in Sicily, in 1801.

CHAMBER-POT, *n.* A vessel used in bedrooms.

CHANCE-MEDLEY, *n.* In *law*, the killing of a person by chance, when the killer is doing a lawful act; for if he is doing an unlawful act, it is felony. As

CERES. Ceres is a dwarf planet, according to a new classification scheme adopted by astronomers in 2006. It had been called an asteroid for more than 150 years—the largest in the solar system—and a planet upon its discovery by Giuseppe Piazzi (not Piozzi), an Italian astronomer who named it "Ceres" a year after he found it. Webster may have conflated the discoverer with Hester Lynch Piozzi, formerly Thrale, in whose household Samuel Johnson was "domesticated" for over sixteen years, and where Mrs. Thrale's salon attracted the likes of Edmund Burke, David Garrick, and Sir Joshua Reynolds, all of them friends of Johnson.

CHANCE-MEDLEY. Johnson's example is of a man "lopping trees by an highway-side."

if a man, when throwing bricks from a house into a street where people are continually passing, after giving warning to passengers to take care, should kill a person, this is chance-medley. But if he gives no warning, and kills a man, it is manslaughter.

CHAOS, *n.* That confusion, or confused mass, in which matter is supposed to have existed, before it was separated into its different kinds and reduced to order, by the creating power of God.

CHAPEL, *n.* 2. A printer's workhouse; said to be so called because printing was first carried on in a chapel. *Bailey. Encyc.*

CHASTE, *n.* 3. In *language,* pure; genuine; uncorrupt; free from barbarous words and phrases, and from quaint, affected, extravagant expressions.

CHEAP, *a.* 1. Bearing a low price, in market; that may be purchased at a low price; that is, at a price as low or lower than the usual price of the article or commodity, or at a price less than the real value. The sense is always comparative; for a price deemed *cheap* at one time is considered *dear* at another.

It is a principle which the progress of political science has clearly established; a principle that illustrates at once the wisdom of the creator and the blindness of human cupidity, that it is *cheaper* to hire the labor of freemen than to compel the labor of slaves. *L. Bacon*

CHESAPEAK, *n.* A bay of the U. States, whose entrance is between Cape Charles and Cape Henry, in Virginia, and which extends northerly into Maryland 270 miles. It receives the waters of the Susquehannah, Potomack, Rappahannock, York, and James Rivers.

CHIMISTRY, *n.* Chimistry is a science, the object of which is to discover the nature and properties of all bodies by analysis and synthesis. *Macquer.*

Chimistry is that science which explains the intimate mutual action of all natural bodies. *Fourcroy.*

Analysis or decomposition, and synthesis or combination, are the two methods which chimistry uses to accomplish its purposes.
Fourcroy. Hooper.

Chimistry may be defined, the science which investigates the composition of material substances, and the permanent changes of constitution which their mutual actions produce. *Ure.*

Chimistry may be defined, that science, the object of which is to discover and explain the changes of composition that occur among the integrant and constituent parts of different bodies. *Henry.*

Chimistry is the science which treats of those events and changes in natural bodies, which are not accompanied by sensible motions.
Thomson.

Chimistry is justly considered as a science, but the practical operations may be denominated an art.

CHIMNEY-CORNER, *n.* The corner of a fire-place, or the space between the fire and the sides of the fire-place. In the Northern States of America, fire-places were formerly made six or eight feet wide, or even more, and a stool was placed by the side of the fire, as a seat for children, and this often furnished a comfortable situation for idlers. As fuel has become scarce, our fire-places are contracted, till in many or most of our dwellings, we have no chimney-corners.

2. In *a more enlarged sense,* the fire-side, or a place near the fire.

CHIMPANZEE, *n.* An animal of the ape kind, a variety of the ourang-outang.
Dict. Nat. Hist.
It is now considered a distinct species. *Cuvier.*

CHORE, *n.* In America, this word denotes small work of a domestic kind, as distinguished from the principal work of the day. It is generally used in the plural, *chores,* which includes the daily or occasional business of feeding cattle and other animals, preparing fuel, sweeping the house, cleaning furniture, &c.

CHOWDER, *n.* In *New England,* a dish of fish boiled with biscuit, &c. In Spanish, *chode* is a paste made of milk, eggs, sugar and flour. In the west of England, *chowder-beer* is a liquor made by boiling black spruce in water and mixing with it melasses.

CHUCKLE-HEAD, *n.* A vulgar word in America, denoting a person with a large head, a dunce. Bailey says, a rattling, noisy, empty fellow.

CIPHER, *n.* 1. In *arithmetic,* an Arabian or Oriental character, of this form 0, which, standing by itself, expresses nothing, but increases or diminishes the value of other figures, according to its position. In whole numbers, when placed at the right hand of a figure, it increases its value ten fold; but in decimal fractions, placed at the left hand of a figure, it diminishes the value of that figure ten fold.

CIRCLE, *n.* 1. In *geometry,* a plane figure comprehended by a single curve line, called its circumference, every part of which is equally distant from a point called the center. Of course all lines drawn from the center to the circumference or periphery, are equal to each other.

CIRCUMFORANEAN, CIRCUMFORANEOUS, *a.* Going about; walking or wandering from house to house; as a *circumforaneous* fidler or piper; *circum-foraneous* wits. *Addison, Spect.* 47.

Circumforaneous musicians, male and female, are daily seen at the doors of hotels, in France; and sometimes they enter the room, where a company is dining, and entertain them with music; expecting a franc or a few sous as a reward. *W.*

CITIZEN, *n. In the U. States,* a person, native or naturalized, who has the privilege of exercising the elective franchise, or the qualifications which enable him to vote for rulers, and to purchase and hold real estate.

If the *citizens* of the U. States should not be free and happy, the fault will be entirely their own. *Washington.*

CIVILIZATION, *n.* The act of civilizing, or the state of being civilized; the state of being refined in manners, from the grossness of savage life, and improved in arts and learning.

CLASSICAL, *a.* Relating to ancient Greek and Roman authors of the first rank or estimation, which, in modern times, have been and still are studied as the best models of fine writing. Thus, Aristotle, Plato, Demosthenes, Thucydides, &c, among the Greeks, and Cicero, Virgil, Livy, Sallust, Cesar, and Tacitus, among the Latins, are *classical* authors. Hence, 2. Pertaining to writers of the first rank among the moderns; being of the first order; constituting the best model or authority as an author; as, Addison and Johnson are English *classical* writers. Hence *classical* denotes pure, chaste, correct, refined; as a *classical* taste; a *classical* style.

At Liverpool, Roscoe is like Pompey's column at Alexandria, towering alone in *classic* dignity. *Irving.*

CLEVER, *a.* 1. Fit; suitable; convenient; proper; commodious. *Pope.*
2. Dextrous; adroit; ready; that performs with skill or address.
Addison.
3. In *New England,* good-natured, possessing an agreeable mind or disposition. In *Great Britain,* this word is applied to the body or its movements, in its literal sense; in *America,* it is applied chiefly to the mind, temper, disposition. In Great Britain, a *clever man* is a dextrous man, one who performs an act with skill or address. In *New-England,* a clever man is a man of a pleasing obliging disposition, and amiable manners, but often implying a moderate share of talents. Fitness, suitableness, gives both senses analogically; the former applied to the body; the latter, to the mind, or its qualities. It is a colloquial word, but sometimes found in respectable writings.

In some of the United States, it is said this word is applied to the intellect, denoting ingenious, knowing, discerning.

CLOCK, *n.* A machine, consisting of wheels moved by weights, so constructed that by a uniform vibration of a pendulum, it measures time, and its divisions, hours, minutes and seconds, with great exactness. It indicates the hour by the stroke of a small hammer on a bell.

The phrases, *what o'clock is it? it is nine o'clock*, seem to be contracted from *what of the clock? it is nine of the clock*.

2. A figure or figured work in the ankle of a stocking. *Swift.*

CLOTHIER, *n.* In English authors, a man who makes cloths; a maker of cloth. *Johnson.*

In this sense, I believe it is not used in the U. States; certainly not in New England.

2. In *America*, a man whose occupation is to full and dress cloth.

CLOVE, *n.* A cleft; a fissure; a gap; a ravine. This word, though properly an appellative, is not often used as such in English; but is appropriated to particular places, that are real clefts, or which appear as such; as the *Clove* of Kaaterskill, in the state of New-York, and the Stony *Clove*. It is properly a Dutch word. *Journ. of Science.*

COACH, *n.* [. . . This word seems to be radically a couch or bed, (Fr. *couche, coucher*) a covered bed on wheels, for conveying the infirm.] A close vehicle for commodious traveling, borne on four wheels, and drawn by horses or other animals. It differs from a chariot in having seats in front, as well as behind. It is a carriage of state, or for pleasure, or for travelling.

Hackney-coach, a coach kept for hire. In some cities, they are licensed by authority, and numbered, and the rates of fare fixed by law.

Mail-coach, a coach that carries the public mails.

Stage-coach, a coach that regularly conveys passengers from town to town. [See STAGE.]

COCK-FIGHT, COCK-FIGHTING, *n.* A match or contest of cocks; a barbarous sport of the ancients, and moderns, in which cocks are set to fight with each other, till one or the other is conquered. *Bacon. Addison.*

COFFEE, *n.* 2. A drink made from the berry of the coffee-tree, by decoction. The berry is first roasted, and then ground in a mill, and boiled. The use of it is said to have been introduced into France by Thevenot, the traveler, and into England, in 1652, by a Greek servant, called Pasqua. The best coffee is said to be the Mocha coffee from Arabia Felix. The coffee of Java, Bourbon and the West Indies constitutes an important article of commerce.

COLONY, *n.* 1. A company or body of people transplanted from their mother country to a remote province or country to cultivate and inhabit it, and remaining subject to the jurisdiction of the parent state; as the British *colonies* in America or the Indies; the Spanish *colonies* in South America.

When such settlements cease to be subject to the parent state, they are no longer denominated *colonies*.

The first settlers of New England were the best of Englishmen, well educated, devout christians, and zealous lovers of liberty. There was never a *colony* formed of better materials.   *Ames.*

Colored people, black people, Africans or their descendants, mixed or unmixed.

COLUMBIUM, *n.* [from *Columbia,* America.] A metal first discovered in an ore or oxyd, found in Connecticut, at New-London, near the house of Gov. Winthrop, and by him transmitted to Sir Hans Sloane, by whom it was deposited in the British museum. The same metal was afterwards discovered in Sweden, and called *tantalum,* and its ore *tantalite.*   *Cleaveland.*

COMET, *n.* An opake, spherical, solid body, like a planet, but accompanied with a train of light, performing revolutions about the sun, in an elliptical orbit, having the sun in one of its foci. In its approach to its perihelion, it becomes visible, and after passing its perihelion, it departs into remote regions and disappears. In popular language, comets are *tailed, bearded* or *hairy,* but these terms are taken from the appearance of the light which attends them, which, in different positions with respect to the sun, exhibits the form of a tail or train, a beard, or a border of hair. When the comet is westward of the sun and rises or sets before it, the light appears in the morning like a train beginning at the body of the comet and extending westward and diverging in proportion to its extent. Thus the comet of 1769, [which I saw,] when it rose in the morning, presented a luminous train that extended nearly from the horizon to the meridian. When the comet and the sun are opposite, the earth being between them, the comet is, to the view, immersed in its train and the light appears around its body like a fringe or border of hair. From the train of a comet, this body has obtained the popular name of a *blazing star.*

Herschel observed several comets, which appeared to have no nucleus, but to be merely collections of vapor condensed about a center.   *Cyc.*

COMMEMORATION, *n.* The act of calling to remembrance, by some solemnity; the act of honoring the memory of some person or event, by solemn celebration. The feast of shells at Plymouth in Massachusetts is an annual *commemoration* of the first landing of our ancestors in 1620.

Commonplace-book, a book in which are registered such facts, opinions or observations as are deemed worthy of notice or remembrance, so disposed that any one may be easily found. Hence *commonplace* is used as an epithet to denote what is common or often repeated, or trite; as a *commonplace* observation.

COMPENSATE, *v.t.* 1. To give equal value to; to recompense; to give an equivalent for services, or an amount lost or bestowed; to return or bestow that which makes good a loss, or is estimated a sufficient remuneration; as, to *compensate* a laborer for his work, or a merchant for his losses.

2. To be equivalent in value or effect to; to counterbalance; to make amends for.

> The length of the night and the dews do *compensate* the heat of the day.
>
> *Bacon.*

> The pleasures of sin never compensate the sinner for the miseries he suffers, even in this life.
>
> *Anon.*

COMPLETE, *a.* In strict propriety, this word admits of no comparison; for that which is *complete,* cannot be more or less so. But as the word, like many others, is used with some indefiniteness of signification, it is customary to qualify it with *more, most, less* and *least. More complete, most complete, less complete,* are common expressions.

CONCUBINAGE, *n.* In some countries, concubinage is a marriage of an inferior kind, or performed with less solemnity than a true or formal marriage; or marriage with a woman of inferior condition, to whom the husband does not convey his rank or quality. This is said to be still in use in Germany. *Encyc.*

CONCUPISCENCE, *n.* Lust; unlawful or irregular desire of sexual pleasure. In a more general sense, the coveting of carnal things, or an irregular appetite for worldly good; inclination for unlawful enjoyments.

> We know even secret *concupiscence* to be sin.
>
> *Hooker.*

CONDESCENSION, *n.* Voluntary descent from rank, dignity or just claims; relinquishment of strict right; submission to inferiors in granting requests or performing acts which strict justice does not require. Hence, courtesy.

CONDOR, *n.* The largest species of fowl hitherto discovered; a native of South America. Some naturalists class it with the vulture; others, with the eagle. The wings of the largest, when expanded, are said to extend 15 or 18 feet; and the fowl has strength to bear off a calf or a deer.

> *Dict. Nat. Hist.*

> The size of the Condor has been greatly exaggerated. It is about the size of the *Lämmer-geyer* or vulture of the Alps, which it resembles in its habits. It is properly a vulture. *Humboldt. Cuvier.*

CONGRESS, *n.* 1. A meeting of individuals; an assembly of envoys, commissioners, deputies, &c., particularly a meeting of the representatives of several courts, to concert measures for their common good, or to adjust their mutual concerns. *Europe.*

2. The assembly of delegates of the several British Colonies in America, which united to resist the claims of Great Britain in 1774, and which declared the colonies independent.

3. The assembly of the delegates of the several United States, after the declaration of Independence, and until the adoption of the present constitution, and the organization of the government in 1789. During these periods, the congress consisted of one house only.

4. The assembly of senators and representatives of the several states of North America, according to the present constitution, or political compact, by which they are united in a federal republic; the legislature of the United States, consisting of two houses, a senate and a house of representatives. Members of the senate are elected for six years, but the members of the house of representatives are chosen for two years only. Hence the united body of senators and representatives for the two years, during which the representatives hold their seats, is called *one congress.* Thus we say the first or second session of the *sixteenth* congress.

CONJURE, *v.t.* To expel, to drive or to affect, in some manner, by magic arts, as by invoking the Supreme Being, or by the use of certain words, characters or ceremonies to engage supernatural influence; as, to *conjure up* evil spirits, or to *conjure down* a tempest; to *conjure* the stars.

Note. It is not easy to define this word, nor any word of like import; as the practices of conjurors are little known, or various and indefinite. The use of this word indicates that an oath or solemn invocation originally formed a part of the ceremonies.

CONSCIENCE, *n.* . . . Conscience is called by some writers the *moral sense,* and considered as an original faculty of our nature. Others question the propriety of considering conscience as a distinct faculty or principle. They consider it rather as the general principle of moral approbation or disapprobation, applied to one's own conduct and affections; alledging that our notions of right and wrong are not to be deduced from a single principle or faculty, but from various powers of the understanding and will.
Encyc.   Hucheson.   Reid.   Edin. Encyc.

CONTEMPT, *n.* 1.The act of despising; the act of viewing or considering and treating as mean, vile and worthless; disdain; hatred of what is mean or deemed vile. This word is one of the strongest expressions of a mean opinion which the language affords.

Nothing, says Longinus, can be great, the *contempt* of which is great.
Addison.

CONTEMPTIBLE, *a.* 1. Worthy of contempt; that deserves scorn, or disdain; despicable; mean; vile. Intemperance is a *contemptible* vice. No plant or animal is so *contemptible* as not to exhibit evidence of the wonderful power and wisdom of the Creator.

    The pride that leads to duelling is a *contemptible* passion.

CONTINENTAL, *a.* Pertaining or relating to a continent; as the *continental powers* of Europe. In America, pertaining to the United States, as *continental money*, in distinction from what pertains to the separate states; *a word much used during the revolution.*

CONTRAST, *n.* Opposition or dissimilitude of figures, by which one contributes to the visibility or effect of the other.   *Johnson.*

    Contrast, in this sense, is applicable to things of a similar kind. We never speak of a *contrast* between a man and a mountain, or between a dog and a tree; but we observe the *contrast* between an oak and a shrub, and between a palace and a cottage.

    3. Opposition of things or qualities; or the placing of opposite things in view, to exhibit the superior excellence of one to more advantage. What a *contrast* between modesty and impudence, or between a wellbred man and a clown!

COOP, *n.* 1. A box of boards, grated or barred on one side, for keeping fowls in confinement. It is usually applied to long boxes for keeping poultry for fattening or conveyance on board of ships, as *cage* is used for a small box to keep singing birds in houses. I do not know that it is ever used in America for a *pen* to confine other animals.

COPYRIGHT, *n.* The sole right which an author has in his own original literary compositions; the exclusive right of an author to print, publish and vend his own literary works, for his own benefit; the like right in the hands of an assignee.

CORAL, *n.* 1. In *zoology*, a genus belonging to the order of vermes zoophyta. The trunk is radicated, jointed and calcarious. The species are distinguished by the form of their branches, and are found in the ocean adhering to stones, bones, shells, &c. Coral was formerly supposed to be a vegetable substance, but is now known to be composed of a congeries of animals. Coral is red, white and black. It is properly the shells of marine animals of the polype kind, consisting of calcarious earth combined with gelatine and other animal matter. In the South Sea, the isles are mostly coral rocks covered with earth.

                               Encyc.   Nicholson.

CORSET, *n.* A boddice; jumps; something worn to give shape to the body; used by ladies and dandies.

COSCINOMANCY, *n.* The art or practice of divination, by suspending a sieve and taking it between two fingers, or by fixing it to the point of a pair of shears, then repeating a formula of words, and the names of persons suspected. If the sieve trembles, shakes or turns, when any name is repeated, the person is deemed guilty. This divination is mentioned by Theocritus, and is said to be still practiced in some parts of England. The practice and the name are strangers in America.

COTTON-GIN, *n.* A machine to separate the seeds from cotton, invented by that celebrated mechanician, E. Whitney.

COTTON-PLANT, COTTON-SHRUB, *n.* . . . In the southern states of America, the cotton cultivated is distinguished into three kinds; the *nankeen cotton,* so called from its color; the *green seed cotton,* producing white cotton with green seeds. These grow in the middle and upper country, and are called short staple cotton. The *black seed cotton,* cultivated in the lower country near the sea, and on the isles near the shore, produces cotton of a fine, white, silky appearance, very strong and of a long staple. The seeds of the long staple cotton are separated by roller-gins. The seeds of the short staple cotton are separated with more difficulty, by a saw-gin invented by E. Whitney.   *Ramsay. Drayton.*

COUNTERBALANCE, *v.t.* To weigh against; to weigh against with an equal weight; to act against with equal power or effect; to countervail. A column of thirty inches of quicksilver, and a column of thirty-two feet of water, *counterbalance* the weight of a like column of the whole atmosphere. The pleasures of sin never *counterbalance* the pain, misery and shame which follow the commission of it.

COUPLE, *n.* 1. Two of the same species or kind, and near in place, or considered together; as a *couple* of men; a *couple* of oranges. I have planted a *couple* of cherry trees. We cannot call a horse and an ox a couple, unless we add a generic term. Of a horse and ox feeding in a pasture, we should say, *a couple of animals.* Among huntsmen and soldiers, *brace* is used for couple; as a *brace* of ducks; a *brace* of pistols. *Couple* differs from *pair,* which implies strictly, not only things of the same kind, but likeness, equality or customary association. A *pair* is a *couple;* but a *couple* may or may not be a *pair.*

COURT, *n.* 10. In *the U. States,* a legislature consisting of two houses; as the *General Court* of Massachusetts. The original constitution of Connecticut established a *General Court* in 1639.   *B. Trumbull.*

COW, *n.* The female of the bovine genus of animals; a quadruped with cloven hoofs, whose milk furnishes an abundance of food and profit to the farmer.

CRANIOSCOPY, *n.* The science of the eminences produced in the cranium by the brain, intended to discover the particular part of the brain in which reside the organs which influence particular passions or faculties.

Ed. Encyc.

CREATE, *v.t.* 5. To make or produce, by new combinations of matter already created, and by investing these combinations with new forms, constitutions and qualities; to shape and organize.

God *created* man in his own image. Gen. i.

CREATURE, *n.* That which is created; every being besides the Creator, or every thing not self-existent. The sun, moon and stars; the earth, animals, plants, light, darkness, air, water, &c., are the *creatures* of God.

CREDENTIALS, *n. plu.* [*Rarely or never used in the singular.*] That which gives credit; that which gives a title or claim to confidence; the warrant on which belief, credit or authority is claimed, among strangers; as the letters of commendation and power given by a government to an embassador or envoy, which give him credit at a foreign court. So the power of working miracles given to the apostles may be considered as their *credentials,* authorizing them to propagate the gospel, and entitling them to credit.

CREEPER, *n.* 5. A genus of birds, the *Certhia,* or ox-eye, of many species. These birds run along the body or branch of a tree, and when they observe a person near, they run to the side opposite, so as to keep out of sight. *Encyc.*

CREOLE, *n.* In the *West Indies* and *Spanish America,* a native of those countries descended from European ancestors.

CRETIN, *n.* A name given to certain deformed and helpless idiots in the Alps.

CRIB, *n.* 5. A small building, raised on posts, for storing Indian corn.

U. States.

CRITIC, *n.* 1. A person skilled in judging of the merit of literary works; one who is able to discern and distinguish the beauties and faults of writing. In a more general sense, a person skilled in judging with propriety of any combination of objects, or of any work of art; and particularly of what are denominated the *Fine Arts.* A critic is one who, from experience, knowledge, habit or taste, can perceive the difference between propriety and impropriety, in objects or works presented to his view; between the natural and unnatural; the high and the low, or lofty and mean; the congruous and incongruous; the correct and incorrect, according to the established rules of the art.

CROCK, *n.* An earthen vessel; a pot or pitcher; a cup.   *Obs.*

CRUISE, *v.i.* To sail back and forth, or to rove on the ocean in search of an enemy's ships for capture, or for protecting commerce; or to rove for plunder as a pirate. The admiral *cruised* between the Bahama isles and Cuba. We *cruised* off Cape Finisterre. A pirate was *cruising* in the gulf of Mexico.

CRUSTY, *a.* 2. Peevish; snappish; morose; surly; *a word used in familiar discourse, but not deemed elegant.*

CUBE, *n.* 2. In arithmetic, the product of a number multiplied into itself, and that product multiplied into the same number; or it is formed by multiplying any number twice by itself; as, 4X4=16, and 16X4=64, the cube of 4.

CUCKINGSTOOL, *n.* An engine for punishing scolds and refractory women; also brewers and bakers; called also a *tumbrel* and a *trebuchet.* The culprit was seated on the stool and thus immersed in water.   *Old Eng. Law.*

CULTIVATION, *n.* The art or practice of tilling and preparing for crops; husbandry; the management of land. Land is often made better by *cultivation.* Ten acres under good *cultivation* will produce more than twenty when badly tilled.
    2. Study, care and practice directed to improvement, correction, enlargement or increase; the application of the means of improvement; as, men may grow wiser by the *cultivation* of talents; they may grow better by *cultivation* of the mind, of virtue, and of piety.

CUPIDITY, *n.* An eager desire to possess something; an ardent wishing or longing; inordinate or unlawful desire of wealth or power. It is not used, I believe, for the animal appetite, like lust or concupiscence, but for desire of the mind.
        No property is secure when it becomes large enough to tempt the *cupidity* of
        indigent power.   *Burke.*

CURFEW, *n.* The ringing of a bell or bells at night, as a signal to the inhabitants to rake up their fires and retire to rest. This practice originated in England from an order of William the conqueror, who directed that at the ringing of the bell, at eight o'clock every one should put out his light and go to bed. This word is not used in America; although the practice of ringing a bell, at nine o'clock, continues in many places, and is considered in New England, as a signal for people to retire from company to their own abodes; and in general, the signal is obeyed.

CURIOSITY, *n.* A strong desire to see something novel, or to discover something unknown, either by research or inquiry; a desire to gratify the senses with a sight of what is new or unusual, or to gratify the mind with new discoveries; inquisitiveness. A man's *curiosity* leads him to view the ruins of Balbec, to investigate the origin of Homer, to discover the component parts of a mineral, or the motives of another's actions.

CURTAIN-LECTURE, *n.* Reproof given in bed by a wife to her husband.
Addison.

CUSTOMER, *n.* 2. One who frequents or visits any place for procuring what he wants. We say, a mill has many *customers.* Hence a person who receives supplies is called a *customer;* the smith, the shoemaker and the tailor have their *customers;* and the coffee-house has its *customers.*

CYMBAL, *n.* 1. A musical instrument used by the ancients, hollow and made of brass, somewhat like a kettle-drum; but the precise form is not ascertained.
    2. A mean instrument used by gypsies and vagrants, made of a steel wire, in a triangular form, on which are passed five rings, which are touched and shifted along the triangle with an iron rod held in the left hand, while it is supported in the right by a ring, to give it free motion.   *Encyc.*

CYPRESS, *n.* A genus of plants or trees. The most remarkable are the sempervirens or common cypress, the evergreen American cypress or white cedar, and the disticha or deciduous American cypress. The wood of these trees is remarkable for its durability. The coffins in which the Athenian heroes and the mummies of Egypt were deposited, are said to have been made of the first species.   *Encyc.*
    2. The emblem of mourning for the dead, cypress branches having been anciently used at funerals.
      Had success attended the Americans, the death of Warren would have been sufficient to damp the joys of victory, and the *cypress* would have been united with the laurel.   *Eliot's Biog.*

CZAR, *n.* A king; a chief; a title of the emperor of Russia; pronounced *tzar,* and so written by good authors.

C

CURTAIN-LECTURE. This is straight out of Johnson, but too good to leave out.

D

DABBLER, *n.* One who plays in water or mud. 2. One who dips slightly into any thing; one who meddles, without going to the bottom; a superficial meddler; as a *dabbler* in politics.

DACTYLOLOGY, *n.* The act or the art of communicating ideas or thoughts by the fingers. Deaf and dumb persons acquire a wonderful dexterity in this art.

DAD, DADDY, *n.* Father; a word used by infants, from whom it is taken. The first articulations of infants or young children are *dental* or *labial;* dental, in *tad, dad,* and labial, in *mamma, papa.*

DAMAGE, *n.* Any hurt, injury or harm to one's estate; any loss of property sustained; any hinderance to the increase of property; or any obstruction to the success of an enterprise. A man suffers *damage* by the destruction of his corn, by the burning of his house, by the detention of a ship which defeats a profitable voyage, or by the failure of a profitable undertaking. *Damage* then is any actual loss, or the prevention of profit. It is usually and properly applied to property, but sometimes to reputation and other things which are valuable. But in the latter case, *injury* is more correctly used.

DAMSEL, *n.* A young woman. Formerly, a young man or woman of noble or genteel extraction; as *Damsel* Pepin; *Damsel* Richard, prince of Wales. It is now used only of young women, and is applied to any class of young unmarried women, unless to the most vulgar, and sometimes to country girls.

This word is rarely used in conversation, or even in prose writings of the present day; but it occurs frequently in the scriptures, and in poetry.

☞ D. It is never quiescent in English words, except in a rapid utterance of such words as *handkerchief.* ☜

DANCE, *n.* In a general sense, a leaping and frisking about. Appropriately, a leaping or stepping with motions of the body adjusted to the measure of a tune, particularly by two or more in concert. A lively brisk exercise or amusement, in which the movements of the persons are regulated by art, in figure, and by the sound of instruments, in measure.

2. A tune by which dancing is regulated, as the minuet, the waltz, the cotillon, &c.

DANDY, *n.* In *modern usage,* a male of the human species, who dresses himself like a doll, and who carries his character on his back.

DARK, *a.* 3. Gloomy; disheartening; having unfavorable prospects; as a *dark* time in political affairs.

> There is in every true woman's heart a spark of heavenly fire, which beams and blazes in the *dark* hour of adversity. *Irving.*

DAY, *n.* 1. That part of the time of the earth's revolution on its axis, in which its surface is presented to the sun; the part of the twenty four hours when it is light; or the space of time between the rising and setting of the sun; called the *artificial* day.

> And God called the light *day.* Gen. i.

2. The whole time or period of one revolution of the earth on its axis, or twenty four hours; called the *natural* day.

> And the evening and the morning were the first *day.* Gen. i.

In this sense, the day may commence at any period of the revolution. The Babylonians began the day at sun-rising; the Jews, at sun-setting; the Egyptians, at midnight, as do several nations in modern times, the British, French, Spanish, American, &c. This day, in reference to civil transactions, is called the *civil* day. Thus with us the day when a legal instrument is dated, begins and ends at midnight.

7. Time of commemorating an event; anniversary; the same day of the month, in any future year. We celebrate the *day* of our Savior's birth.

DEAF, *n.* [. . . The true English pronunciation of this word is *deef,* as appears from the poetry of Chaucer, who uniformly makes it rhyme with *leaf;* and this proof is confirmed by poetry in the works of Sir W. Temple. Such was the pronunciation which our ancestors brought from England. The word is in analogy with *leaf, sheaf,* and the long sound of the vowels naturally precedes the semi-vowel *f. Def,* from the Danish and Swedish pronunciation, is an anomaly in English of a singular kind, there being not another word like it in the language. See Chaucer's Wife of Bath's Prologue.]

DEBACLE, *n.* The geological deluge, which is supposed to have swept the surface of the earth, and to have conveyed the fragments of rocks, and the

DEAF. Sir William Temple (1628–99) was a celebrated English statesman and sometime poet. The critic Henry Hallam said of him, "if his thoughts are not very striking, they are commonly just." Hallam may have been thinking of Temple's line "the greatest pleasure of life is love." ☞

remains of animals and vegetables, to a distance from their native localities.
Ed. Encyc.

DEBT, *n.* 1. That which is due from one person to another, whether money, goods, or services; that which one person is bound to pay or perform to another; as the *debts* of a bankrupt; the *debts* of a nobleman. It is a common misfortune or vice to be in *debt*.
> When you run in *debt*, you give to another power over your liberty.
> *Franklin.*

DECAY, *n.* Gradual failure of health, strength, soundness, prosperity, or any species of excellence or perfection; decline to a worse or less perfect state; tendency towards dissolution or extinction; a state of depravation or diminution. Old men feel the *decay* of the body. We perceive the *decay* of the faculties in age. We lament the *decay* of virtue and patriotism in the state. The northern nations invaded the Roman Empire, when in a state of *decay*.

DECLARATION, *n.* 4. A public annunciation; proclamation; as the *Declaration* of Independence, July 4, 1776.

DECORUM, *n.* 1. Propriety of speech or behavior; suitableness of speech and behavior, to one's own character, and to the characters present, or to the place and occasion; seemliness; decency; opposed to rudeness, licentiousness, or levity.
> To speak and behave with *decorum* is essential to good breeding.

DEFIANCE, *n.* 1. A daring; a challenge to fight; invitation to combat; a call to an adversary to encounter, if he dare. Goliath bid *defiance* to the army of Israel. 3. Contempt of opposition or danger; a daring or resistance that implies the contempt of an adversary, or of any opposing power. Men often transgress the law and act in *defiance* of authority.

DEFINE, *v.t.* 4. To determine or ascertain the extent of the meaning of a word; to ascertain the signification of a term; to explain what a word is understood to express; as, to *define* the words, *virtue, courage, belief,* or *charity.*

DEFORM, *v.t.* 1. To mar or injure the form; to alter that form or disposition of parts which is natural and esteemed beautiful, and thus to render it displeasing to the eye; to disfigure; as, a hump on the back *deforms* the body.

2. To render ugly or displeasing, by exterior applications or appendages; as, to *deform* the face by paint, or the person by unbecoming dress.

4. To injure and render displeasing or disgusting; to disgrace; to disfigure moral beauty; as, all vices *deform* the character of rational beings.

DEFRAUD, *v.t.* 1. To deprive of right, either by obtaining something by deception or artifice, or by taking something wrongfully without the knowledge or consent of the owner; to cheat; to cozen; followed by *of* before the thing taken; as, to *defraud* a man *of* his right.

The agent who embezzles public property, *defrauds* the state.

The man who by deception obtains a price for a commodity above its value, *defrauds* the purchaser.

2. To withhold wrongfully from another what is due to him. *Defraud* not the hireling of his wages.

3. To prevent one wrongfully from obtaining what he may justly claim.

A man of fortune who permits his son to consume the season of education in hunting, shooting, or in frequenting horse-races, assemblies, &c., *defrauds* the community of a benefactor, and bequeaths them a nuisance.   *Paley.*

DEGENERACY, *n.* 2. In *morals*, decay of virtue; a growing worse; departure from the virtues of ancestors; desertion of that which is good. We speak of the *degeneracy* of men in modern times, or of the *degeneracy* of manners, of the age, of virtue, &c., sometimes without reason.

DELEGATE, *v.t.* 1. To send away; appropriately, to send on an embassy; to send with power to transact business, as a representative. The President *delegated* three commissioners to the court of St. Cloud.

DELIGHT, *v.t.* 1. To affect with great pleasure; to please highly; to give or afford high satisfaction or joy; as, a beautiful landscape *delights* the eye; harmony *delights* the ear; the good conduct of children, and especially their piety, *delights* their parents.

DELUGE, *n.* 1. Any overflowing of water; an inundation; a flood; a swell of water over the natural banks of a river or shore of the ocean, spreading over the adjacent land. But appropriately, the great flood or overflowing of the earth by water, in the days of Noah; according to the common chronology, Anno Mundi, 1656.   Gen. vi.

DEMOCRACY, *n.* Government by the people; a form of government, in which the supreme power is lodged in the hands of the people collectively, or in which the people exercise the powers of legislation. Such was the government of Athens.

DEMOCRAT, *n.* One who adheres to a government by the people, or favors the extension of the right of suffrage to all classes of men.

DENTIFRICE, *n.* A powder or other substance to be used in cleaning the teeth. Burnt shells and charcoal pulverized make an excellent dentifrice.

DELUGE. Following Bishop Ussher, Webster knows the date of the biblical flood to be 2348 B.C., i.e., the 1,656th year in the history of the world. ☞

DEPEND, *v.i.* 2. To be connected with any thing, as the cause of its existence or of its operation and effects; to rely on; to have such connection with any thing as a cause, that without it, the effect would not be produced; followed by *on* or *upon*. We *depend on* God for existence; we *depend on* air for respiration; vegetation *depends on* heat and moisture; the infant *depends on* its parents for support; the peace of society *depends on* good laws and a faithful administration.

5. To rely; to rest with confidence; to trust; to confide; to have full confidence or belief. We *depend on* the word or assurance of our friends. We *depend on* the arrival of the mail at the usual hour. *Depend on* it, the knave will deceive us.

DEPENDENCE, DEPENDENCY, *n.* 5. Reliance; confidence; trust; a resting on; as, we may have a firm *dependence* on the promises of God.

DEPHLOGISTICATED, *pp.* Deprived of phlogiston. *Dephlogisticated air*, is an elastic fluid capable of supporting animal life and flame much longer than common air. It is now called *oxygen, oxygen gas,* or *vital air.*

DEROGATORY, *a.* Detracting or tending to lessen by taking something from; that lessens the extent, effect or value: with *to.* Let us entertain no opinions *derogatory to* the honor of God, or his moral government. Let us say nothing *derogatory to* the merit of our neighbor.

DESIDERATUM, *n.* That which is desired; that which is not possessed, but which is desirable; any perfection or improvement which is wanted. The longitude is a *desideratum* in navigation. A tribunal to settle national disputes without war is a great *desideratum.*

DESIRE, *n.* 1. An emotion or excitement of the mind, directed to the attainment or possession of an object from which pleasure, sensual, intellectual or spiritual, is expected; a passion excited by the love of an object, or uneasiness at the want of it, and directed to its attainment or possession. *Desire* is a wish to possess some gratification or source of happiness which is supposed to be *obtainable.* A *wish* may exist for some thing that is or is not *obtainable.* Desire, when directed solely to sensual enjoyment, differs little from appetite. In other languages, desire is expressed by longing or reaching towards, and when it is ardent or intense, it approaches to longing, but the word in English usually expresses less than longing.

DETER, *v.t.* To discourage and stop by fear; to stop or prevent from acting or proceeding, by danger, difficulty or other consideration which disheartens, or countervails the motive for an act. We are often *deterred* from our duty by trivial difficulties. The state of the road or a cloudy sky may *deter* a man from undertaking a journey.

A million of frustrated hopes will not *deter* us from new experiments.

M. Mason.

DIALECT, *n.* The form or idiom of a language, peculiar to a province, or to a kingdom or state; consisting chiefly in differences of orthography or pronunciation. The Greek language is remarkable for four dialects, the Attic, Ionic, Doric and Eolic. A dialect is the branch of a parent language, with such local alterations as time, accident and revolutions may have introduced among descendants of the same stock or family, living in separate or remote situations. But in regard to a large portion of words, many languages, which are considered as distinct, are really dialects of one common language.

DIAMOND, *n.* A mineral, gem or precious stone, of the most valuable kind, remarkable for its hardness, as it scratches all other minerals. When pure, the diamond is usually clear and transparent, but it is sometimes colored. In its rough state, it is commonly in the form of a roundish pebble, or of octahedral crystals. It consists of carbon, and when heated to 14° Wedgewood, and exposed to a current of air, it is gradually, but completely combustible. When pure and transparent, it is said to be of the first water.

Encyc. Kirwan. Cleaveland.

DIET, *n.* 2. Food regulated by a physician, or by medical rules; food prescribed for the prevention or cure of disease, and limited in kind or quantity. I restrained myself to a regular *diet* of flesh once a day.

DIFFUSE, *v.t.* 2. To spread; to send out or extend in all directions; to disperse. Flowers *diffuse* their odors. The fame of Washington is *diffused* over Europe. The knowledge of the true God will be *diffused* over the earth.

DIGAMMA, *n.* The name of F, most absurdly given to that letter, when first invented or used by the Eolians, on account of its figure. A letter should be named from its sound, and not from its shape. The letter is *ef*.

DIGNITY, *n.* True honor; nobleness or elevation of mind, consisting in a high sense of propriety, truth and justice, with an abhorrence of mean and sinful actions; opposed to *meanness*. In this sense, we speak of the *dignity* of mind, and *dignity* of sentiments. This dignity is based on moral rectitude; all vice is incompatible with true *dignity* of mind. The man who deliberately injures another, whether male or female, has no true *dignity* of soul.

DILETTANTE, *n.* One who delights in promoting science or the fine arts.

Burke.

DINE, *v.i.* To eat the chief meal of the day. This meal seems originally to have been taken about the middle of the day, at least in northern climates, as it still is by laboring people. Among people in the higher walks of life, and in commercial towns, the time of dining is from two to five or six o'clock in the afternoon.

DIPHTHONG, *n.* [The pronunciation *dipthong* is vulgar.]

DIPPING-NEEDLE, *n.* A needle that dips; a magnetic needle which dips or inclines to the earth; an instrument which shows the inclination of the magnet, at the different points of the earth's surface. In the equatorial regions, the needle takes a horizontal position; but as we recede from the equator towards either pole, it dips or inclines one end to the earth, the north end, as we proceed northward, and the south end, as we proceed southward, and the farther north or south we proceed, the greater is the dip or inclination. This is on the supposition that the poles of the earth and the magnetic poles coincide, which is not the case. The above statement is strictly true, only of the magnetic equator and its poles.   *Cavallo. Cyc.*

DISABUSE, *v.t.* To free from mistake; to undeceive; to disengage from fallacy or deception; to set right. It is our duty to *disabuse* ourselves of false notions and prejudices.

> If men are now sufficiently enlightened to *disabuse* themselves of artifice, hypocrisy and superstition, they will consider this event as an era in their history.   *J. Adams.*

DISCERNMENT, *n.* The act of discerning; also, the power or faculty of the mind, by which it distinguishes one thing from another, as truth from falsehood, virtue from vice; acuteness of judgment; power of perceiving differences of things or ideas, and their relations and tendencies. The errors of youth often proceed from the want of *discernment*.

DISCOURAGEMENT, *n.* 2. That which destroys or abates courage; that which depresses confidence or hope; that which deters or tends to deter from an undertaking, or from the prosecution of any thing. Evil examples are great *discouragements* to virtue. The revolution was commenced under every possible *discouragement*.

DISCOVERABLE, *a.* 3. That may be found out, or made known; as, the scriptures reveal many things not *discoverable* by the light of reason.

DISCOVERY, *n.* The action of disclosing to view, or bringing to light; as, by the *discovery* of a plot, the public peace is preserved.
    2. Disclosure; a making known; as, a bankrupt is bound to make a full *discovery* of his estate and effects.

DIPPING-NEEDLE. Tiberius Cavallo (1749–1809), an Anglo-Italian physicist, wrote *History and Practice of Aerostation* (1785) and *Medical Properties of Factitious Air* (1798). Cavallo's multiplier, celebrated in its time, amplified small electric charges so that they could be seen and measured in an electroscope.

3. The action of finding something hidden; as the *discovery* of lead or silver in the earth.

4. The act of finding out, or coming to the knowledge of; as the *discovery* of truth; the *discovery* of magnetism.

5. The act of espying; first sight of; as the *discovery* of America by Columbus, or of the Continent by Cabot.

6. That which is discovered, found out or revealed; that which is first brought to light, seen or known. The properties of the magnet were an important *discovery*. Redemption from sin was a *discovery* beyond the power of human philosophy.

7. In *dramatic poetry*, the unraveling of a plot, or the manner of unfolding the plot or fable of a comedy or tragedy.

DISCRETIONARY, DISCRETIONAL, *a.* Left to discretion; unrestrained except by discretion or judgment; that is to be directed or managed by discretion only. Thus, the President of the U. States is, in certain cases, invested with *discretionary* powers, to act according to circumstances.

DISDAIN, *n.* Contempt; scorn; a passion excited in noble minds, by the hatred or detestation of what is mean and dishonorable, and implying a consciousness of superiority of mind, or a supposed superiority. In ignoble minds, *disdain* may spring from unwarrantable pride or haughtiness, and be directed toward objects of worth. It implies hatred, and sometimes anger.

DISEASE, *n.* 5. Political or civil disorder, or vices in a state; any practice which tends to disturb the peace of society, or impede or prevent the regular administration of government.

> The instability, injustice and confusion introduced into the public councils have, in truth, been the mortal *diseases* under which popular governments have every where perished.   *Federalist, Madison.*

DISGRACEFUL, *a.* Shameful; reproachful; dishonorable; procuring shame; sinking reputation. Cowardice is *disgraceful* to a soldier. Intemperance and profaneness are *disgraceful* to a man, but more *disgraceful* to a woman.

DISOBEY, *v.t.* To neglect or refuse to obey; to omit or refuse to do what is commanded, or to do what is forbid; to transgress or violate an order or injunction. Refractory children *disobey* their parents; men *disobey* their maker and the laws; and we all *disobey* the precepts of the gospel. [*The word is applicable both to the command and to the person commanding.*]

DISPENSE, *v.t.* 1. To deal or divide out in parts or portions; to distribute. The steward *dispenses* provisions to every man, according to his directions. The society *dispenses* medicines to the poor gratuitously or at first cost. God *dispenses* his favors according to his good pleasure.

DISPLAY, *v.t.* 2. To spread before the view; to show; to exhibit to the eyes, or to the mind; to make manifest. The works of nature *display* the power and wisdom of the Supreme Being. Christian charity *displays* the effects of true piety. A dress, simple and elegant, *displays* female taste and beauty to advantage.

DISPUTE, *n.* Strife or contest in words or by arguments; an attempt to prove and maintain one's own opinions or claims, by arguments or statements, in opposition to the opinions, arguments or claims of another; controversy in words. They had a *dispute* on the lawfulness of slavery, a subject which, one would think, could admit of no *dispute.*

DISPUTE, *v.i.* 1. To contend in argument; to reason or argue in opposition; to debate; to altercate; and to *dispute violently* is to wrangle. Paul *disputed* with the Jews in the synagogue. The disciples of Christ *disputed* among themselves who should be the greatest. Men often *dispute* about trifles.

DISSEMINATE, *v.t.* 1. Literally, to sow; to scatter seed; but seldom or never used in its literal sense. But hence,
 2. To scatter for growth and propagation, like seed; to spread. Thus, principles, opinions and errors are *disseminated,* when they are spread and propagated. To *disseminate* truth or the gospel is highly laudable.
 4. To spread; to disperse.
 The Jews are disseminated through all the trading parts of the world.
Addison.
 [The second is the most proper application of the word, as it should always include the idea of growth or taking root. The fourth sense is hardly vindicable.]

DISSIDENT, *n.* A dissenter; one who separates from the established religion; a word applied to the members of the Lutheran, Calvinistic and Greek churches in Poland. *Encyc.*

DISSIMULATION, *n.* The act of dissembling; a hiding under a false appearance; a feigning; false pretension; hypocrisy. Dissimulation may be simply concealment of the opinions, sentiments or purpose; but it includes also the assuming of a false or counterfeit appearance which conceals the real opinions or purpose. *Dissimulation* among statesmen is sometimes regarded as a necessary vice, or as no vice at all.

DISSIPATION, *n.* 4. A dissolute, irregular course of life; a wandering from object to object in pursuit of pleasure; a course of life usually attended with careless and exorbitant expenditures of money, and indulgence in vices, which impair or ruin both health and fortune.
 What! is it proposed then to reclaim the spendthrift from his *dissipation* and extravagance, by filling his pockets with money? *P. Henry, Wirt's Sketches.*

DISTINGUISH, *v.t.* 2. To separate one thing from another by some mark or quality; to know or ascertain difference.

First, by sight; as, to *distinguish* one's own children from others by their features.

Secondly, by feeling. A blind man *distinguishes* an egg from an orange, but rarely *distinguishes* colors.

Thirdly, by smell; as, it is easy to *distinguish* the smell of a peach from that of an apple.

Fourthly, by taste; as, to *distinguish* a plum from a pear.

Fifthly, by hearing; as, to *distinguish* the sound of a drum from that of a violin.

Sixthly, by the understanding; as, to *distinguish* vice from virtue, truth from falsehood.

DISTRICT, *n.* 1. Properly, a limited extent of country; a circuit within which power, right or authority may be exercised, and to which it is restrained; a word applicable to any portion of land or country, or to any part of a city or town, which is defined by law or agreement. A governor, a prefect, or a judge may have his *district.* Some of the states are divided into *districts* for the choice of senators, representatives or electors. Cities and towns are divided into *districts* for various purposes, as for schools, &c. The United States are divided into *districts* for the collection of the revenue.

DISTRUST, *v.t.* 2. To doubt; to suspect not to be real, true, sincere or firm. We *distrust* a man's courage, friendship, veracity, declarations, intentions or promises, when we question their reality or sincerity. We cannot *distrust* the declarations of God. We often have reason to *distrust* our own resolutions.

DISTURB, *v.t.* 3. To move from any regular course or operation; to interrupt regular order; to make irregular. It has been supposed that the approach of a comet may *disturb* the motions of the planets in their orbits. An unexpected cause may *disturb* a chimical operation, or the operation of medicine.

4. To interrupt; to hinder; to incommode. Care *disturbs* study. Let no person *disturb* my franchise.

DIVERT, *v.t.* 2. To turn the mind from business or study; hence, to please; to amuse; to entertain; to exhilarate. Children are *diverted* with sports; men are *diverted* with works of wit and humor; low minds are *diverted* with buffoonery in stage-playing.

DIVING-BELL, *n.* A hollow vessel in form of a truncated cone or pyramid, with the smaller base close, and the larger one open, in which a person may descend into deep water and remain, till the inclosed air ceases to be respirable.

DOCK, *n.* A broad deep trench on the side of a harbor, or bank of a river, in which ships are built or repaired. A *dry dock* has flood-gates to admit the tide, and to prevent the influx, as occasion may require.

Wet docks have no flood-gates, but ships may be repaired in them during the recess of the tide. *Wet docks* are also constructed with gates to keep the water in at ebb tide, so that vessels may lie constantly afloat in them.

Mar. Dict.   Cyc.

In America, the spaces between wharves are called *docks.*

D

DOCTOR, *n.* 2. One who has passed all the degrees of a faculty, and is empowered to practice and teach it, as a *doctor* in divinity, in physic, in law; or according to modern usage, a person who has received the highest degree in a faculty. The degree of *doctor* is conferred by universities and colleges, as an honorary mark of literary distinction. It is also conferred on physicians, as a professional degree.

DODGE, *v.t.* To evade by a sudden shift of place; to escape by starting aside; as, to *dodge* a blow aimed; to *dodge* a cannon ball. [*This is a common word, very expressive and useful, but not admissible in solemn discourse or elegant composition.*]

DODO, *n.* The Didus, a genus of fowls of the gallinaceous order. The hooded dodo is larger than a swan, with a strong hooked bill. The general color of the plumage is cinereous; the belly and thighs whitish. The head is large, and seems as if covered with a hood. The solitary dodo is a large fowl, and is said to weigh sometimes forty five pounds. The plumage is gray and brown mixed.

Encyc.

DODO. Webster does not realize that the bird is extinct and probably had been since late in the seventeenth century.

DOLL, *n.* A puppet or baby for a child; a small image in the human form, for the amusement of little girls.

DOLLAR, *n.* [. . . said to be from *Dale,* the town where it was first coined.] A silver coin of Spain and of the United States, of the value of one hundred cents, or four shillings and sixpence sterling. The dollar seems to have been originally a German coin, and in different parts of Germany, the name is given to coins of different values.

DOODLE, *n.* A trifler; a simple fellow.

DOOM, *n.* 3. The state to which one is doomed, or destined. To suffer misery is the *doom* of sinners. To toil for subsistence is the *doom* of most men.

DOUBLE, *v.i.* To increase to twice the sum, number, value, quantity or length; to increase or grow to twice as much. A sum of money *doubles* by compound interest in a little more than eleven years. The inhabitants of the United States *double* in about twenty five years.

DOUBT, *n.* A fluctuation of mind respecting truth or propriety, arising from defect of knowledge or evidence; uncertainty of mind; suspense; unsettled state of opinion; as, to have *doubts* respecting the theory of the tides.

DOVE, *n.* The œnas, or domestic pigeon, a species of Columba. Its color is a deep bluish ash color; the breast is dashed with a fine changeable green and purple; the sides of the neck, with a copper color. In a wild state, it builds its nest in holes of rocks or in hollow trees, but it is easily domesticated, and forms one of the luxuries of the table.
    2. A word of endearment, or an emblem of innocence.   *Cant.* ii. 14.

DRAGON, *n.* [. . . . The origin of this word is not obvious. . . . In Scotch, the word signifies a paper kite, as also in Danish; probably from the notion of flying or shooting along, like a fiery meteor. In Welsh, *draig* is rendered by Owen a procreator or generating principle, a fiery serpent, a dragon, and the Supreme; and the plural *dreigiau,* silent lightnings, *dreigiaw,* to lighten silently. Hence I infer that the word originally signified a shooting meteor in the atmosphere, a fiery meteor, and hence a fiery or flying serpent, from a root which signified to shoot or draw out.]

DRAMA, *n.* A poem or composition representing a picture of human life, and accommodated to action. The principal species of the drama are tragedy and comedy; inferior species are tragi-comedy, opera, &c.   *Encyc.*

DRAW, *v.t.* 1. To pull along; to haul; to cause to move forward by force applied in advance of the thing moved or at the fore-end, as by a rope or chain. It differs from *drag* only in this, that *drag* is more generally applied to things moved along the ground by sliding, or moved with greater toil or difficulty, and *draw* is applied to all bodies moved by force in advance, whatever may be the degree of force. *Draw* is the more general or generic term, and *drag,* more specific. We say, the horses *draw* a coach or wagon, but they *drag* it through mire; yet *draw* is properly used in both cases.

DRAW, *v.i. Draw,* in most of its uses, retains some shade of its original sense, to pull, to move forward by the application of force in advance, or to extend in length. And Johnson justly observes, that it expresses an action gradual or continuous, and leisurely. We *pour* liquor quick, but we *draw* it in a continued stream. We *force* compliance by threats, but we *draw* it by gradual prevalence. We write a letter in haste, but we *draw* a bill with slow caution, and regard to a precise form. We *draw* a bar of metal by continued beating.

DRAWING-ROOM, *n.* A room appropriated for the reception of company; a room in which distinguished personages hold levees, or private persons receive parties. It is written by Coxe, withdrawing-room, a room to which company *withdraws* from the dining-room.

DREAM, *n.* 1. The thought or series of thoughts of a person in sleep. We apply *dream,* in the singular, to a series of thoughts, which occupy the mind of a sleeping person, in which he imagines he has a view of real things or transactions. A *dream* is a series of thoughts not under the command of reason, and hence wild and irregular. *Stewart.*

2. In scripture, *dreams* were sometimes impressions on the minds of sleeping persons, made by divine agency. God came to Abimelech in a *dream.* Joseph was warned by God in a *dream.*

3. A vain fancy; a wild conceit; an unfounded suspicion.

DRUGGIST, *n.* One who deals in drugs; properly, one whose occupation is merely to buy and sell drugs, without compounding or preparation. In America, the same person often carries on the business of the druggist and the apothecary.

DRUID, *n.* [. . . The Welsh derivation accords with that of Pliny, who supposes the druids were so called, because they frequented or instructed in the forest, or sacrificed under an oak. But some uncertainty rests on this subject.] A priest or minister of religion, among the ancient Celtic nations in Gaul, Britain and Germany. The Druids possessed some knowledge of geometry, natural philosophy, &c., superintended the affairs of religion and morality, and performed the office of judges. *Owen. Encyc.*

DRUM, *n.* 1. A martial instrument of music, in form of a hollow cylinder, and covered at the ends with vellum, which is stretched or slackened at pleasure.

DRUNKENNESS, *n.* Intoxication; inebriation; a state in which a person is overwhelmed or overpowered with spirituous liquors, so that his reason is disordered, and be reels or staggers in walking. Drunkenness renders some persons stupid, others gay, others sullen, others furious.

DUDS, *n.* Old clothes; tattered garments. [*A vulgar word.*]

DUMB, *a.* 2. Destitute of the power of speech; unable to utter articulate sounds; as the *dumb* brutes. The asylum at Hartford in Connecticut was the first institution in America for teaching the deaf and *dumb* to read and write.

DUMP, *n.* 1. A dull gloomy state of the mind; sadness; melancholy; sorrow; heaviness of heart.

In doleful *dumps*.   *Gay.*
2. Absence of mind; reverie.   *Locke.*
3. A melancholy tune or air.   *Shak.*
[This is not an elegant word, and in America, I believe, is always used in the plural; as, the woman is in the *dumps*.]

DUNNING, *ppr. or n.* [from *dun*, a color.] The operation of curing codfish, in such a manner as to give it a particular color and quality. Fish for dunning are caught early in spring, and often in February. At the Isles of Shoals, off Portsmouth, in New Hampshire, the cod are taken in deep water, split and slack-salted; then laid in a pile for two or three months, in a dark store, covered, for the greatest part of the time, with salt-hay or eel-grass, and pressed with some weight. In April or May, they are opened and piled again as close as possible in the same dark store, till July or August, when they are fit for use.   *J. Haven.*

DUTY, *n.* That which a person owes to another; that which a person is bound, by any natural, moral or legal obligation, to pay, do or perform. Obedience to princes, magistrates and the laws is the *duty* of every citizen and subject; obedience, respect and kindness to parents are *duties* of children; fidelity to friends is a *duty;* reverence, obedience and prayer to God are indispensable *duties;* the government and religious instruction of children are *duties* of parents which they cannot neglect without guilt.
   2. Forbearance of that which is forbid by morality, law, justice or propriety. It is our *duty* to refrain from lewdness, intemperance, profaneness and injustice.
   3. Obedience; submission.

E

EAVES-DROPPER, *n.* One who stands under the eaves or near the window or door of a house, to listen and hear what is said within doors, whether from curiosity, or for the purpose of tattling and making mischief.   *Shak.*

EDUCATION, *n.* The bringing up, as of a child; instruction; formation of manners. Education comprehends all that series of instruction and discipline which is intended to enlighten the understanding, correct the temper, and form the manners and habits of youth, and fit them for usefulness in their future stations. To give children a good *education* in manners, arts and science, is important; to give them a religious *education* is indispensable; and an immense responsibility rests on parents and guardians who neglect these duties.

EFFOSSION, *n.* The act of digging out of the earth; as the *effossion* of coins.   *Arbuthnot.*

EFFRONTERY, *n.* Impudence; assurance; shameless boldness; sauciness; boldness transgressing the bounds of modesty and decorum. *Effrontery* is a sure mark of ill breeding.

EGOIST, *n.* A name given to certain followers of Des Cartes, who held the opinion that they were uncertain of every thing except their own existence and the operations and ideas of their own minds.   *Reid.*

EFFOSSION. In Bierce's *Devil's Dictionary,* under "Efferous, Effigiate, Efflagitate, Effodient, Effossion," we are told, "See some other dictionary."

☞ E. In a numerous class of words, indeed in almost every word, except a few from the Greek, the final *e* is silent, serving no purpose whatever. . . . In some of these words, the use of *e* is borrowed from the French; in most or all cases, it is not authorized by the Latin originals; it is worse than useless, as it leads to a wrong pronunciation; and the retaining of it in such words is, beyond measure, absurd. 🕮

BIERCE VS. WEBSTER

☞ Ambrose Bierce's *The Devil's Dictionary* would not have been conceived had not earnest dictionaries like Webster's preceded it. Bierce certainly didn't like Webster's moralism and pomposity, and an especially annoying encounter one day with one of Webster's definitions may have planted the seed for Bierce's own book. Even some of Bierce's fake quotes can be seen as parodies of Webster's. (Under his definition of *abridge*, v.t., to shorten, there is a "quote" from Oliver Cromwell that begins "When in the course of human events it becomes necessary for a people to abridge their king. . . .") But it is Bierce's definitions that more often seem aimed at him. For Bierce, *faith* is "belief without evidence [see Webster's SUPERSTITION] in what is told by one who speaks without knowledge, of things without parallel." Killing two lexicographers with one gibe, he reminds us that "in Dr. Johnson's famous dictionary, *patriotism* is defined as the last resort of a scoundrel. With all due respect to an enlightened but inferior lexicographer, I beg to submit that it is the first." And a *dictionary* is a "malevolent literary device for cramping the growth of language and making it hard and inelastic." Webster would have been dumbfounded by these definitions of *faith* and *patriotism*. He was sure that *his* dictionary, far from cramping the growth of language, would end up fostering it—notwithstanding Bierce's definition of *hell* as "the residence of the late Dr. Noah Webster, dictionary-maker." ▨

EGOTIST, *n.* One who repeats the word *I* very often in conversation or writing; one who speaks much of himself, or magnifies his own achievements; one who makes himself the hero of every tale.

ELECTRICITY, *n.* The operations of a very subtil fluid, which appears to be diffused through most bodies, remarkable for the rapidity of its motion, and one of the most powerful agents in nature. The name is given to the operations of this fluid, and to the fluid itself. As it exists in bodies, it is denominated a property of those bodies, though it may be a distinct substance, invisible, intangible and imponderable. When an electric body is rubbed with a soft dry substance, as with woolen cloth, silk or fur, it attracts or repels light substances, at a greater or less distance, according to the strength of the electric virtue; and the friction may be continued, or increased, till the electric body will emit sparks or flashes resembling fire, accompanied with a sharp sound. When the electric fluid passes from cloud to cloud, from the clouds to the earth, or from the earth to the clouds, it is called *lightning*, and produces thunder. Bodies which, when rubbed, exhibit this property, are called *electrics* or *non-conductors*. Bodies, which, when excited, do not exhibit this property, as water and metals, are called *non-electrics* or *conductors*, as they readily convey electricity from one body to another, at any distance, and such is the rapidity of the electric fluid in motion, that no perceptible space of time is required for its passage to any known distance.   *Cavallo. Encyc.*

It is doubted by modern philosophers whether electricity is a fluid or material substance. Electricity, according to Professor Silliman, is a power which causes repulsion and attraction between the masses of bodies under its influence; a power which causes the *heterogeneous particles* of bodies to separate, thus producing chimical decomposition; one of the causes of magnetism.

ELEGANCE, ELEGANCY, *n*. In its primary sense, this word signifies that which is choice or select, as distinguished from what is common.

1. "The beauty of propriety, not of greatness," says Johnson.

Applied to manners or behavior, elegance is that fine polish, politeness or grace, which is acquired by a genteel education, and an association with wellbred company.

Applied to language, elegance respects the manner of speaking or of writing. *Elegance of speaking* is the propriety of diction and utterance, and the gracefulness of action or gesture; comprehending correct, appropriate and rich expressions, delivered in an agreeable manner. *Elegance of composition* consists in correct, appropriate and rich expressions, or well chosen words, arranged in a happy manner. Elegance implies neatness, purity, and correct, perspicuous arrangement, and is calculated to please a delicate taste, rather than to excite admiration or strong feeling. Elegance is applied also to form. Elegance in *architecture,* consists in the due symmetry and distribution of the parts of an edifice, or in regular proportions and arrangement. And in a similar sense, the word is applied to the person or human body. It is applied also to penmanship, denoting that form of letters which is most agreeable to the eye. In short, in a looser sense, it is applied to many works of art or nature remarkable for their beauty; as *elegance* of dress or furniture.

ELEMENT, *n*. 1. The first or constituent principle or minutest part of any thing; as the *elements* of earth, water, salt, or wood; the *elements* of the world; the *elements* of animal or vegetable bodies. So letters are called the *elements* of language.

2. An ingredient; a constituent part of any composition.

3. In *a chimical sense,* an atom; the minutest particle of a substance; that which cannot be divided by chimical analysis, and therefore considered as a simple substance, as oxygen, hydrogen, nitrogen, &c.

An *element* is strictly the last result of chimical analysis; that which cannot be decomposed by any means now employed. An *atom* is the last result of mechanical division; that which cannot be any farther divided, without decomposition: hence there may be both *elementary* and *compound* atoms.

4. In *the plural*, the first rules or principles of an art or science; rudiments; as the *elements* of geometry; the *elements* of music; the *elements* of painting; the *elements* of a theory.

5. In *popular language*, fire, air, earth and water, are called the four *elements*, as formerly it was supposed that these are simple bodies, of which the world is composed. Later discoveries prove air, earth and water to be compound bodies, and fire to be only the extrication of light and heat during *combustion*.

ELEPHANT, *n.* 1. The largest of all quadrupeds, belonging to the order of Bruta. This animal has no foreteeth in either jaw; the canine-teeth are very long; and he has a long proboscis or trunk, by which he conveys food and drink to his mouth. The largest of these animals is about 16 feet long and 14 feet high; but smaller varieties are not more than seven feet high. The eyes are small and the feet short, round, clumsy, and distinguishable only by the toes. The trunk is a cartilaginous and muscular tube, extending from the upper jaw, and is seven or eight feet in length. The general shape of his body resembles that of swine. His skin is rugged, and his hair thin. The two large tusks are of a yellowish color, and extremely hard. The bony substance of these is called *ivory*. The elephant is 30 years in coming to his full growth, and he lives to 150 or 200 years of age. Elephants are natives of the warm climates of Africa and Asia, where they are employed as beasts of burden. They were formerly used in war. *Encyc.*

ELF, *n.* 1. A wandering spirit; a fairy; a hobgoblin; an imaginary being which our rude ancestors supposed to inhabit unfrequented places, and in various ways to affect mankind. Hence in Scottish, *elf-shot* is an elf-arrow; an arrowhead of flint, supposed to be shot by elfs; and it signifies also a disease supposed to be produced by the agency of spirits.

Every *elf*, and fairy sprite,
Hop as light as bird from brier.   *Shak.*

ELM, *n.* A tree of the genus Ulmus. The common elm is one of the largest and most majestic trees of the forest, and is cultivated for shade and ornament. Another species, the fulva, is called slippery elm, from the quality of its inner bark. One species seems to have been used to support vines.

The treaty which William Penn made with the natives in 1682 was negotiated under a large *Elm* which grew on the spot now called Kensington, just above Philadelphia. It was prostrated by a storm in 1810, at which time its stem measured 24 feet in circumference.   *Memoirs of Hist. Soc. Penn.*

ELOPE, *v.i.* 1. To run away; to depart from one's proper place or station privately or without permission; to quit, without permission or right, the station in which one is placed by law or duty. Particularly and appropriately, to run away or depart from a husband, and live with an adulterer, as a married woman; or to quit a father's house, privately or without permission, and marry or live with a gallant, as an unmarried woman.

2. To run away; to escape privately; to depart, without permission, as a son from a father's house, or an apprentice from his master's service.

EMBALM, *v.t.* 3. To preserve, with care and affection, from loss or decay.
The memory of my beloved daughter is *embalmed* in my heart.   *N. W.*

EMBEZZLEMENT, *n.* The act of fraudulently appropriating to one's own use, the money or goods entrusted to one's care and management. An accurate account of the *embezzlements* of public money would form a curious history.

EMIGRATE, *v.i.* To quit one country, state or region and settle in another; to remove from one country or state to another for the purpose of residence. Germans, Swiss, Irish and Scotch, *emigrate*, in great numbers, to America. Inhabitants of New England *emigrate* to the Western States.

EMPIRICISM, *n.* Dependence of a physician on his experience in practice, without the aid of a regular medical education.

2. The practice of medicine without a medical education. Hence, quackery; the pretensions of an ignorant man to medical skill.
Shudder to destroy life, either by the naked knife, or by the surer and safer medium of *empiricism*.   *Dwight.*

CHANGE OF MEANING

☞ Words often change their meanings over time. Still, it can be startling to realize that words we are familiar and comfortable with today meant something quite different not so long ago. For Webster, **EMPIRICISM** meant quackery; a **PRAGMATIST**, a meddler; a **HYPOCHONDRIAC**, one who was weak or melancholic; to **WALLOP**, to boil noisily; **PRESTIGIOUS**, juggling or practicing tricks; **REPERTORY**, the index of a book, or a treasury or magazine; and **IMBECILITY**, weakness of body as well as of mind, or impotence in males. It is not only for scholars to bear in mind, when confronting (say) a nineteenth-century text, that words that look like old friends might not have carried the same meaning then as they do now. ☜

EMPORIUM, *n.* 1. A place of merchandize; a town or city of trade; particularly, a city or town of extensive commerce, or in which the commerce of an extensive country centers, or to which sellers and buyers resort from different countries. Such are London, Amsterdam and Hamburg. New York will be an *emporium.*

ENCROACH, *v.i.* [Fr. *accrocher,* to catch, to grapple, from *croc,* a hook.] Primarily, to catch as with a hook. Hence,
1. To enter on the rights and possessions of another; to intrude; to take possession of what belongs to another, by gradual advances into his limits or jurisdiction, and usurping a part of his rights or prerogatives; with *on.* The farmer who runs a fence on his neighbor's land, and incloses a piece with his own, *encroaches on* his neighbor's property. Men often *encroach,* in this manner, *on* the highway. The sea is said to *encroach* on the land, when it wears it away gradually; and the land *encroaches* on the sea, when it is extended into it by alluvion. It is important to prevent one branch of government from *encroaching* on the jurisdiction of another.
2. To creep on gradually without right.
    Superstition—a creeping and *encroaching* evil.   *Hooker.*

ENCYCLOPEDIA, ENCYCLOPEDY, *n.* The circle of sciences; a general system of instruction or knowledge. More particularly, a collection of the principal facts, principles and discoveries, in all branches of the sciences and the arts, digested under proper titles and arranged in alphabetical order, as the French *Encyclopedia;* the *Encyclopedia* Brittanica.

ENIGMATOGRAPHY, ENIGMATOLOGY, *n.* The art of making riddles; or the art of solving them.

ENOUGH, *a.* [Note. This word, in vulgar language, is sometimes placed before its noun, like most other adjectives. But in elegant discourse or composition, it always follows the noun, to which it refers; as, bread *enough;* money *enough.*]

ENSLAVE, *v.t.* To reduce to slavery or bondage; to deprive of liberty and subject to the will of a master. Barbarous nations *enslave* their prisoners of war, but civilized men barbarously and wickedly purchase men to *enslave* them.
2. To reduce to servitude or subjection. Men often suffer their passions and appetites to *enslave* them. They are *enslaved* to lust, to anger, to intemperance, to avarice.

ENVIOUS, *a.* Feeling or harboring envy; repining or feeling uneasiness, at a view of the excellence, prosperity or happiness of another; pained by the desire of possessing some superior good which another possesses, and usually disposed to deprive him of that good, to lessen it or to depreciate it in common estimation. Sometimes followed by *against*, but generally and properly by *at*, before the person envied.

EPIDEMIC, *n.* A popular disease; a disease generally prevailing. The influenza of October and November 1789, that of March and April 1790, that of the winter 1824–5, and that of 1825–6, were very severe *epidemics*.

ERGOTISM, *n.* [L. *ergo.*] A logical inference; a conclusion. *Brown.*

ERROR, *n.* 2. A mistake made in writing or other performance. It is no easy task to correct the *errors* of the press. Authors sometimes charge their own *errors* to the printer.

ERUDITION, *n.* Learning; knowledge gained by study, or from books and instruction; particularly, learning in literature, as distinct from the sciences, as in history, antiquity and languages. The Scaligers were men of deep *erudition.*

      The most useful *erudition* for republicans is that which exposes the causes of discords.   *J. Adams.*

ESCAPADE, *n.* The fling of a horse. In Spanish, flight, escape.

ESCHEAT, *v.i.* 2. In *America,* to fall or come, as land, to the state, through failure of heirs or owners, or by forfeiture for treason. In the feudal sense, no *escheat* can exist in the United States; but the word is used in statutes confiscating the estates of those who abandoned their country, during the revolution, and in statutes giving to the state the lands for which no owner can be found.

ETERNITY, *n.* We speak of eternal duration preceding the present time. God has existed from *eternity.* We also speak of endless or everlasting duration in future, and dating from present time or the present state of things. Some men doubt the *eternity* of future punishment, though they have less difficulty in admitting the *eternity* of future rewards.

ETHER, *n.* A thin, subtil matter, much finer and rarer than air, which, some philosophers suppose, begins from the limits of the atmosphere and occupies the heavenly space.   *Newton.*

EVACUATE, *v.t.* 4. To quit; to withdraw from a place. The British army *evacuated* the city of New-York, November 25, 1783.

EVE, *n.* The consort of Adam, and mother of the human race; so called by Adam, because she was the mother of all living. In this case, the word would properly belong to the Heb. חיה. But the Hebrew name is חוה havah or chavah, coinciding with the verb, to shew, to discover, and Parkhurst hence denominates Eve, the manifester. In the Septuagint, *Eve,* in Gen. iii. 20, is rendered **Ζωη**, life; but in Gen. iv. 1, it is rendered **Ευαν**, *Euan* or *Evan.* The reason of this variation is not obvious, as the Hebrew is the same in both passages. In Russ. Eve is *Evva.* In the Chickasaw language of America, a wife is called *awah,* says Adair.

EVEN, *a.* 9. Capable of being divided into equal parts, without a remainder; opposed to odd. 4, 6, 8, 10, are even numbers.
> Let him tell me whether the number of the stars is even or odd.   *Taylor.*

EVOLVE, *v.t.* To unfold; to open and expand.
> The animal soul sooner *evolves* itself to its full orb and extent than the human soul.   *Hale.*

EXCESSIVE, *a.* 2. Beyond the established laws of morality and religion, or beyond the bounds of justice, fitness, propriety, expedience or utility; as *excessive* indulgence of any kind.
> *Excessive* bail shall not be required.   *Bill of Rights.*

EXECUTIVE, *a.* Having the quality of executing or performing; as executive power or authority; an *executive* officer. Hence, in government, *executive* is used in distinction from *legislative* and *judicial.* The body that deliberates and enacts laws, is *legislative;* the body that judges, or applies the laws to particular cases, is *judicial;* the body or person who carries the laws into effect, or superintends the enforcement of them, is *executive.*
> It is of the nature of war to increase the *executive,* at the expense of the legislative authority.   *Federalist, Hamilton.*

EXHAUSTION, *n.* 3. In *mathematics,* a method of proving the equality of two magnitudes by a *reductio ad absurdum,* or showing that if one is supposed either greater or less than the other, there will arise a contradiction.   *Encyc.*

EXORCISM, *n.* The expulsion of evil spirits from persons or places by certain adjurations and ceremonies. *Exorcism* was common among the Jews, and still makes a part of the superstitions of some churches.   *Encyc.*

EXPECTATION, *n.* The act of expecting or looking forward to a future event with at least some reason to believe the event will happen. *Expectation* differs from *hope.* *Hope* originates in desire, and may exist with little or no ground of belief that the desired event will arrive. *Expectation* is founded on some reasons which render the event probable. *Hope* is directed to some good; *expectation* is directed to good or evil.

The same weakness of mind which indulges absurd *expectations,* produces petulance in disappointment.   *Irving.*

EXPERIENCE, *n.* 1. Trial, or a series of trials or experiments; active effort or attempt to do or to prove something, or repeated efforts. A man attempts to raise wheat on moist or clayey ground; his attempt fails of success; *experience* proves that wheat will not flourish on such a soil. He repeats the trial, and his *experience* proves the same fact. A single trial is usually denominated an *experiment; experience* may be a series of trials, or the result of such trials.

EXPERIMENT, *n.* A trial; an act or operation designed to discover some unknown truth, principle or effect, or to establish it when discovered. *Experiments* in chimistry disclose the qualities of natural bodies. A series of *experiments* proves the uniformity of the laws of matter. It is not always safe to trust to a single *experiment.* It is not expedient to try many *experiments* in legislation.

A political *experiment* cannot be made in a laboratory, nor determined in a few hours.   *J. Adams.*

EXPORT, *v.t.* To carry out; but appropriately, and perhaps exclusively, to convey or transport, in traffick, produce and goods from one country to another, or from one state or jurisdiction to another, either by water or land. We *export* wares and merchandize from the United States to Europe. The Northern States *export* manufactures to South Carolina and Georgia. Goods are *exported* from Persia to Syria and Egypt on camels.

F

FACT, *n.* 1. Any thing done, or that comes to pass; an act; a deed; an effect produced or achieved; an event. Witnesses are introduced into court to prove a *fact*. *Facts* are stubborn things. To deny a *fact* knowingly is to lie.

FACTION, *n.* 1. A party, in political society, combined or acting in union, in opposition to the prince, government or state; usually applied to a minority, but it may be applied to a majority. Sometimes a state is divided into *factions* nearly equal. Rome was almost always disturbed by *factions*. Republics are proverbial for *factions*, and *factions* in monarchies have often effected revolutions.

A feeble government produces more *factions* than an oppressive one.
Ames.

By a *faction*, I understand a number of citizens, whether amounting to a majority or minority of the whole, who are united and actuated by some common impulse of passion, or of interest, adverse to the rights of other citizens, or to the permanent and aggregate interests of the community.   *Federalist, Madison.*

FACTOR, *n.* In *commerce*, an agent employed by merchants, residing in other places, to buy and sell, and to negotiate bills of exchange, or to transact other business on their account.

FACTORY, *n.* A house or place where factors reside, to transact business for their employers. The English merchants have factories in the East Indies, Turkey, Portugal, Hamburg, &c.

FACULTY, *n.* 1. That power of the mind or intellect which enables it to receive, revive or modify perceptions; as the *faculty* of seeing, of hearing, of imagining, of remembering, &c.; or in general, the faculties may be called the powers or capacities of the mind.

2. The power of doing any thing; ability. There is no *faculty* or power in creatures, which can rightly perform its functions, without the perpetual aid of the Supreme Being.   *Hooker.*

10. In colleges, the masters and professors of the several sciences.
Johnson.

One of the members or departments of a university. In most universities there are four *faculties;* of arts, including humanity and philosophy; of theology; of medicine; and of law.   *Encyc.*

In *America,* the *faculty* of a college or university consists of the president, professors and tutors.

FAIN, *a.* 1. Glad; pleased; rejoiced. But the appropriate sense of the word is, glad or pleased to do something under some kind of necessity; that is, glad to evade evil or secure good. Thus, says Locke, "The learned Castalio was *fain* to make trenches at Basil, to keep himself from starving." This appropriation of the word, which is modern, led Dr. Johnson into a mistake in defining the word. The proper signification is glad, joyful.

FAIR, *n.* A stated market in a particular town or city; a stated meeting of buyers and sellers for trade. A fair is annual or more frequent. The privilege of holding fairs is granted by the king or supreme power. Among the most celebrated *fairs* in Europe are those of Francfort and Leipsic in Germany; of Novi in the Milanese; of Riga and Archangel in Russia; of Lyons and St. Germain in France. In Great Britain many towns enjoy this privilege.   *Encyc.*

FAIRY, *n.* [. . . The origin of this word is not obvious, and the radical letters are uncertain. The conjectures of Baxter, Jamieson and others throw no satisfactory light on the subject.] A *fay;* an imaginary being or spirit, supposed to assume a human form, dance in meadows, steal infants and play a variety of pranks.   *Locke. Pope.*

FAITH, *n.* 4. *Evangelical, justifying,* or *saving faith,* is the assent of the mind to the truth of divine revelation, on the authority of God's testimony, accompanied with a cordial assent of the will or approbation of the heart; an entire confidence or trust in God's character and declarations, and in the character and doctrines of Christ, with an unreserved surrender of the will to his guidance, and dependence on his merits for salvation. In other words, that firm belief of God's testimony, and of the truth of the gospel, which influences the will, and leads to an entire reliance on Christ for salvation.

FAKIR, FAQUIR, *n.* A monk in India. The fakirs subject themselves to severe austerities and mortifications. Some of them condemn themselves to a standing posture all their lives, supported only by a stick or rope under their arm-pits. Some mangle their bodies with scourges or knives. Others wander about in companies, telling fortunes, and these are said to be arrant villains.   *Encyc.*

FALL, *n.* 10. Descent of water; a cascade; a cataract; a rush of water down a steep place; usually in the plural; sometimes in the singular; as the *falls* of

Niagara, or the Mohawk; the *fall* of the Hoosatonuc at Canaan. *Fall* is applied to a perpendicular descent, or to one that is very steep. When the descent is moderate, we name it *rapids*. Custom however sometimes deviates from this rule, and the *rapids* of rivers are called *falls*.

FAMILY, *n.* The collective body of persons who live in one house and under one head or manager; a household, including parents, children and servants, and as the case may be, lodgers or boarders.

2. Those who descend from one common progenitor; a tribe or race; kindred; lineage. Thus the Israelites were a branch of the *family* of Abraham; and the descendants of Reuben, of Manasseh, &c., were called their *families*. The whole human race are the *family* of Adam, the human *family*.

FAN, *n.* An instrument used by ladies to agitate the air and cool the face in warm weather. It is made of feathers, or of thin skin, paper or taffety mounted on sticks, &c.

FANATIC, FANATICAL, *n.* A person affected by excessive enthusiasm, particularly on religious subjects; one who indulges wild and extravagant notions of religion, and sometimes exhibits strange motions and postures, and vehement vociferation in religious worship. Fanatics sometimes affect to be inspired or to have intercourse with superior beings.

FANCY, *n.* 1. The faculty by which the mind forms images or representations of things at pleasure. It is often used as synonymous with *imagination;* but imagination is rather the power of combining and modifying our conceptions.
Stewart.

FARCE, *n.* [. . . Literally, seasoning, stuffing or mixture, like the stuffing of a roasted fowl; *force-meat*]. A dramatic composition, originally exhibited by charlatans or buffoons, in the open street, for the amusement of the crowd, but now introduced upon the stage. It is written without regularity, and filled with ludicrous conceits. The dialogue is usually low, the persons of inferior rank, and the fable or action trivial or ridiculous.   *Encyc.*

Farce is that in poetry which grotesque is in a picture: the persons and actions of a farce are all unnatural, and the manners false.   *Dryden.*

FARM, *n.* 2. In the United States, a portion or tract of land, consisting usually of grass land, meadow, pasture, tillage and woodland, cultivated by one man and usually owned by him in fee. A like tract of land under lease is called a *farm;* but most cultivators are proprietors of the land, and called *farmers*.

A tract of new land, covered with forest, if intended to be cultivated by one man as owner, is also called a *farm*. A man goes into the new States, or into the unsettled country, to buy a *farm*, that is, land for a farm.

FASCINATE, *v.t.* 2. To charm; to captivate; to excite and allure irresistibly or powerfully. The young are *fascinated* by love; female beauty *fascinates* the unguarded youth; gaming is a *fascinating* vice.

FATHER, *n.* 6. He who creates, invents, makes or composes any thing; the author, former or contriver; a founder, director or instructor. . . . Washington, as a defender and an affectionate and wise counselor, is called the *father* of his country.

FEAR, *v.t.* 1. To feel a painful apprehension of some impending evil; to be afraid of; to consider or expect with emotions of alarm or solicitude. We *fear* the approach of an enemy or of a storm. We have reason to *fear* the punishment of our sins.

FEATHER, FETHER, *n.* A plume; a general name of the covering of fowls. The smaller fethers are used for the filling of beds; the larger ones, called quills, are used for ornaments of the head, for writing pens, &c. The fether consists of a shaft or stem, corneous, round, strong and hollow at the lower part, and at the upper part, filled with pith. On each side of the shaft are the vanes, broad on one side and narrow on the other, consisting of thin lamins. The fethers which cover the body are called the *plumage;* the fethers of the wings are adapted to flight.

FEMALE, *a.* Noting the sex which produces young; not male; as a *female* bee.
    2. Pertaining to females; as a *female* hand or heart; *female* tenderness.
        To the generous decision of a *female* mind, we owe the discovery of America.   *Belknap.*
    3. Feminine; soft; delicate; weak.

FENCE, *n.* A wall, hedge, ditch, bank, or line of posts and rails, or of boards or pickets, intended to confine beasts from straying, and to guard a field from being entered by cattle, or from other encroachment. A good farmer has good *fences* about his farm; an insufficient *fence* is evidence of bad management. Broken windows and poor *fences* are evidences of idleness or poverty or of both.

FERMENTATION, *n.* The sensible internal motion of the constituent particles of animal and vegetable substances, occasioned by a certain degree of heat and moisture, and accompanied by an extrication of gas and heat. Fermentation is followed by a change of properties in the substances fermented, arising from new combinations of their principles. It may be defined, in its most general sense, any spontaneous change which takes place in animal or vegetable substances, after life has ceased. It is of three kinds, *vinous, acetous* and *putrefactive.* The term is also applied to other processes, as the *panary* fermentation, or the raising of bread; but it is limited, by some authors, to the vinous and acetous fermentations, which terminate in the production of alcohol or vinegar. Fermentation differs from effervescence. The former is confined to animal and vegetable substances; the latter is applicable to mineral substances. The former is spontaneous; the latter produced by the mixture.   *Encyc. Parr. Thomson.*

FERRET, *n.* An animal of the genus Mustela, or Weasel kind, about 14 inches in length, of a pale yellow color with red eyes. It is a native of Africa, but has been introduced into Europe. It cannot however bear cold, and cannot subsist even in France, except in a domestic state. Ferrets are used to catch rabbits.   *Encyc.*

FERRY, *n.* 2. The place or passage where boats pass over water to convey passengers.

    3. The right of transporting passengers over a lake or stream. A. B. owns the *ferry* at Windsor. [*In New England, this word is used in the two latter senses.*]

FETICHISM, FETICISM, *n.* The worship of idols among the negroes of Africa, among whom *fetich* is an idol, any tree, stone or other thing worshipped.

FIDELITY, *n.* 1. Faithfulness; careful and exact observance of duty, or performance of obligations. We expect *fidelity* in a public minister, in an agent or trustee, in a domestic servant, in a friend.

    The best security for the *fidelity* of men, is to make interest coincide with duty.   *Federalist, Hamilton.*

FILLIP, *v.t.* To strike with the nail of the finger, first placed against the ball of the thumb, and forced from that position with some violence.

Fine Arts, or polite arts, are the arts which depend chiefly on the labors of the mind or imagination, and whose object is pleasure; as poetry, music, painting and sculpture.

FIRE, *n.* 3. The burning of a house or town; a conflagration. Newburyport and Savannah have suffered immense losses by *fire*. The great *fire* in Boston in 1711 consumed a large part of the town.

FISH, *n.* [. . . This animal may be named from its rapid motion. In W. *fysg* is hasty, impetuous.] An animal that lives in water. *Fish* is a general name for a class of animals subsisting in water, which were distributed by Linne into six orders. They breathe by means of gills, swim by the aid of fins, and are oviparous. Some of them have the skeleton bony, and others cartilaginous. Most of the former have the opening of the gills closed by a peculiar cover-

FERRY. Webster mentions *ferry boat* under SCOW, but fails to define it here.

ing, called the gill-lid; many of the latter have no gill-lid, and are hence said to breathe through apertures. Cetaceous animals, as the whale and dolphin, are, in popular language, called fishes, and have been so classed by some naturalists; but they breathe by lungs, and are viviparous, like quadrupeds. The term *fish* has been also extended to other aquatic animals, such as shell-fish, lobsters, &c. We use *fish,* in the singular, for *fishes* in general or the whole race.

FLATTER, *v.t.* 1. To soothe by praise; to gratify self-love by praise or obsequiousness; to please a person by applause or favorable notice, by respectful attention, or by any thing that exalts him in his own estimation, or confirms his good opinion of himself. We *flatter* a woman when we praise her children.
    7. To wheedle; to coax; to attempt to win by blandishments, praise or enticements. How many young and credulous persons are *flattered* out of their innocence and their property, by seducing arts!

FLAUNT, *v.i.* To throw or spread out; to flutter; to display ostentatiously; as a *flaunting* show.
        You *flaunt* about the streets in your new gilt chariot.   *Arbuthnot.*
        One *flaunts* in rags, one flutters in brocade.   *Pope.*
    [This correctly expresses the author's meaning, which is, that the proud often attempt to make a show and parade of their importance, even in poverty. Johnson's remark on the use of the word seems therefore to be unfounded.]

FLAWY, *a.* Full of flaws or cracks; broken; defective; faulty.
    2. Subject to sudden gusts of wind.

FLEA, *n.* An insect of the genus Pulex. It has two eyes, and six feet; the feelers are like threads; the rostrum is inflected, setaceous, and armed with a sting. The flea is remarkable for its agility, leaping to a surprising distance, and its bite is very troublesome.

FLITTERMOUSE, *n.* A bat; an animal that has the fur of a mouse, and membranes which answer the purpose of wings, and enable the animal to sustain itself in a fluttering flight.

FLOCK, *n.* 2. A company or collection of fowls of any kind, and when applied to birds on the wing, a flight; as a *flock* of wild-geese; a *flock* of ducks; a *flock* of blackbirds. In the U. States, *flocks* of wild-pigeons sometimes darken the air.

FLOOD, *n.* 1. A great flow of water; a body of moving water; particularly, a body of water, rising, swelling and overflowing land not usually covered with water. Thus there is a *flood,* every spring, in the Connecticut, which inundates the adjacent meadows. There is an annual *flood* in the Nile, and in the Missisippi.

2. *The flood*, by way of eminence, the deluge; the great body of water which inundated the earth in the days of Noah. Before the *flood*, men lived to a great age.

FLOUR, *n.* The edible part of corn; meal.   *Johnson.*

In the United States, the modern practice is to make a distinction between *flour* and *meal;* the word *flour* being more usually applied to the finer part of *meal*, separated from the bran, as wheat *flour*, rye *flour*. This is a just and useful distinction.

FLOW, *v.i.* 1. To move along an inclined plane, or on descending ground, by the operation of gravity, and with a continual change of place among the particles or parts, as a fluid. A solid body descends or moves in mass, as a ball or a wheel; but in the *flowing* of liquid substances, and others consisting of very fine particles, there is a constant change of the relative position of some parts of the substance, as is the case with a stream of water, of quicksilver, and of sand. Particles at the bottom and sides of the stream, being somewhat checked by friction, move slower than those in the middle and near the surface of the current. Rivers *flow* from springs and lakes; tears *flow* from the eyes.

FOLK, *n.* [. . . Originally and properly it had no plural, being a collective noun; but in modern use, in America, it has lost its singular number, and we hear it only in the plural. It is a colloquial word, not admissible into elegant style.] 1. People in general, or any part of them without distinction. What do *folks* say respecting the war? Men love to talk about the affairs of other *folks*. Certain people, discriminated from others; as old *folks*, and young *folks*. Children sometimes call their parents, the old *folks*. So we say sick *folks;* poor *folks;* proud *folks*.

FORBID, *v.t.* Literally, to bid or command against. Hence, 1. To prohibit; to interdict; to command to forbear or not to do. The laws of God *forbid* us to swear. Good manners also *forbid* us to use profane language. All servile labor and idle amusements on the sabbath are *forbidden*.

FOREGO, *v.t.* To forbear to possess or enjoy; voluntarily to avoid the enjoyment of good. Let us *forego* the pleasures of sense, to secure immortal bliss.

FOREST, *n.* [. . . This enables us to understand the radical meaning of other words which signify *strange, wild, barbarous*, &c. They all express distance from cities and civilization, and are from roots expressing departure or wandering.] 1. An extensive wood, or a large tract of land covered with trees. In *America*, the word is usually applied to a wood of native growth, or a tract of woodland which has never been cultivated. It differs from wood or woods chiefly in extent. We read of the Hercynian *forest,* in Germany, and the *forest* of Ardennes, in France or Gaul.

FORFEIT, v.t To lose or render confiscable, by some fault, offense or crime; to lose the right to some species of property or that which belongs to one; to alienate the right to possess by some neglect or crime; as, to *forfeit* an estate by a breach of the condition of tenure or by treason. By the ancient laws of England, a man *forfeited* his estate by neglecting or refusing to fulfill the conditions on which it was granted to him, or by a breach of fealty. A man now *forfeits* his estate by committing treason. A man *forfeits* his honor or reputation by a breach of promise, and by any criminal or disgraceful act. Statutes declare that by certain acts a man shall *forfeit* a certain sum of money. Under the feudal system, the right to the land *forfeited,* vested in the lord or superior. In modern times, the right to things *forfeited* is generally regulated by statutes; it is vested in the state, in corporations, or in prosecutors or informers, or partly in the state or a corporation, and partly in an individual.

The duelist, to secure the reputation of bravery, *forfeits* the esteem of good men, and the favor of heaven.

FORGERY, *n.* 3. That which is forged or counterfeited. Certain letters, purporting to be written by Gen. Washington, during the revolution, were *forgeries.*

FORGIVE, *v.t.* 1. To pardon; to remit, as an offense or debt; to overlook an offense, and treat the offender as not guilty. The original and proper phrase is to *forgive the offense,* to send it away, to reject it, that is, not to *impute it,* [put it to] the offender. But by an easy transition, we also use the phrase, to *forgive the person* offending.

As savages never forget a favor, so they never *forgive* an injury.

N. Chipman.

It is to be noted that *pardon,* like *forgive,* may be followed by the name or person and by the offense; but *remit* can be followed by the offense only. We forgive or pardon the man, but we do not *remit* him.

FORMERLY, *adv.* In time past, either in time immediately preceding, or at any indefinite distance; of old; heretofore. We *formerly* imported slaves from Africa. Nations *formerly* made slaves of prisoners taken in war.

FORTITUDE, *n.* That strength or firmness of mind or soul which enables a person to encounter danger with coolness and courage, or to bear pain or adversity without murmuring, depression or despondency. Fortitude is the basis or source of genuine courage or intrepidity in danger, of patience in suffering, of forbearance under injuries, and of magnanimity in all conditions

of life. We sometimes confound the effect with the cause, and use fortitude as synonymous with courage or patience; but *courage* is an active virtue or vice, and patience is the effect of *fortitude*.
 Fortitude is the guard and support of the other virtues.   *Locke.*

FORTUITOUS, *a.* Accidental; casual; happening by chance; coming or occurring unexpectedly, or without any known cause. We speak of *fortuitous* events, when they occur without our foreseeing or expecting them, and of a *fortuitous* concourse of atoms, when we suppose the concourse not to result from the design and power of a controlling agent. But an event cannot be in fact *fortuitous*.

FOSSIL, *n.* A substance dug from the earth, or penetrated with earthy or metallic particles.
 Fossils are *native* or *extraneous. Native fossils* are minerals, properly so called, as earths, salts, combustibles and metallic bodies. *Extraneous fossils* are bodies of vegetable or animal origin accidentally buried in the earth, as plants, shells, bones and other substances, many of which are petrified.
                   Encyc.

FRANKLINITE, *n.* A mineral compound of iron, zink and manganese, found in New Jersey, and named from Dr. Franklin.   *Cleaveland.*

FREEDOM, *n.* A state of exemption from the power or control of another; liberty; exemption from slavery, servitude or confinement. *Freedom* is *personal, civil, political,* and *religious.* [See *Liberty.*]
 4. Exemption from fate, necessity, or any constraint in consequence of predetermination or otherwise; as the *freedom* of the will.
 5. Any exemption from constraint or control.
 8. License; improper familiarity; violation of the rules of decorum; with a plural. Beware of what are called innocent *freedoms.*

FREETHINKER, *n.* A softer name for a deist; an unbeliever; one who discards revelation.

FRENCH-HORN, *n.* A wind instrument of music made of metal.

FREQUENCY, *n.* A return or occurrence of a thing often repeated at short intervals. The *frequency* of crimes abates our horror at the commission; the *frequency* of capital punishments tends to destroy their proper effect.

FREQUENT, *v.t.* To visit often; to resort to often or habitually. The man who *frequents* a dram-shop, an ale house, or a gaming table, is in the road to poverty, disgrace and ruin.

FRESHET, *n.* A flood or overflowing of a river, by means of heavy rains or melted snow; an inundation.   *New England.*

FRIENDLY, *a.* 5. Favorable; propitious; salutary; promoting the good of; as a *friendly* breeze or gale. Excessive rains are not *friendly* to the ripening fruits. Temperance is *friendly* to longevity.

FRIENDSHIP, *n.* An attachment to a person, proceeding from intimate acquaintance, and a reciprocation of kind offices, or from a favorable opinion of the amiable and respectable qualities of his mind. *Friendship* differs from benevolence, which is good will to mankind in general, and from that *love* which springs from animal appetite. *True* friendship is a noble and virtuous attachment, springing from a pure source, a respect for worth or amiable qualities. *False* friendship may subsist between bad men, as between thieves and pirates. This is a temporary attachment springing from interest, and may change in a moment to enmity and rancor.

There can be no *friendship* without confidence, and no confidence without integrity.   *Rambler.*

FROLICK, *n.* 2. A scene of gayety and mirth, as in dancing or play. [*This is a popular use of the word in America.*]

FRONTIER, *a.* Lying on the exterior part; bordering; conterminous; as a *frontier* town.

FROSTNAIL, *n.* A nail driven into a horse-shoe, to prevent the horse from slipping on ice. In some of the United States, the ends of the shoe are pointed for this purpose, and these points are called *calks.*

FRUGAL, *a.* Economical in the use or appropriation of money, goods or provisions of any kind; saving unnecessary expense, either of money or of any thing else which is to be used or consumed; sparing; not profuse, prodigal or lavish. We ought to be *frugal* not only in the expenditure of money and of goods, but in the employment of time. It is followed by *of,* before the thing saved; as *frugal of* time. It is not synonymous with *parsimonious,* nor with *thrifty,* as now used.

FUGUE, *n.* In *music,* a chase or succession in the parts; that which expresses the capital thought or sentiment of the piece, in causing it to pass successively and alternately from one part to another.   *Encyc.*

FULSOME, *a.* Nauseous; offensive.
2. Rank; offensive to the smell; as a rank and *fulsome* smell.   *Bacon.*
3. Lustful; as *fulsome* ewes.   *Shak.*
4. Tending to obscenity; as a *fulsome* epigram.   *Dryden.*

FRIENDSHIP. ☞
Samuel Johnson wrote essays for his periodical, the *Rambler,* from 1750 to 1752. Samuel Richardson was among its admirers, considering it at least as good as Steele and Addison's *Spectator.* Webster here quotes one of his Franklinesque aphorisms; others appear at MEMORY, POISON, SHAME, and WOMAN.

These are the English definitions of *fulsome*, but I have never witnessed such applications of the word in the United States. It seems then that *full* and *foul* are radically the same word, the primary sense of which is stuffed, crowded, from the sense of putting on or in. In the United States, the compound *fulsome* takes its signification from *full*, in the sense of cloying or satiating, and in England, *fulsome* takes its predominant sense from *foulness*.

FUR, *n.* 1. The short, fine, soft hair of certain animals, growing thick on the skin, and distinguished from the hair, which is longer and coarser. Fur is one of the most perfect non-conductors of heat, and serves to keep animals warm in cold climates.

FURLOW, *n.* [. . . The common orthography *furlough* is corrupt, as the last syllable exhibits false radical consonants. The true orthography is *furlow*.] Leave of absence; a word used only in military affairs. Leave or license given by a commanding officer to an officer or soldier to be absent from service for a certain time.

G

GAB, *n.* The mouth; as in the phrase, the gift of the *gab*, that is, loquaciousness. But the word is so vulgar as rarely to be used.

GAIN, *v.t.* 1. To obtain by industry or the employment of capital; to get as profit or advantage; to acquire. Any industrious person may *gain* a good living in America; but it is less difficult to *gain* property, than it is to use it with prudence. Money at interest may *gain* five, six, or seven per cent.

GALAXY, *n.* The milky way; that long, white, luminous track which seems to encompass the heavens like a girdle. This luminous appearance is found by the telescope to be occasioned by a multitude of stars, so small as not to be distinguished by the naked eye.   *Encyc.*

GALE, *n.* A current of air; a strong wind. The sense of this word is very indefinite. The poets use it in the sense of a moderate breeze or current of air, as a *gentle gale*. A stronger wind is called a *fresh gale*.
  In the language of seamen, the word *gale*, unaccompanied by an epithet, signifies a vehement wind, a storm or tempest. They say, the ship carried away her top-mast in a *gale*, or *gale* of wind; the ship rode out the *gale*. But the word is often qualified, as a *hard* or *strong gale*, a *violent gale*. A current of wind somewhat less violent is denominated a *stiff gale*. A less vehement wind is called a *fresh gale*, which is a wind not too strong for a ship to carry single reefed top-sails, when close hauled. When the wind is not so violent

---

☞ G. The Celtic nations had a peculiar manner of beginning the sound of *u* or *w* with the articulation *g*, or rather prefixing this articulation to that vowel. Thus *guard* for *ward*, *gwain* for *wain*, *guerre* for *war*, *gwell* for *well*. Whether this *g* has been added by the Celtic races, or whether the Teutonic nations have lost it, is a question I have not examined with particular attention. ☜

---

but that a ship will carry her top-sails a-trip or full spread, it is called a *loom-gale*.   *Mar. Dict.   Encyc.*

GALLANT, *n.* 2. A man who is polite and attentive to ladies; one who attends upon ladies at parties, or to places of amusement.
   3. A wooer; a lover; a suitor.
   4. In an *ill sense*, one who caresses a woman for lewd purposes.

GALLOP, *n.* The movement or pace of a quadruped, particularly of a horse, by springs, reaches or leaps. The animal lifts his fore feet nearly at the same time, and as these descend and are just ready to touch the ground, the hind feet are lifted at once. The gallop is the swiftest pace of a horse, but it is also a moderate pace, at the pleasure of a rider.

GALOCHE.   ☞   GALOCHE, *n.* [Fr. from Sp. *galocha*, a clog or wooden shoe.] A patten, clog
Webster had to know   or wooden shoe, or a shoe to be worn over another shoe to keep the foot dry.
that this and GOLOE-   It is written also *galoshe*.
SHOE were the same
word, but he assigns   GALVANISM, *n.* [from *Galvani* of Bologna, the discoverer.] Electrical phenom-
them different etymolo-   ena in which the electricity is developed without the aid of friction, and in
gies.   which a chimical action takes place between certain bodies.   *Edin. Encyc.*
   Galvanism is heat, light, electricity and magnetism, united in combination or in simultaneous action; sometimes one and sometimes another of them predominating, and thus producing more or less all the effects of each: usual means of excitement, contact of dissimilar bodies, especially of metals and fluids.   *Hare.   Silliman.*

GAMBLER, *n.* One who games or plays for money or other stake. *Gamblers* often or usually become cheats and knaves.

GAME, *n.* 3. An exercise or play for amusement or winning a stake; as a *game* of cricket; a *game* of chess; a *game* of whist. Some *games* depend on skill; others on hazard.
   9. In *antiquity*, games were public diversions or contests exhibited as spectacles for the gratification of the people. These *games* consisted of running, leaping, wrestling, riding, &c. Such were the Olympic games, the Pythian, the Isthmian, the Nemean, &c. among the Greeks; and among the Romans, the Apollinarian, the Circensian, the Capitoline, &c.   *Encyc.*

GANTLOPE, *n.* A military punishment inflicted on criminals for some hainous offense. It is executed in this manner; soldiers are arranged in two rows, face to face, each armed with a switch or instrument of punishment; between these rows, the offender, stripped to his waist, is compelled to pass a certain number of times, and each man gives him a stroke. A similar punishment is used on board of ships. Hence this word is chiefly used in the phrase, *to run the gantlet* or *gantlope*.   *Dryden.   Mar. Dict.*

GARDEN, *n.* 2. A rich, well cultivated spot or tract of country; a delightful spot. The intervals on the river Connecticut are all a *garden*. Lombardy is the *garden* of Italy.

GARRETEER, *n.* An inhabitant of a garret; a poor author.

GAS, *n.* In *chimistry*, a permanently elastic aeriform fluid, or a substance reduced to the state of an aeriform fluid by its permanent combination with caloric.   *Dict. Nat. Hist.*
     Gases are invisible except when colored, which happens in two or three instances.

GASLIGHT, *n.* Light produced by the combustion of carbureted hydrogen gas. Gaslights are now substituted for oil lights, in illuminating streets and apartments in houses.

GASTRILOQUIST, *n.* Literally, one who speaks from his belly or stomach; hence, one who so modifies his voice that it seems to come from another person or place.   *Reid.*

GAVOT, *n.* A kind of dance, the air of which has two brisk and lively strains in common time, each of which is played twice over. The first has usually four or eight bars, and the second contains eight, twelve or more.   *Encyc.*

GAWKY, *a.* Foolish; awkward; clumsy; clownish. [In this sense it is retained in vulgar use in America.] [Is not this allied to the Fr. *gauche*, left, untoward, unhandy, Eng. *awk*, awkward; *gauchir*, to shrink back or turn aside, to use shifts, to double, to dodge. This verb well expresses the actions of a jester or buffoon.]

GAZEL, *n.* An animal of Africa and India, of the genus Antilope. It partakes of the nature of the goat and the deer. Like the goat, the gazel has hollow permanent horns, and it feeds on shrubs; but in size and delicacy, and in the nature and color of its hair, it resembles the roe-buck. It has cylindrical horns, most frequently annulated at the base, and bunches of hair on its fore legs. It has a most brilliant, beautiful eye.   *Goldsmith.   Ed. Encyc.*

GAZETTE, *n.* [. . . *Gazetta* is said to have been a Venetian coin, which was the price of the first newspaper, and hence the name.] A newspaper; a sheet or half sheet of paper containing an account of transactions and events of public or private concern, which are deemed important and interesting. The first gazette in England was published at Oxford in 1665. On the removal of the court to London, the title was changed to the *London Gazette*. It is now the official newspaper, and published on Tuesdays and Saturdays. *Encyc.*

GENEVA, *n.* A spirit distilled from grain or malt, with the addition of juniper berries. But instead of these berries, the spirit is now flavored with the oil of turpentine. The word is usually contracted and pronounced *gin*. *Encyc.*

GENTLEMAN, *n.* 2. In *the United States*, where titles and distinctions of rank do not exist, the term is applied to men of education and of good breeding, of every occupation. Indeed this is also the popular practice in Great Britain. Hence,

3. A man of good breeding, politeness, and civil manners, as distinguished from the vulgar and clownish.

A plowman on his legs is higher than a *gentleman* on his knees.
Franklin.

4. A term of complaisance. In the plural, the appellation by which men are addressed in popular assemblies, whatever may be their condition or character.

GEORAMA.
Between 1825 and 1832 Parisians marveled at this globe in an octagonal building that today would lie in front of the Opera. Visitors could go up inside the globe on a spiral staircase.

GEORAMA, *n.* An instrument or machine which exhibits a very complete view of the earth, lately invented in Paris. It is a hollow sphere of forty feet diameter, formed by thirty six bars of iron representing the parallels and meridians, and covered with a bluish cloth, intended to represent seas and lakes. The land, mountains and rivers are painted on paper and pasted on this cover. *Journ. of Science.*

GIBBSITE, *n.* A mineral found at Richmond, in Massachusetts, and named in honor of George Gibbs, Esq. It occurs in irregular stalactical masses, which present an aggregation of elongated, tuberous branches, parallel and united. Its structure is fibrous, the fibers radiating from an axis. Its colors are a dirty white, greenish white and grayish. *Cleaveland.*

GIDDY, *a.* Vertiginous; reeling; whirling; having in the head a sensation of a circular motion or swimming; or having lost the power of preserving the balance of the body, and therefore wavering and inclined to fall, as in the case of some diseases and of drunkenness. In walking on timber aloft, or looking down a precipice, we are apt to be *giddy*.

GIN, *n.* [A contraction of *engine.*] A machine or instrument by which the mechanical powers are employed in aid of human strength. The word is applied to various engines, as a machine for driving piles, another for raising weights, &c.; and a machine for separating the seeds from cotton, invented by E. Whitney, is called a *cotton-gin*. It is also the name given to an engine of torture, and to a pump moved by rotary sails.

GINSENG, *n.* [This word is probably Chinese, and it is said by Grosier, to signify the resemblance of a man, or man's thigh. He observes also that the root in the language of the Iroquois is called *garentoquen*, which signifies *legs and thighs separated.* Grosier's China, i. 534.1]. A plant, of the genus Panax, the root of which is in great demand among the Chinese. It is found in the Northern parts of Asia and America, and is an article of export from America to China. It has a jointed, fleshy, taper root, as large as a man's finger, which when dry is of a yellowish white color, with a mucilaginous sweetness in the taste, somewhat resembling that of liquorice, accompanied with a slight bitterness.   *Encyc.*

GIPSEY, *n.* The Gipseys are a race of vagabonds which infest Europe, Africa and Asia, strolling about and subsisting mostly by theft, robbery and fortune-telling. The name is supposed to be corrupted from *Egyptian*, as they were thought to have come from Egypt. But their language indicates that they originated in Hindoostan.   *Grellman.*

GLAND, *n.* 1. In *anatomy*, a distinct soft body, formed by the convolution of a great number of vessels, either constituting a part of the lymphatic system, or destined to secrete some fluid from the blood. Glands have been divided into *conglobate* and *conglomerate*, from their structure; but a more proper division is into *lymphatic* and *secretory*. The former are found in the course of the lymphatic vessels, and are conglobate. The latter are of various structure. They include the mucous follicles, the conglomerate glands, properly so called, such as the parotid glands and the pancreas, the liver, kidneys, &c. The term has also been applied to other bodies of a similar appearance, neither lymphatic nor secretory; such as the thymus and thyroid glands, whose use is not certainly known, certain portions of the brain, as the pineal and pituitary glands, &c.   *Encyc. Parr. Coxe.*

GLOSSARY, *n.* A dictionary or vocabulary, explaining obscure or antiquated words found in old authors; such as Du Cange's Glossary; Spelman's Glossary.

GLUE, *v.t.* To join with glue or a viscous substance. Cabinet makers *glue* together some parts of furniture.
2. To unite; to hold together.   *Newton*
[This word is now seldom used in a figurative sense. The phrases, to *glue* friends together, vices *glue* us to low pursuits or pleasures, found in writers of the last century, are not now used, or are deemed inelegant.]

GNOME, *n.* An imaginary being, supposed by the cabalists, to inhabit the inner parts of the earth, and to be the guardian of mines, quarries, &c.   *Encyc.*

GOAT, *n.* An animal or quadruped of the genus Capra. The horns are hollow, turned upwards, erect and scabrous. Goats are nearly of the size of sheep, but

GLOSSARY. Charles du Fresne, sieur du Cange (1610–88), was a French medieval historian and philologist. His 1678 glossary is of medieval and late Latin. Sir Henry Spelman (1562–1641) wrote an important law glossary.

stronger, less timid and more agile. They delight to frequent rocks and mountains, and subsist on scanty coarse food. The milk of the goat is sweet, nourishing and medicinal, and the flesh furnishes provisions to the occupants of countries where they abound.

GOLF, *n.* A game with ball and bat, in which he who drives the ball into a hole with the fewest strokes is the winner.   *Strutt.*

GOLOESHOE, *n.* [Arm. *golo* or *golei,* to cover.] An over-shoe; a shoe worn over another to keep the foot dry.

GOOD, *n.* That which contributes to diminish or remove pain, or to increase happiness or prosperity; benefit; advantage; opposed to *evil* or *misery.* The medicine will do neither *good* nor harm. It does my heart *good* to see you so happy.
   2. Welfare; prosperity; advancement of interest or happiness. He labored for the *good* of the state.
      The *good* of the whole community can be promoted only by advancing the *good* of each of the members composing it.   *Federalist, Jay.*

GOOM, *n.* A man recently married, or who is attending his proposed spouse for the purpose of marriage; used in composition, as in *bridegoom.* It has been corrupted into *groom.*

GOTHAM. Washington Irving, in *Salmagundi,* gave this name to New York "because the inhabitants were such wiseacres" (*Webster's New International Dictionary,* 3rd edition). Webster gives the American pronunciation, forgetting that the Brits call it "got 'em." See HAM.

GOTHAMIST, *n.* A person deficient in wisdom, so called from Gotham in Nottinghamshire, noted for some pleasant blunders.   *Bp. Morton.*

GOVERNMENT, *n.* 5. The system of polity in a state; that form of fundamental rules and principles by which a nation or state is governed, or by which individual members of a body politic are to regulate their social actions; a constitution, either written or unwritten, by which the rights and duties of citizens and public officers are prescribed and defined; as a monarchial *government,* or a republican *government.*
      Thirteen *governments* thus founded on the natural authority of the people alone, without the pretence of miracle or mystery, are a great point gained in favor of the rights of mankind.   *J. Adams.*

GRANDJUROR, *n.* One of a grand jury. In Connecticut, a peace-officer.

GRATITUDE, *n.* An emotion of the heart, excited by a favor or benefit received; a sentiment of kindness or good will towards a benefactor; thankfulness. Gratitude is an agreeable emotion, consisting in or accompanied with good will to a benefactor, and a disposition to make a suitable return of benefits or services, or when no return can be made, with a desire to see the benefactor prosperous and happy. Gratitude is a virtue of the highest excellence, as it implies a feeling and generous heart, and a proper sense of duty.

The love of God is the sublimest *gratitude*.   *Paley.*

GRAVE, *n.* 3. Any place where the dead are reposited; a place of great slaughter or mortality. Flanders was formerly the *grave* of English armies. Russia proved to be the *grave* of the French army under Bonaparte. The tropical climates are the *grave* of American seamen and of British soldiers.

Specific gravity, the weight belonging to an equal bulk of every different substance. Thus the exact weight of a cubic inch of gold, compared with that of a cubic inch of water or tin, is called its specific gravity. The specific gravity of bodies is usually ascertained by weighing them in distilled water. *Encyc.*

GREEN, *v.t.* To make green. This is used by Thomson and by Barlow, but is not an elegant word, nor indeed hardly legitimate, in the sense in which these writers use it. "Spring *greens* the year." "God *greens* the groves." The only legitimate sense of this verb, if used, would be, to dye green, or to change to a green color. A plant growing in a dark room is yellow; let this plant be carried into the open air, and the rays of the sun will *green* it. This use would correspond with the use of *whiten, blacken, redden.*

GREEN, *n.* 4. The leaves and stems of young plants used in cookery or dressed for food in the spring; *in the plural.*   *New England.*

GRIEF, *n.* 2. The pain of mind occasioned by our own misconduct; sorrow or regret that we have done wrong; pain accompanying repentance. We feel *grief* when we have offended or injured a friend, and the consciousness of having offended the Supreme Being, fills the penitent heart with the most poignant *grief.*

GROCER, *n.* [This is usually considered as formed from *gross,* but in other languages, the corresponding word is from the name of plants, herbs or spices. . . . The French, Spanish and Portuguese use words formed from the name of spice, and the Italian is from the same word as drug. It would seem then that a *grocer,* whatever may be the origin of the name, was originally a seller of spices and other vegetables.]

GROG-BLOSSOM, *n.* A rum bud; a redness on the nose or face of men who drink ardent spirits to excess; a deformity that marks the beastly vice of intemperance.

GROUND-FLOOR, *n.* The first or lower floor of a house. But the English call the *second* floor from the ground the *first* floor.

GUARANTY, *v.t.* 2. To undertake to secure to another, at all events, as claims, rights or possessions. Thus in the treaty of 1778, France *guarantied* to the United States their liberty, sovereignty and independence, and their possessions; and the United States *guarantied* to France its possessions in America.

The United States shall *guaranty* to every state in the Union a republican form of government.   *Const. of U. States*

GUITAR, *n.* A stringed instrument of music; in England and the United States, used chiefly by ladies, but in Spain and Italy, much used by men.
Encyc.

GUMPTION, n Care; skill; understanding. [*Vulgar.*]

GUN, *n.* An instrument consisting of a barrel or tube of iron or other metal fixed in a stock, from which balls, shot or other deadly weapons are discharged by the explosion of gunpowder. The larger species of guns are called cannon; and the smaller species are called muskets, carbines, fowling pieces, &c. But one species of fire-arms, the pistol, is never called a gun.

GYMNOSOPHIST, *n.* A philosopher of India, so called from his going with bare feet, or with little clothing. The Gymnosophists in India lived in the woods and on mountains, subsisting on wild productions of the earth. They never drank wine nor married. Some of them traveled about, and practiced physic. They believed the immortality and transmigration of the soul. They placed the chief happiness of man in a contempt of the goods of fortune, and of the pleasures of sense.   *Encyc.*

H

HABERDASHER, *n.* [perhaps from G. *habe*, D. *have*, goods, and G. *tauschen*, to barter, to truck. If not, I can give no account of its origin.] A seller of small wares; *a word little used or not at all in the U. States.*

HABIT, *n.* 4. A disposition or condition of the mind or body acquired by custom or a frequent repetition of the same act. *Habit* is that which is held or retained, the effect of custom or frequent repetition. Hence we speak of good *habits* and bad *habits.* Frequent drinking of spirits leads to a *habit* of intemperance. We should endeavor to correct evil *habits* by a change of practice. A great point in the education of children, is to prevent the formation of bad *habits.*

HAIL, *n.* Masses of ice or frozen vapor, falling from the clouds in showers or storms. These masses consist of little spherules united, but not all of the same consistence; some being as hard and solid as perfect ice; others soft, like frozen snow. Hailstones assume various figures; some are round, others angular, others pyramidical, others flat, and sometimes they are stellated with six radii, like crystals of snow.   *Encyc.*

HAIL, *v.t.* To call; to call to a person at a distance, to arrest his attention. It is properly used in any case where the person accosted is distant, but is appropriately used by seamen. *Hoa* or *hoi*, the ship *ahoay*, is the usual manner of hailing; to which the answer is *holloa*, or *hollo.* Then follow the usual questions, whence came ye? where are you bound? &c.

HALLELUIAH, *n.* [This word is improperly written with *j*, in conformity with the German and other continental languages, in which *j* has the sound

---

H. It is pronounced with an expiration of breath, which, preceding a vowel, is perceptible by the ear at a considerable distance.

of *y*. But to pronounce the word with the English sound of *j* destroys its beauty. The like mistake of the sound of *j* in *Jehovah, Jordan, Joseph,* has perverted the true pronunciation, which was *Yehovah, Yordan. Yoseph.* This perversion must now be submitted to, but in *Halleluiah* it ought not to be tolerated.]

HALLUCINATION. ☞ Erasmus Darwin (1731–1802), a source that Webster often turned to (see PRECLUDE), was an English physician and poet. His *Zoonomia* explained organic life according to evolutionary principles, and so anticipated later theories. Charles Darwin and Francis Galton were his grandsons.

HALLUCINATION, *n.* 2. In *medicine,* faulty sense [*dysœsthesia,*] or erroneous imagination. *Hallucinations of the senses* arise from some defect in the organs of sense, or from some unusual circumstances attending the object, as when it is seen by moonlight; and they are sometimes symptoms of general disease, as in fevers. *Maniacal hallucinations* arise from some imaginary or mistaken idea. Similar hallucinations occur in *revery.*   *Darwin. Parr.*

HAM, Sax. *ham,* a house, is our modern word *home,* G. *heim.* It is used in *hamlet* and in the names of places, as in *Walt-ham,* wood-house, *walt,* a wood, and *ham,* a house, [not Wal-tham, as it is often pronounced,] *Buckingham, Notting-ham, Wrent-ham, Dur-ham,* &c.

HAREM, *n.* A seraglio; a place where Eastern princes confine their women, who are prohibited from the society of others.

HARLEQUIN, *n.* A buffoon, dressed in party-colored clothes, who plays tricks, like a merry-andrew, to divert the populace. This character was first introduced into Italian comedy, but is now a standing character in English pantomime entertainments.   *Encyc.*

HARLOT, *n.* [W. *herlawd,* a stripling; *herlodes,* a hoiden; a word composed of *her,* a push, or challenge, and *llawd,* a lad. This word was formerly applied to males as well as females.
        A sturdie *harlot*—that was her hostes man.   *Chaucer, Tales.*
        He was a gentil *harlot* and a kind.   *Ibid.*
    The word originally signified a bold stripling, or a hoiden. But the W. *llawd* signifies not only a *lad,* that is, a shoot, or growing youth, but as an adjective, tending forward, craving, *lewd.*]

Harmonical mean, in arithmetic and algebra, a term used to express certain relations of numbers and quantities, which are supposed to bear an analogy to musical consonances.

Harmonical proportion, in arithmetic and algebra, is said to obtain between three quantities, or four quantities, in certain cases.

HARNESS, *n.* The furniture of a draught horse, whether for a wagon, coach, gig, chaise, &c.; called in some of the American states, *tackle* or *tackling,* with which, in its primary sense, it is synonymous.   *Dryden.*

HARP, *n.* 1. An instrument of music of the stringed kind, of a triangular figure, held upright and commonly touched with the fingers.

Encyc.   Johnson.

HARVEST, *n.* [. . . This word signifies autumn, and primarily had no reference to the collection of the fruits of the earth; but in German, *herbstzeit* is harvest-time . . . and primarily it refers to the cold, chilly weather in autumn in the north of Europe. This being the time when crops are collected in northern climates, the word came to signify *harvest.*] 1. The season of reaping and gathering in corn or other crops. It especially refers to the time of collecting corn or grain, which is the chief food of men, as wheat and rye. In Egypt and Syria, the wheat harvest is in April and May; in the south of Europe and of the United States, in June; in the Northern states of America, in July; and in the north of Europe, in August and September. In the United States, the harvest of maiz is mostly in October.

HASTE, *n.* Celerity of motion; speed; swiftness; dispatch; expedition; applied only to voluntary beings, as men and other animals; never to other bodies. We never say, a ball flies with *haste.*

HAT, *n.* 1. A covering for the head; a garment made of different materials, and worn by men or women for defending the head from rain or heat, or for ornament. Hats for men are usually made of fur or wool, and formed with a crown and brim. Hats for females are made of straw or grass braid, and various other materials. Of these the ever varying forms admit of no description that can long be correct.

HATRED, *n.* Great dislike or aversion; hate; enmity. *Hatred* is an aversion to evil, and may spring from utter disapprobation, as the *hatred* of vice or meanness; or it may spring from offenses or injuries done by fellow men, or from envy or jealousy, in which case it is usually accompanied with malevolence or malignity. Extreme hatred is abhorrence or detestation.

HAUNT, *v.t.* 3. It is particularly applied to specters or apparitions, which are represented by fear and credulity as frequenting or inhabiting old, decayed and deserted houses.

HAVE, *v.t.* 6. To be urged by necessity or obligation; to be under necessity, or impelled by duty. I *have* to visit twenty patients every day. We *have* to strive against temptations. We *have* to encounter strong prejudices. The nation *has* to pay the interest of an immense debt.

HAYWARD, *n.* A person who keeps the common herd or cattle of a town, and guards hedges or fences. In New England, the *hayward* is a town officer whose duty is to impound cattle, and particularly swine which are found running at large in the highways, contrary to law.

HAZARD, *v.t.* To expose to chance; to put in danger of loss or injury; to venture; to risk; as, to *hazard* life to save a friend; to *hazard* an estate on the throw of a die; to *hazard* salvation for temporal pleasure.

Men *hazard* nothing by a course of evangelical obedience.   *Clarke.*

2. To venture to incur, or bring on; as, to *hazard* the loss of reputation.

HEART, *n.* 4. The seat of the affections and passions, as of love, joy, grief, enmity, courage, pleasure, &c.

The *heart* is deceitful above all things. Every imagination of the thoughts of the *heart* is evil continually. We read of an honest and good *heart,* and an evil *heart* of unbelief, a willing *heart,* a heavy *heart,* sorrow of *heart,* a hard *heart,* a proud *heart,* a pure *heart.* The *heart* faints in adversity, or under discouragement, that is, courage fails; the *heart* is deceived, enlarged, reproved, lifted up, fixed, established, moved, &c.   *Scripture.*

7. The seat of the will; hence, secret purposes, intentions or designs. There are many devices in a man's *heart.* The *heart* of kings is unsearchable. The Lord tries and searches the *heart.* David had it in his *heart* to build a house of rest for the ark.   *Scripture.*

HEAT, *n.* 1. Heat, as a cause of sensation, that is, the matter of heat, is considered to be a subtil fluid, contained in a greater or less degree in all bodies. In modern chimistry, it is called *caloric.* It expands all bodies in different proportions, and is the cause of fluidity and evaporation. A certain degree of it is also essential to animal and vegetable life. Heat is *latent,* when so combined with other matter as not to be perceptible. It is *sensible,* when it is evolved and perceptible.   *Lavoisier.   Encyc.*

2. Heat, as a sensation, is the effect produced on the sentient organs of animals, by the passage of caloric, disengaged from surrounding bodies, to the organs. When we touch or approach a hot body, the caloric or heat passes *from* that body *to* our organs of feeling, and gives the sensation of heat. On the contrary, when we touch a cold body, the caloric passes *from* the hand *to* that body, and causes a sensation of cold.   *Lavoisier.*

Note. This theory of heat seems not to be fully settled.

HEATHEN, *n.* [. . . that is, one who lives in the country or woods, as *pagan* from *pagus,* a village.] A pagan; a Gentile; one who worships idols, or is unacquainted with the true God. In the Scriptures, the word seems to comprehend all nations except the Jews or Israelites, as they were all strangers to the true religion, and all addicted to idolatry. The word may now be applied perhaps to all nations, except to Christians and Mohammedans.

Heathen, without the plural termination, is used plurally or collectively, for Gentiles or heathen nations.

HEAVEN, *n*. 6. Modern philosophers divide the expanse above and around the earth into two parts, the atmosphere or aerial heaven, and the etherial heaven beyond the region of the air, in which there is supposed to be a thin, unresisting medium called ether. *Encyc.*

HELIOSCOPE, *n*. A sort of telescope fitted for viewing the sun without pain or injury to the eyes, as when made with colored glasses, or glasses blackened with smoke. *Encyc.*

HELTER-SKELTER, cant words denoting hurry and confusion. [*Vulgar.*]

HEMLOCK, *n*. 3. A poison, an infusion or decoction of the poisonous plant.
Popular liberty might then have escaped the indelible reproach of decreeing to the same citizens the *hemlock* on one day, and statues on the next. *Federalist, Madison.*

HEMP, *n*. 1. A fibrous plant constituting the genus Cannabis, whose skin or bark is used for cloth and cordage. Hence *canvas*, the coarse strong cloth used for sails.
2. The skin or rind of the plant, prepared for spinning. Large quantities of *hemp* are exported from Russia.

HEPTAGONAL, *a*. Having seven angles or sides. *Heptagonal numbers*, in arithmetic, a sort of polygonal numbers, wherein the difference of the terms of the corresponding arithmetical progression is 5. One of the properties of these numbers is, that if they are multiplied by 40, and 9 is added to the product, the sum will be a square number. *Encyc.*

> HEPTAGONAL. Webster fails to define *polygonal numbers.*

HERRING, *n*. A fish of the genus Clupea. Herrings, when they migrate, move in vast shoals, and it is said that the name is formed from the Teutonic *here, heer,* an army or multitude. They come from high northern latitudes in the spring, and visit the shores of Europe and America, where they are taken and salted in great quantities.

HERSCHEL, *n*. A planet discovered by Dr. Herschel, in 1781.

> HERSCHEL. This planet is now called *Uranus.*

HETEROSCIAN, *n*. Those inhabitants of the earth are called *Heteroscians,* whose shadows fall one way only. Such are those who live between the tropics and the polar circles. The shadows of those who live north of the tropic of Cancer, fall northward; those of the inhabitants south of the tropic of Capricorn, fall southward; whereas the shadows of those who dwell between the tropics fall sometimes to the north and sometimes to the south.

HEXAGON, *n*. In *geometry*, a figure of six sides and six angles. If the sides and angles are equal, it is a *regular hexagon*. The cells of honeycomb are hexagons, and it is remarkable that bees instinctively form their cells of this figure which fills any given space without any interstice or loss of room.

HIDE, *v.t.* 1. To conceal; to withhold or withdraw from sight; to place in any state or position in which the view is intercepted from the object. The intervention of the moon between the earth and the sun *hides* the latter from our sight. The people in Turkey hide their grain in the earth. No human being can *hide* his crimes or his neglect of duty from his Maker.

HIGHLAND, *n.* Elevated land; a mountainous region.
Highlands of Scotland, mountainous regions inhabited by the descendants of the ancient Celts, who retain their primitive language.
Highlands on the Hudson, sixty miles from New York. These afford most sublime and romantic scenery, and here is West Point, a fortified post during the revolution, and now the seat of one of the best military schools of the age.

HIPPOPOTAMUS, *n.* The river-horse, an animal that inhabits the Nile and other rivers in Africa. This animal resembles a hog rather than a horse, and was named perhaps from his neighing voice. He has been found of the length of 17 feet. He delights in the water, but feeds on herbage on land.   *Encyc.*

HISTORY, *n.* [. . . *History* and *story* are the same word differently written.] An account of facts, particularly of facts respecting nations or states; a narration of events in the order in which they happened, with their causes and effects. *History* differs from *annals. Annals* relate simply the facts and events of each year, in strict chronological order, without any observations of the annalist. *History* regards less strictly the arrangement of events under each year, and admits the observations of the writer. This distinction however is not always regarded with strictness.
History is of different kinds, or treats of different subjects; as a *history* of government, or political *history; history* of the christian church, or ecclesiastical *history; history* of war and conquests, or military *history; history* of law; *history* of commerce; *history* of the crusades, &c. In these and similar examples, *history* is *written* narrative or relation. What is the *history* of nations, but a narrative of the follies, crimes and miseries of man?
2. Narration; verbal relation of facts or events; story. We listen with pleasure to the soldier or the seaman, giving a *history* of his adventures.
4. Description; an account of things that exist; as natural *history,* which comprehends a description of the works of nature, particularly of animals, plants and minerals; a *history* of animals, or zoology; a *history* of plants.
5. An account of the origin, life and actions of an individual person. We say, we have a concise *history* of the prisoner in the testimony offered to the court.
A formal written account of an individual's life, is called *biography.*

HOB, HUB, *n.* The nave of a wheel; a solid piece of timber in which the spokes are inserted.   *Washington.*

HOIST, *v.t.* 3. To lift and move the leg backwards; a word of command used by milkmaids to cows, when they wish them to lift and set back the right leg.

HOMICIDE, *n.* 1. The killing of one man or human being by another. Homicide is of three kinds, *justifiable, excusable,* and *felonious; justifiable,* when it proceeds from unavoidable necessity, without an intention to kill, and without negligence; *excusable,* when it happens from misadventure, or in self-defense; *felonious,* when it proceeds from malice, or is done in the prosecution of some unlawful act, or in a sudden passion. Homicide committed with premeditated malice, is murder. Suicide also, or self-murder, is felonious homicide. Homicide comprehends murder and manslaughter.
                                                             Blackstone.

HOMMONY, *n.* [Indian.] In *America,* maiz hulled and broken, but coarse, prepared for food by being mixed with water and boiled.   *Adair.*

HOORA, HOORAW, *exclam.* A shout of joy or exultation. [*This is the genuine English word, for which we find in books most absurdly written, huzza,* a foreign word never or rarely used.]

HOORA. *Huzza* may be absurd, but see ACCLAMATION.

HOPE, *n.* 1. A desire of some good, accompanied with at least some expectation of obtaining it, or a belief that it is obtainable. *Hope* differs from *wish* and *desire* in this, that it implies some expectation of obtaining the good desired, or the possibility of possessing it. *Hope* therefore always gives pleasure or joy; whereas *wish* and *desire* may produce or be accompanied with pain and anxiety.
    He that lives upon *hope,* will die fasting.   *Franklin.*

HORD, HORDE, *n.* A company of wandering people dwelling in tents or wagons, and migrating from place to place to procure pasturage for their cattle. Such are some tribes of the Tartars in the north of Asia. A hord usually consists of fifty or sixty tents.   *Encyc. Mitford.*

HORE, *n.* [. . . The common orthography *whore* is corrupt.] A woman, married or single, who indulges unlawful sexual intercourse; also, a prostitute; a common woman; a harlot; a woman of ill fame. [This word comprehends *adultress* and *fornicatrix,* and all lewd women whether paid for prostitution or not.]

HORIZON, *n.* [. . . This word, like *contest, aspect,* and others in Milton, must be read in poetry with the accent on the second syllable; a harsh, unnatural pronunciation, in direct opposition to the regular analogy of English words. With the accent on the first syllable, as in common usage, it is an elegant word.]

HORNBOOK, *n.* The first book of children, or that in which they learn their letters and rudiments; so called from its cover of horn. [*Now little used.*]
Locke.

HOSPITAL, *n.* A building appropriated for the reception of sick, infirm and helpless paupers, who are supported and nursed by charity; also, a house for the reception of insane persons, whether paupers or not, or for seamen, soldiers, foundlings, &c. who are supported by the public, or by private charity, or for infected persons, &c.

HOUSE-BREAKING, *n.* The breaking, or opening and entering of a house by daylight, with the intent to commit a felony, or to steal or rob. The same crime committed at night is *burglary.* Blackstone.

HOVER, *v.i.* 4. To wander about from place to place in the neighborhood; to move back and forth; as an army *hovering* on our borders; a ship *hovering* on our coast. Cranch's Rep.

HUMOR, *n.* 4. That quality of the imagination which gives to ideas a wild or fantastic turn, and tends to excite laughter or mirth by ludicrous images or representations. *Humor* is less poignant and brilliant than *wit;* hence it is always agreeable. Wit, directed against folly, often offends by its severity; humor makes a man ashamed of his follies, without exciting his resentment. Humor may be employed solely to raise mirth and render conversation pleasant, or it may contain a delicate kind of satire.

HUNTING, *n.* The act or practice of pursuing wild animals, for catching or killing them. Hunting was originally practiced by men for the purpose of procuring food, as it still is by uncivilized nations. But among civilized men, it is practiced mostly for exercise or diversion, or for the destruction of noxious animals, as in America.

HURDY-GURDY, *n.* An instrument of music, said to be used in the streets of London. Todd.

HYDROGEN, *n.* [. . . so called as being considered the generator of water.] In *chimistry,* a gas which constitutes one of the elements of water, of which it is said by Lavoisier to form fifteen parts in a hundred; but according to Berzelius and Dulong, hydrogen gas is 11.1 parts in a hundred, and oxygen 88.9. Hydrogen gas is an aeriform fluid, the lightest body known, and though extremely inflammable itself, it extinguishes burning bodies, and is fatal to animal life. Its specific gravity is 0.0694, that of air being 1.00. In consequence of its extreme lightness, it is employed for filling air balloons.

Lavoisier.   Webster's Manual.

HYPOCHONDRIAC, *n.* A person affected with debility, lowness of spirits or melancholy.

HYPOCRITE, *n.* 1. One who feigns to be what he is not; one who has the form of godliness without the power, or who assumes an appearance of piety and virtue, when he is destitute of true religion.

HYSTERICS, *n.* A disease of women, proceeding from the womb, and characterized by fits or spasmodic affections of the nervous system.   *Encyc.*

HYSTERICS. Johnson says this is "supposed to proceed from disorders in the womb." Webster doesn't appear to doubt it.

I

IDIOT, *n.* 1. A natural fool, or fool from his birth; a human being in form, but destitute of reason, or the ordinary intellectual powers of man.

A person who has understanding enough to measure a yard of cloth, number twenty correctly, tell the days of the week, &c., is not an *idiot* in the eye of the law.   *Encyc.*

IDLENESS, *n.* Abstinence from labor or employment; the state of a person who is unemployed in labor, or unoccupied in business; the state of doing nothing. *Idleness* is the parent of vice.

IELAND, *n.* [. . . Sax. *ealond, iegland;* composed of *ie, ea,* water, . . . and land. This is the genuine English word, always used in discourse, but for which is used *island,* an absurd compound of Fr. *isle* and land, which signifies *land-in water-land,* or rather *ieland-land.*] 1. A portion of land surrounded by water; as Bermuda, Barbadoes, Cuba, Great Britain, Borneo.

IGNIS FATUUS, *n.* A meteor or light that appears in the night, over marshy grounds, supposed to be occasioned by phosphoric matter extricated from putrefying animal or vegetable substances, or by some inflammable gas; vulgarly called *Will with the wisp,* and *Jack with a lantern.*   *Ed. Encyc.*

ILLEGIBLE, *a.* That cannot be read; obscure or defaced so that the words cannot be known. It is a disgrace to a gentleman to write an *illegible* hand. The manuscripts found in the ruins of Herculaneum are mostly *illegible.*

☞ I. The sound of *i* long, as in *fine, kind, arise,* is diphthongal; it begins with a sound approaching that of broad *a,* but it is not exactly the same, as the organs are not open to the same extent, and therefore the sound begins a little above that of *aw.* The sound, if continued, closes with one that nearly approaches to that of *e* long. This sound can be learned only by the ear. ☜

161

ILL-NATURED, *a.* Cross; crabbed; surly; intractable; of habitual bad temper; peevish; fractious. An *ill-natured* person may disturb the harmony of a whole parish.

IMBECILITY, *n.* 1.Want of strength; weakness; feebleness of body or of mind. We speak of the *imbecility* of the body or of the intellect, when either does not possess the usual strength and vigor that belongs to men and which is necessary to a due performance of its functions. This may be natural, or induced by violence or disease.

2. Impotence of males; inability to procreate children.

IMITABLE, *a.* That may be imitated or copied. Let us follow our Savior in all his *imitable* conduct and traits of character. There are some works of the ancients that are hardly *imitable*. The dignified style of Johnson is scarcely *imitable.*

IMMODEST, *a.* 2. Appropriately, wanting in the reserve or restraint which decency requires; wanting in decency and delicacy. It is *immodest* to treat superiors with the familiarity that is customary among equals.

IMMORAL, *a.* Inconsistent with moral rectitude; contrary to the moral or divine law; wicked; unjust; dishonest; vicious. Every action is *immoral* which contravenes any divine precept, or which is contrary to the duties which men owe to each other.

2. Wicked or unjust in practice; vicious; dishonest; as an *immoral* man. Every man who violates a divine law or a social duty, is *immoral,* but we particularly apply the term to a person who habitually violates the laws.

IMPATIENT, *a.* Uneasy or fretful under suffering; not bearing pain with composure; not enduring evil without fretfulness, uneasiness, and a desire or effort to get rid of the evil. Young men are *impatient* of restraint. We are all apt to be *impatient* under wrongs; but it is a christian duty not to be *impatient* in sickness, or under any afflictive dispensation of Providence.

2. Not suffering quietly; not enduring.

3. Hasty; eager; not enduring delay. The *impatient* man will not wait for information; he often acts with precipitance. Be not *impatient* for the return of spring.

This word is followed by *of, at, for,* or *under.* We are *impatient of* restraint, or *of* wrongs; *impatient at* the delay of expected good; *impatient for* the return of a friend, or *for* the arrival of the mail; *impatient under* evils of any kind. The proper use of these particles can be learnt only by practice or observation.

IMPIETY, *n.* Ungodliness; irreverence towards the Supreme Being; contempt of the divine character and authority; neglect of the divine precepts. These constitute different degrees of *impiety.*

2. Any act of wickedness, as blasphemy and scoffing at the Supreme Being, or at his authority; profaneness. Any expression of contempt for God or his laws, constitutes an *impiety* of the highest degree of criminality. Disobedience to the divine commands or neglect of duty implies contempt for his authority, and is therefore *impiety*. *Impiety*, when it expresses the temper or disposition, has no plural; but it is otherwise when it expresses an act of wickedness, for all such acts are *impieties*.

IMPORT, *v.t.* To bring from a foreign country or jurisdiction, or from another state, into one's own country, jurisdiction or state; opposed to *export*. We *import* teas and silks from China, wines from Spain and France, and dry goods from Great Britain. Great Britain *imports* cotton from America and India. We may say also that Connecticut, Massachusetts and Maine *import* flour from the middle states.

IMPORTANCE, *n.* Weight; consequence; a bearing on some interest; that quality of any thing by which it may affect a measure, interest or result. The education of youth is of great *importance* to a free government. A religious education is of infinite *importance* to every human being.

IMPOSTOR, *n.* One who imposes on others; a person who assumes a character for the purpose of deception; a deceiver under a false character. It seems to be yet unsettled, whether Perkin Warbeck was an *impostor*.   *Encyc.*

IMPRINT, *v.t.* 3. To fix on the mind or memory; to impress. Let your father's admonitions and instructions be *imprinted* on your mind.

IMPRUDENCE, *n.* Want of prudence; indiscretion; want of caution, circumspection, or a due regard to the consequences of words to be uttered or actions to be performed, or their probable effects on the interest, safety, reputation or happiness of one's self or others; heedlessness; inconsiderateness; rashness. Let a man of sixty attempt to enumerate the evils which his *imprudence* has brought on himself, his family, or his neighbors.

INCOMPATIBILITY, *n.* 2. Irreconcilable disagreement. During the revolution in France, *incompatibility* of temper was deemed a sufficient cause for divorcing man and wife.

INDEBTED, *a.* 2. Obliged by something received, for which restitution or gratitude is due. We are *indebted to* our parents *for* their care of us in infancy and youth. We are *indebted to* God for life. We are *indebted to* the christian religion *for* many of the advantages, and much of the refinement of modern times.

INDECENCY, *n.* That which is unbecoming in language or manners; any action or behavior which is deemed a violation of modesty, or an offense to

IMPOSTOR. Few Americans today would recognize the name of Perkin Warbeck, a pretender to the English throne (1474–99). He confessed to being an impostor, and the current edition of the *Encyclopædia Britannica* calls him "vain, foolish, and incompetent."

delicacy, as rude or wanton actions, obscene language, and whatever tends to excite a blush in a spectator. Extreme assurance or impudence may also be deemed *indecency* of behavior towards superiors.

Declaration of Independence, the solemn declaration of the Congress of the United States of America, on the 4th of July 1776, by which they formally renounced their subjection to the government of Great Britain.

INDIA *Rubber, n.* The caoutchouc, a substance of extraordinary elasticity, called also *elastic gum* or *resin.* It is produced by incision from the syringe tree of Cayenne.

INDICATIVE, *a.* Showing; giving intimation or knowledge of something not visible or obvious. Reserve is not always *indicative* of modesty; it may be *indicative* of prudence.

INDIGENCY, *n.* Want of estate, or means of comfortable subsistence; penury; poverty. A large portion of the human race live in *indigence,* while others possess more than they can enjoy.

INDIVISIBLE, *a.* That cannot be divided, separated or broken; not separable into parts. Perhaps the particles of matter, however small, cannot be considered as *indivisible.* The mind or soul must be *indivisible.* A mathematical point is *indivisible.*

INDULGENCE, INDULGENCY, *n.* Free permission to the appetites, humor, desires, passions or will to act or operate; forbearance of restraint or control. How many children are ruined by *indulgence! Indulgence* is not kindness or tenderness, but it may be the effect of one or the other, or of negligence.

INESTIMABLE, *a.* Too valuable or excellent to be rated; being above all price; as *inestimable* rights. The privileges of American citizens, civil and religious, are *inestimable.*

INFANCY, *n.* The first part of life, beginning at the birth. In common usage, *infancy* extends not beyond the first year or two of life, but there is not a defined limit where *infancy* ends, and childhood begins.

INFATUATION, *n.* 2. A state of mind in which the intellectual powers are weakened, either generally or in regard to particular objects, so that the person affected acts without his usual judgment, and contrary to the dictates of reason. All men who waste their substance in gaming, intemperance or any other vice, are chargeable with *infatuation.*

INFER, *v.t.* 2. To deduce; to draw or derive, as a fact or consequence. From the character of God, as creator and governor of the world, we *infer* the indispensable obligation of all his creatures to obey his commands. We *infer* one proposition or truth from another, when we perceive that if one is true, the other must be true also.

INFERIOR, *a.* 2. Lower in station, age, or rank in life. Pay due respect to those who are superior in station, and due civility to those who are *inferior.*

INFLUENZA, *n.* An epidemic catarrh. The *influenza* of October and November, 1789, and that of April and May, 1790, were very general or universal in the United States, and unusually severe. A like *influenza* prevailed in the winters of 1825 and 1826.

INHERENT, *a.* 2. Innate; naturally pertaining to; as the *inherent* qualities of the magnet; the *inherent* right of men to life, liberty and protection.

INHERIT, *v.t.* 2. To receive by nature from a progenitor. The son *inherits* the virtues of his father; the daughter *inherits* the temper of her mother, and children often *inherit* the constitutional infirmities of their parents.

INKHORN, *n.* [*ink* and *horn;* horns being formerly used for holding ink.] 1. A small vessel used to hold ink on a writing table or desk, or for carrying it about the person. Inkhorns are made of horn, glass or stone.

INNATE, *a.* Inborn; native; natural. *Innate* ideas are such as are supposed to be stamped on the mind, at the moment when existence begins. Mr. Locke has taken great pains to prove that no such ideas exist. *Encyc.*

INNING, *n.* The ingathering of grain.
    2. A term in cricket, a turn for using the bat.

INNKEEPER, *n.* An inn-holder. In *America,* the innkeeper is often a tavern keeper or taverner, as well as an innkeeper, the inn for furnishing lodgings and provisions being usually united with the tavern for the sale of liquors.

INNOCENCE, *n.* 4. Freedom from the guilt of a particular sin or crime. This is the sense in which the word is most generally used, for perfect *innocence* cannot be predicated to man.

INNOVATION, *n.* Change made by the introduction of something new; change in established laws, customs, rites or practices. *Innovation* is expedient, when it remedies an evil, and safe, when men are prepared to receive it.

Innovation is often used in an ill sense, for a change that disturbs settled opinions and practices without an equivalent advantage.

INOCULATE, *v.t.* 2. To communicate a disease to a person by inserting infectious matter in his skin or flesh; as, to *inoculate* a person with the matter of small pox or cow pox. When the latter disease is communicated, it is called *vaccination*.

INSPIRATION, *n.* The infusion of ideas into the mind by the Holy Spirit; the conveying into the minds of men, ideas, notices or monitions by extraordinary or supernatural influence or the communication of the divine will to the understanding by suggestions or impressions on the mind, which leave no room to doubt the reality of their supernatural origin.

INSTANCE, *n.* Example; a case occurring; a case offered. Howard furnished a remarkable *instance* of disinterested benevolence. The world may never witness a second *instance* of the success of daring enterprise and usurpation, equal to that of Buonaparte.

Suppose the earth should be removed nearer to the sun, and revolve, for *instance,* in the orbit of Mercury, the whole ocean would boil with heat.

Bentley.

INSTINCT, *n.* A certain power or disposition of mind by which, independent of all instruction or experience, without deliberation and without having any end in view, animals are unerringly directed to do spontaneously whatever is necessary for the preservation of the individual, or the continuation of the kind. Such, in the human species, is the instinct of sucking exerted immediately after birth, and that of insects in depositing their eggs in situations most favorable for hatching. *Encyc.*

INSTRUCT, *v.t.* 1. To teach; to inform the mind; to educate; to impart knowledge to one who was destitute of it. The first duty of parents is to *instruct* their children in the principles of religion and morality.

INSTRUMENT, *n.* 1. A tool; that by which work is performed or any thing is effected; as a knife, a hammer, a saw, a plow, &c. Swords, muskets and cannon are *instruments* of destruction. A telescope is an astronomical *instrument.*

2. That which is subservient to the execution of a plan or purpose, or to the production of any effect; means used or contributing to an effect; *applicable to persons or things.* Bad men are often *instruments* of ruin to others. The distribution of the Scriptures may be the *instrument* of a vastly extensive reformation in morals and religion.

INSULT, *v.t.* To treat with gross abuse, insolence or contempt, by words or actions; as, to call a man a coward or a liar, or to sneer at him, is to *insult* him.

INTERPOSITION, *n.* 2. Intervenient agency; as the *interposition* of the magistrate in quieting sedition. How many evidences have we of divine *interposition* in favor of good men!

INTESTINE, *a.* 2. Internal with regard to a state or country; domestic, not foreign; as *intestine* feuds; *intestine* war; *intestine* enemies. It is to be remarked that this word is usually or always applied to evils. We never say, *intestine* happiness or prosperity; *intestine* trade, manufactures or bills; but *intestine* broils, trouble, disorders, calamities, war, &c. We say, *internal* peace, welfare, prosperity, or *internal* broils, war, trade, &c. This restricted use of *intestine* seems to be entirely arbitrary.

INTRUDE, *v.i.* To thrust one's self in; to come or go in without invitation or welcome; to enter, as into company, against the will of the company or the host; as, to *intrude* on families at unseasonable hours. Never *intrude* where your company is not desired.

INVALID, *n.* 2. A person who is infirm, wounded, maimed, or otherwise disabled for active service; a soldier or seaman worn out in service. The hospitals for *invalids* at Chelsea and Greenwich, in England, are institutions honorable to the English nation.

INVENTION, *n.* 1. The action or operation of finding out something new; the contrivance of that which did not before exist; as the *invention* of logarithms; the *invention* of the art of printing; the *invention* of the orrery. *Invention* differs from *discovery*. *Invention* is applied to the contrivance and production of something that did not before exist. *Discovery* brings to light that which existed before, but which was not known. We are indebted to *invention* for the thermometer and barometer. We are indebted to *discovery* for the knowledge of the isles in the Pacific ocean, and for the knowledge of galvanism, and many species of earth not formerly known. This distinction is important, though not always observed.
2. That which is invented. The cotton gin is the *invention* of Whitney; the steam boat is the *invention* of Fulton. The Doric, Ionic and Corinthian orders are said to be *inventions* of the Greeks; the Tuscan and Composite are *inventions* of the Latins.
3. Forgery; fiction. Fables are the *inventions* of ingenious men.

INVISIBLE, *a.* That cannot be seen; imperceptible by the sight. Millions of stars, *invisible* to the naked eye, may be seen by the telescope.

IRONY, *n.* A mode of speech expressing a sense contrary to that which the speaker intends to convey; as, Nero was a very virtuous prince; Pope Hildebrand was remarkable for his meekness and humility. When irony is uttered, the dissimulation is generally apparent from the manner of speaking, as by a smile or an arch look, or perhaps by an affected gravity of countenance. Irony in writing may also be detected by the manner of expression.

ISTHMUS, *n.* A neck or narrow slip of land by which two continents are connected, or by which a peninsula is united to the main land. Such is the Neck, so called, which connects Boston with the main land at Roxbury. But the word is applied to land of considerable extent, between seas; as the *isthmus* of Darien, which connects North and South America, and the *isthmus* between the Euxine and Caspian seas.

ISTHMUS. Darien ☞ was the name once used to refer to the entire Isthmus of Panama. See also AMERICA.

IVORY, *n.* The tusk of an elephant, a hard, solid substance, of a fine white color. This tooth is sometimes six or seven feet in length, hollow from the base to a certain highth, and filled with a compact medullary substance, seeming to contain a great number of glands. The ivory of Ceylon and Achem does not become yellow in wearing, and hence is preferred to that of Guinea.

Encyc.

IVORY. Webster's ☞ Achem is Banda Aceh, the Sumatran city devastated by the tsunami of 2004. Guinea, of course, is on the Ivory Coast of Africa.

J

JACOBIN, *n.* The *Jacobins*, in France, during the late revolution, were a society of violent revolutionists, who held secret meetings in which measures were concerted to direct the proceedings of the National Assembly. Hence, a Jacobin is the member of a club, or other person, who opposes government in a secret and unlawful manner or by violent means; a turbulent demagogue.

JANIZARY, *n.* A soldier of the Turkish foot guards. The Janizaries were a body of infantry, and reputed the Grand Seignor's guards. They became turbulent, and rising in arms against the Sultan, were attacked, defeated and destroyed in Constantinople, in June 1826.

JEALOUSY, *n.* 1. That passion or peculiar uneasiness which arises from the fear that a rival may rob us of the affection of one whom we love, or the suspicion that he has already done it; or it is the uneasiness which arises from the fear that another does or will enjoy some advantage which we desire for ourselves. A man's *jealousy* is excited by the attentions of a rival to his favorite lady. A woman's *jealousy* is roused by her husband's attentions to another woman. The candidate for office manifests a *jealousy* of others who seek the same office. The *jealousy* of a student is awakened by the apprehension that his fellow will bear away the palm of praise. In short, *jealousy* is awakened by whatever may exalt others, or give them pleasures and advantages which we desire for ourselves. *Jealousy* is nearly allied to *envy*, for *jealousy*, before a good is lost by ourselves, is, converted into *envy*, after it is obtained by others.

JEOPARDIZE, *v.t.* To expose to loss or injury; to jeopard. [This is a modern word, used by respectable writers in America, but synonymous with *jeopard* and therefore useless.]

JESUITISM, *n.* The arts, principles and practices of the Jesuits.
    2. Cunning; deceit; hypocrisy; prevarication; deceptive practices to effect a purpose.

JOG, *n.* A push; a slight shake; a shake or push intended to give notice or awaken attention. When your friend falls asleep at church, give him a *jog*.

JOINER, *n.* One whose occupation is to construct things by joining pieces of wood; but appropriately and usually, a mechanic who does the wood-work in the covering and finishing of buildings. This is the true and original sense of the word in Great Britain and in New England. This person is called in New York, a *carpenter.* [See *Carpenter.*]

JOURNAL, *n.* 4. A paper published daily, or other newspaper; also, the title of a book or pamphlet published at stated times, containing an account of inventions, discoveries and improvements in arts and sciences; as the *Journal* de Savans; the *Journal* of Science.

JUDAISM, *n.* 1. The religious doctrines and rites of the Jews, as enjoined in the laws of Moses. *Judaism* was a temporary dispensation.

JUDICIARY, *n.* That branch of government which is concerned in the trial and determination of controversies between parties, and of criminal prosecutions; the system of courts of justice in a government. An independent *judiciary* is the firmest bulwark of freedom.   *United States.*

JUGGLER, *n.* 1. One who practices or exhibits tricks by slight of hand; one who makes sport by tricks of extraordinary dexterity, by which the spectator is deceived. *Jugglers* are punishable by law.

JUNGLE, *n.* In Hindoostan, a thick wood of small trees or shrubs.
Asiat. Res.

JUNK, *n.* [L. *juncus,* . . . a bulrush, of which ropes were made in early ages.] 1. Pieces of old cable or old cordage, used for making points, gaskets, mats, &c., and when untwisted and picked to pieces, it forms oakum for filling the seams of ships.   *Mar. Dict.*

JURISPRUDENCE, *n.* The science of law; the knowledge of the laws, customs and rights of men in a state or community, necessary for the due administration of justice. The study of *jurisprudence,* next to that of theology, is the most important and useful to men.

JUSTIFY, *v.t.* To prove or show to be just, or conformable to law, right, justice, propriety or duty; to defend or maintain; to vindicate as right. We cannot *justify* disobedience or ingratitude to our Maker. We cannot *justify* insult or incivility to our fellow men. Intemperance, lewdness, profaneness and dueling are in no case to be *justified.*

K

KANGAROO, *n.* A singular animal found in New Holland, resembling in some respects the opossum. It belongs to the genus Didelphis. It has a small head, neck and shoulders, the body increasing in thickness to the rump. The fore legs are very short, useless in walking, but used for digging or bringing food to the mouth. The hind legs, which are long, are used in moving, particularly in leaping.   *Encyc.*

KETTLE, *n.* A vessel of iron or other metal, with a wide mouth, usually without a cover, used for heating and boiling water or other liquor. Among the *Tartars*, a *kettle* represents a family, or as many as feed from one kettle. Among the *Dutch*, a battery of mortars sunk in the earth, is called a *kettle*.   *Encyc.*

KICKING, *n.* The act of striking with the foot, or of yerking the foot with violence. What cannot be effected by *kicking*, may sometimes be done by coaxing.

KICKSHAW, *n.* 1. Something fantastical or uncommon, or some thing that has no particular name.

KIDNAPPING, *n.* The act of stealing, or forcible abduction of a human being from his own country or state. This crime was capital by the Jewish law, and in modern times is highly penal.

KILOGRAM, *n.* In the new system of French weights and measures, a thousand grams. According to Lunier, the kilogram is equal in weight to a cubic decimeter of water, or two pounds, five drams and a half.

KINGDOM, *n.* 1. The territory or country subject to a king; an undivided territory under the dominion of a king or monarch. The foreign possessions of a king are not usually included in the term *kingdom*. Thus we speak of the *kingdom* of England, of France or of Spain, without including the East or West Indies.

171

KIT-CAT, *n.* A term applied to a club in London, to which Addison and Steele belonged; so called from Christopher Cat, a pastry cook, who served the club with mutton pies; applied also to a portrait three fourths less than a half length, placed in the club-room.   *Todd.*

KITE, *n.* 3. A light frame of wood and paper constructed for flying in the air for the amusement of boys.

KNOWLEDGE, *n.* 1. A clear and certain perception of that which exists, or of truth and fact; the perception of the connection and agreement, or disagreement and repugnancy of our ideas.   *Encyc.   Locke.*

We can have no *knowledge* of that which does not exist. God has a perfect *knowledge* of all his works. Human *knowledge* is very limited, and is mostly gained by observation and experience.

KURILIAN, *a.* The Kurilian isles are a chain in the Pacific, extending from the southern extremity of Kamschatka to Jesso.

L

LABORATORY, *n.* 1. A house or place where operations and experiments in chimistry, pharmacy, pyrotechny, &c., are performed.

2. A place where arms are manufactured or repaired, or fire-works prepared; as the *laboratory* in Springfield, in Massachusetts.

3. A place where work is performed, or any thing is prepared for use. Hence the stomach is called the grand *laboratory* of the human body; the liver, the *laboratory* of the bile.

LADY, *n.* A woman of distinction. Originally, the title of lady was given to the daughters of earls and others in high rank, but by custom, the title belongs to any woman of genteel education.

LAKE, *n.* A large and extensive collection of water contained in a cavity or hollow of the earth. It differs from a *pond* in size, the latter being a collection of small extent; but sometimes a collection of water is called a pond or a lake indifferently. North America contains some of the largest *lakes* on the globe, particularly the *lakes* Ontario, Erie, Huron, Michigan and Superior.

LAMA, *n.* 1. The sovereign pontiff, or rather the god of the Asiatic Tartars.
Encyc.

2. A small species of camel, the Camelus lama of South America.

LAND-OFFICE, *n.* In the *United States,* an office in which the sales of new land are registered, and warrants issued for the location of land, and other business respecting unsettled land is transacted.

LANE, *n.* 1. A narrow way or passage, or a private passage, as distinguished from a public road or highway. A lane may be open to all passengers, or it may be inclosed and appropriated to a man's private use. In *the U. States,* the word is used chiefly in the country, and answers in a degree, to an *alley* in a city. It has sometimes been used for *alley.* In London, the word *lane* is added to the names of streets; as *chancery lane.*

LANGTERALOO, *n.* A game at cards. *Toiler.*

LAND-OFFICE. The adjectival form, as in *land-office business,* was coined by Mark Twain.

173

LANGUAGE, *n.* 3. The speech or expression of ideas peculiar to a particular nation. Men had originally one and the same *language,* but the tribes or families of men, since their dispersion, have distinct *languages.*

5. The inarticulate sounds by which irrational animals express their feelings and wants. Each species of animals has peculiar sounds, which are uttered instinctively, and are understood by its own species, and its own species only.

Magic lantern, an optical machine by which painted images are represented so much magnified as to appear like the effect of magic.

LARCENY, *n.* Theft; the act of taking and carrying away the goods or property of another feloniously. Larceny is of two kinds; *simple larceny,* or theft, not accompanied with any atrocious circumstance; and *mixed* or *compound larceny,* which includes in it the aggravation of taking from one's house or person, as in burglary or robbery. The stealing of any thing below the value of twelve pence, is called *petty larceny;* above that value, it is called *grand larceny.*   *Blackstone.*

LAST, *n.* A load; hence, a certain weight or measure. A *last* of codfish, white herrings, meal, and ashes, is twelve barrels; a *last* of corn is ten quarters or eighty bushels; of gunpowder, twenty four barrels; of red herrings, twenty cades; of hides, twelve dozen; of lether, twenty dickers; of pitch and tar, fourteen barrels; of wool, twelve sacks; of flax or fethers, 1700 lbs.   *Encyc.*

LATIBULIZE, *v.i.* To retire into a den, burrow or cavity, and lie dormant in winter; to retreat and lie hid.

The tortoise *latibulizes* in October.   *Shaw's Zool.*

LATITUDE, *n.* 4. In *geography,* the distance of any place on the globe, north or south of the equator. Boston is situated in the forty third degree of north *latitude.*

LAUGHTER, *n.* Convulsive merriment; an expression of mirth peculiar to man, consisting in a peculiar noise and configuration of features, with a shaking of the sides and expulsion of breath.

LAVA, *n.* 1. A mass or stream of melted minerals or stony matter which bursts or is thrown from the mouth or sides of a volcano, and is sometimes ejected in such quantities as to overwhelm cities. Catana, at the foot of Etna, has often been destroyed by it, and in 1783, a vast tract of land in Iceland was overspread by an eruption of lava from mount Hecla.

LAW, *n.* 1. A rule, particularly an established or permanent rule, prescribed by the supreme power of a state to its subjects, for regulating their actions, particularly their social actions. Laws are *imperative* or *mandatory*, commanding what shall be done *prohibitory*, restraining from what is to be forborn; or *permissive*, declaring what may be done without incurring a penalty. The *laws* which enjoin the duties of piety and morality, are prescribed by God and found in the Scriptures.

> *Law* is beneficence acting by rule.   *Burke.*

3. *Law of nature,* is a rule of conduct arising out of the natural relations of human beings established by the Creator, and existing prior to any positive precept. Thus it is a *law of nature,* that one man should not injure another, and murder and fraud would be crimes, independent of any prohibition from a supreme power.

LAZINESS, *n.* The state or quality of being lazy; indisposition to action or exertion; indolence; sluggishness; heaviness in motion; habitual sloth. *Laziness* differs from *idleness;* the latter being a mere defect or cessation of action, but *laziness* is sloth, with natural or habitual disinclination to action.

> *Laziness* travels so slowly, that poverty soon overtakes him.   *Franklin.*

LEAGUE, *v.i.* To unite, as princes or states in a contract of amity for mutual aid or defense; to confederate. Russia and Austria *leagued* to oppose the ambition of Buonaparte.

LEAGUE, *n.* 1. Originally, a stone erected on the public roads, at certain distances, in the manner of the modern mile-stones. Hence,

2. The distance between two stones. With the English and Americans, a *league* is the length of three miles; but this measure is used chiefly at sea. The *league* on the continent of Europe, is very different among different nations. The Dutch and German *league* contains four geographical miles.

> *Encyc.*

LEARN, *v.t.* 1. To gain knowledge of; to acquire knowledge or ideas of something before unknown. We *learn* the use of letters, the meaning of words and the principles of science. We *learn* things by instruction, by study, and by experience and observation. It is much easier to *learn* what is right, than to unlearn what is wrong.

LEAVE, *v.t.* 1. To withdraw or depart from; to quit for a longer or shorter time indefinitely, or for perpetuity. We left Cowes on our return to the United States, May 10, 1825. We *leave* home for a day or a year. The fever *leaves* the patient daily at a certain hour. The secretary has *left* the business of his office with his first clerk.

LEGISLATE, *v.i.* To make or enact a law or laws. It is a question whether it is expedient to *legislate* at present on the subject. Let us not *legislate,* when we have no power to enforce our laws.

LENGTHY, *a.* Being long or moderately long; not short; not brief; *applied mostly to moral subjects,* as to discourses, writings, arguments, proceedings, &c.; as a *lengthy* sermon; a *lengthy* dissertation; a *lengthy* detail.

Lengthy periods.   *Washington's Letter to Plater.*

No ministerial act in France, in matters of judicial cognizance, is done without a *proces verbal,* in which the facts are stated amidst a great deal of *lengthy* formality, with a degree of minuteness, highly profitable to the verbalizing officers and to the revenue.   *Am. Review, Ap. Oct.* 1811.

P. S. Murray has sent or will send a double copy of the Bride and Giaour; in the last one, some *lengthy* additions; pray accept them, according to old customs—   *Lord Byron's Letter to Dr. Clarke, Dec.* 13, 1813.

Chalmers' Political Annals, in treating of South Carolina—is by no means as *lengthy* as Mr. Hewitt's History.   *Drayton's View of South Carolina.*

LEVEE. Webster ☞ defines *causey* as "a way raised in a common road"; it is our *causeway.* Though both words are centuries old and had long been used interchangeably—even Bailey gives both spellings in his dictionary entry—Webster fails to acknowledge *causeway,* perhaps the more common spelling even in his own time.

LEVEE, *n.* 3. A bank or causey, particularly along a river to prevent inundation; as the *levees* along the Mississippi.

LIBERAL, *a.* 3. Not selfish, narrow or contracted; catholic; enlarged; embracing other interests than one's own; as *liberal* sentiments or views; a *liberal* mind; *liberal* policy.

7. Free; not literal or strict; as a *liberal* construction of law.

Liberal arts, as distinguished from *mechanical arts,* are such as depend more on the exertion of the mind than on the labor of the hands, and regard amusement, curiosity or intellectual improvement, rather than the necessity of subsistence, or manual skill. Such are grammar, rhetoric, painting, sculpture, architecture, music, &c.

LIBERTY, *n.* 2. *Natural liberty,* consists in the power of acting as one thinks fit, without any restraint or control, except from the laws of nature. It is a state of exemption from the control of others, and from positive laws and the institutions of social life. This liberty is abridged by the establishment of government.

3. *Civil liberty,* is the liberty of men in a state of society, or natural liberty, so far only abridged and restrained, as is necessary and expedient for the safety and interest of the society, state or nation. A restraint of natural liberty, not necessary or expedient for the public, is tyranny or oppression. Civil liberty is an exemption from the arbitrary will of others, which exemption is secured by established laws, which restrain every man from injuring or controlling another. Hence the restraints of law are essential to *civil liberty.*

The *liberty* of one depends not so much on the removal of all restraint from him, as on the due restraint upon the *liberty* of others.   *Ames.*

In this sentence, the latter word *liberty* denotes *natural liberty.*

4. *Political liberty* is sometimes used as synonymous with *civil liberty.* But

it more properly designates the *liberty of a nation*, the freedom of a nation or state from all unjust abridgment of its rights and independence by another nation.

5. *Religious liberty*, is the free right of adopting and enjoying opinions of religious subjects, and of worshiping the Supreme Being according to the dictates of conscience, without external control.

Liberty of the press, is freedom from any restriction on the power to publish books; the free power of publishing what one pleases, subject only to punishment for abusing the privilege, or publishing what is mischievous to the public or injurious to individuals.   *Blackstone.*

LICENSE, *n.* Leave; permission; authority or liberty given to do or forbear any act. A *license* may be verbal or written; when *written*, the paper containing the authority is called a *license.* A man is not permitted to retail spirituous liquors till he has obtained a *license.*

LICENTIOUSNESS, *n.* Excessive indulgence of liberty; contempt of the just restraints of law, morality and decorum. The *licentiousness* of authors is justly condemned; the *licentiousness* of the press is punishable by law.

LIFE, *n.* 1. In *a general sense*, that state of animals and plants, or of an organized being, in which its natural functions and motions are performed, or in which its organs are capable of performing their functions. A tree is not destitute of life in winter, when the functions of its organs are suspended; nor man during a swoon or syncope; nor strictly birds, quadrupeds or serpents during their torpitude in winter. They are not strictly dead, till the functions of their organs are incapable of being renewed.

LIFEGUARD, *n.* A guard of the life or person; a guard that attends the person of a prince, or other person.

LIGHT, *n.* 1. That ethereal agent or matter which makes objects perceptible to the sense of seeing, but the particles of which are separately invisible. It is now generally believed that light is a fluid, or real matter, existing independent of other substances, with properties peculiar to itself. Its velocity is astonishing, as it passes through a space of nearly twelve millions of miles in a minute. Light, when decomposed, is found to consist of rays differently colored; as red, orange, yellow, green, blue, indigo, and violet. The sun is the principal source of light in the solar system; but light is also emitted from bodies ignited, or in combustion, and is reflected from enlightened bodies, as the moon. Light is also emitted from certain putrefying substances. It is usually united with heat, but it exists also independent of it.
                              Hooper.   Nicholson.   Encyc.

LIGHTNING, *n.* 1. A sudden discharge of electricity from a cloud to the earth, or from the earth to a cloud, or from one cloud to another, that is, from a body positively charged to one negatively charged, producing a vivid flash of light, and usually a loud report, called thunder. Sometimes lightning is a mere instantaneous flash of light without thunder, as *heat-lightning*, lightning seen by reflection, the flash being beyond the limits of our horizon.

LIKELIHOOD, *n.* Probability; verisimilitude; appearance of truth or reality. There is little *likelihood* that an habitual drunkard will become temperate. There is little *likelihood* that an old offender will be reformed. Prudence directs us not to undertake a design, when there is little or no *likelihood* of success.

LIKELY, *a.* Probable; that may be rationally thought or believed to have taken place in time past, or to be true now or hereafter; such as is more reasonable than the contrary. *A likely* story, is one which evidence, or the circumstances of the case render probable, and therefore credible.

2. Such as may be liked; pleasing; as a *likely* man or woman.

[This use of *likely* is not obsolete, as Johnson affirms, nor is it vulgar. But the English and their descendants in America differ in the application. The English apply the word to external appearance, and with them, *likely* is equivalent to *handsome, well formed;* as a *likely* man, a *likely* horse. In America, the word is usually applied to the endowments of the mind, or to pleasing accomplishments. With us, a *likely* man, is a man of good character and talents, or of good dispositions or accomplishments, that render him pleasing or respectable.]

LINGUIST, *n.* A person skilled in languages; usually applied to a person well versed in the languages taught in colleges, Greek, Latin, and Hebrew.

Milton.

LION, *n.* 1. A quadruped of the genus Felis, very strong, fierce and rapacious. The largest lions are eight or nine feet in length. The male has a thick head, beset with long bushy hair of a yellowish color. The lion is a native of Africa and the warm climates of Asia. His aspect is noble, his gait stately, and his roar tremendous.

LIP, *n.* The edge or border of the mouth. The lips are two fleshy or muscular parts, composing the exterior of the mouth in man and many other animals. In man, the lips, which may be opened or closed at pleasure, form the covering of the teeth, and are organs of speech essential to certain articulations. Hence the lips, by a figure, denote the mouth, or all the organs of speech, and sometimes speech itself.

LIP-DEVOTION, *n.* Prayers uttered by the lips without the desires of the heart.

LITERATURE, *n.* Learning; acquaintance with letters or books. *Literature* comprehends a knowledge of the ancient languages, denominated classical, history, grammar, rhetoric, logic, geography, &c. as well as of the sciences. A knowledge of the world and good breeding give luster to *literature.*

LITHOGRAPHY, *n.* The art of engraving, or of tracing letters, figures or other designs on stone, and of transferring them to paper by impression; an art recently invented by Mr. Sennefelder of Munich, in Bavaria.

Journ. of Science.

LIVESTOCK, *n.* Horses, cattle and smaller domestic animals; a term applied in America, to such animals as may be exported alive for foreign markets.

LOAN-OFFICE, *n.* In *America,* a public office in which loans of money are negotiated for the public, or in which the accounts of loans are kept and the interest paid to the lenders.

LOBSTER, *n.* A crustaceous fish of the genus Cancer. Lobsters have large claws and fangs, and four pair of legs. They are said to change their crust annually, and to be frightened at thunder or other loud report. They constitute an article of food.

Locomotive engine, a steam engine employed in land carriage; chiefly on railways.

LOGARITHM, *n.* Logarithms are the exponents of a series of powers and roots.
Day.
    The logarithm of a number is that exponent of some other number, which renders the power of the latter, denoted by the exponent, equal to the former.
Cyc.
    When the logarithms form a series in arithmetical progression, the corresponding natural numbers form a series in geometrical progression. Thus,

Logarithms	0	1	2	3	4	5
Natural numbers,	1	10	100	1000	10000	100000

    The addition and subtraction of logarithms answer to the multiplication and division of their natural numbers. In like manner, involution is performed by multiplying the logarithm of any number by the number denoting the required power; and evolution, by dividing the logarithm by the number denoting the required root.
    Logarithms are the invention of Baron Napier, lord of Marchiston in Scotland; but the kind now in use, were invented by Henry Briggs, professor of

Locomotive engine. Webster defines neither *railway* nor *railroad.* He could hardly have foreseen, just beyond his horizon, the coming of the iron horse and America's opening to the West.

L

geometry in Gresham college, at Oxford. They are extremely useful in abridging the labor of trigonometrical calculations.

LOGIC, *n.* The art of thinking and reasoning justly.

> *Logic* is the art of using reason well in our inquiries after truth, and the communication of it to others.   *Watts.*

Correct reasoning implies correct thinking and legitimate inferences from premises, which are principles assumed or admitted to be just. *Logic* then includes the art of thinking, as well as the art of reasoning.   *W.*

> The purpose of *logic* is to direct the intellectual powers in the investigation of truth, and in the communication of it to others.   *Hedge.*

LONGITUDE, *n.* 1. Properly, length; as the *longitude* of a room; but in this sense not now used. Appropriately, in geography,

2. The distance of any place on the globe from another place, eastward or westward; or the distance of any place from a given meridian. Boston, in Massachusetts, is situated in the 71st degree of *longitude* west from Greenwich. To be able to ascertain precisely the *longitude* of a ship at sea, is a great desideratum in navigation.

3. The *longitude* of a star, is its distance from the equinoctial points, or the beginning of Aries or Libra.   *Bailey.*

LOSE. A *projector*, ☞ for Webster, is "one who forms wild or impractical schemes."

LOSE, *v.t.* 5. To forfeit, as a penalty. Our first parents *lost* the favor of God by their apostasy.

14. To ruin; to destroy by shipwreck, &c. The Albion was *lost* on the coast of Ireland, April 22, 1822. The admiral *lost* three ships in a tempest.

16. To employ ineffectually; to throw away; to waste. Instruction is often *lost* on the dull; admonition is *lost* on the profligate. It is often the fate of projectors to *lose* their labor.

LOSER, *n.* One that loses, or that is deprived of any thing by defeat, forfeiture or the like; the contrary to *winner* or *gainer*. A *loser* by trade may be honest and moral; this cannot be said of a *loser* by gaming.

LOT, *n.* 6. In *the U. States*, a piece or division of land; perhaps originally assigned by drawing lots, but now any portion, piece or division. So we say, a man has a *lot* of land in Broadway, or in the meadow; he has a *lot* in the plain, or on the mountain; he has a home-*lot*, a house-*lot*, a wood-*lot*.

> The defendants leased a house and *lot* in the city of New York.   *Kent.*
>   *Franklin, Law of Penn.*

LOTTERY, *n.* 1. A scheme for the distribution of prizes by chance, or the distribution itself. *Lotteries* are often authorized by law, but many good men deem them immoral in principle, and almost all men concur in the opinion that their effects are pernicious.

LOVE, *v.t.* 1. In a general sense to be pleased with; to regard with affection, on account of some qualities which excite pleasing sensations or desire of gratification. We *love* a friend, on account of some qualities which give us pleasure in his society. We *love* a man who has done us a favor; in which case, gratitude enters into the composition of our affection. We *love* our parents and our children, on account of their connection with us, and on account of many qualities which please us. We *love* to retire to a cool shade in summer. We *love* a warm room in winter. We *love* to hear an eloquent advocate. The christian *loves* his Bible. In short, we *love* whatever gives us pleasure and delight, whether animal or intellectual; and if our hearts are right, we *love* God above all things, as the sum of all excellence and all the attributes which can communicate happiness to intelligent beings. In other words, the christian *loves* God with the love of complacency in his attributes, the love of benevolence towards the interests of his kingdom, and the love of gratitude for favors received.

LOVE, *n.* An affection of the mind excited by beauty and worth of any kind, or by the qualities of an object which communicate pleasure, sensual or intellectual. It is opposed to *hatred.* *Love* between the sexes, is a compound affection, consisting of esteem, benevolence, and animal desire. *Love* is excited by pleasing qualities of any kind, as by kindness, benevolence, charity, and by the qualities which render social intercourse agreeable. In the latter case, *love* is ardent friendship, or a strong attachment springing from good will and esteem, and the pleasure derived from the company, civilities and kindnesses of others.

Between certain natural relatives, *love* seems to be in some cases instinctive. Such is the *love* of a mother for her child, which manifests itself toward an infant, before any particular qualities in the child are unfolded. This affection is apparently as strong in irrational animals as in human beings.

We speak of the *love* of amusements, the *love* of books, the *love* of money, and the *love* of whatever contributes to our pleasure or supposed profit.

The *love* of God is the first duty of man, and this springs from just views of his attributes or excellencies of character, which afford the highest delight to the sanctified heart. Esteem and reverence constitute ingredients in this affection, and a fear of offending him is its inseparable effect.

LUMBER, *n.* Any thing useless and cumbersome, or things bulky and thrown aside as of no use.

2. In America, timber sawed or split for use; as beams, joists, boards, planks, staves, hoops and the like.

3. Harm; mischief. [*Local.*]   *Pegge.*

LUNCH, LUNCHEON, *n.* Literally, a swallow; but in usage, a portion of food taken at any time, except at a regular meal. It is not unusual to take a *luncheon* before dinner. The passengers in the line-ships regularly have their *lunch.*

LUSCIOUS, *a.* 1. Sweet or rich so as to cloy or nauseate; sweet to excess; as *luscious* food.

4. Fullsome; as *luscious* flattery. 5. Smutty; obscene. [*Unusual.*]   *Steele.*

LUXURY, *n.* 2. That which gratifies a nice and fastidious appetite; a dainty; any delicious food or drink. The canvas-back duck is a *luxury* for an epicure.

M

MACHINE, *n*. An artificial work, simple or complicated, that serves to apply or regulate moving power, or to produce motion, so as to save time or force. The simple machines are the six mechanical powers, viz.; the lever, the pulley, the axis and wheel, the wedge, the screw, and the inclined plane. Complicated machines are such as combine two or more of these powers for the production of motion or force. *Encyc.*

MAD, *a*. 7. Inflamed with anger; very angry. [*This is a common and perhaps the most general sense of the word in America. It is thus used by Arbuthnot, and is perfectly proper.*]
    8. Proceeding from folly or infatuation.
    Mad wars destroy in one year the works of many years of peace.
Franklin.

MADEMOISELLE, *n*. A young woman, or the title given to one; miss; also, the puppet sent from the French metropolis to exhibit the prevailing fashions. *Spectator.*

MADRIGAL, *n*. 1. A little amorous poem, sometimes called a pastoral poem, containing a certain number of free unequal verses, not confined to the scrupulous regularity of a sonnet or the subtilty of the epigram, but containing some tender and delicate, though simple thought, suitably expressed. *Cyc.*
    2. An elaborate vocal composition in five or six parts. *Busby.*

MAGAZINE, *n*. 3. A pamphlet periodically published, containing miscellaneous papers or compositions. The first publication of this kind in England,

---

M. It is called a semi-vowel, as the articulation or compression of the lips is accompanied with a humming sound through the nose, which constitutes a difference between this letter and *b*.

was the *Gentleman's Magazine*, which first appeared in 1731, under the name of *Sylvanus Urban*, by Edward Cave, and which is still continued.

MAGIC, *n*. 1. The art or science of putting into action the power of spirits; or the science of producing wonderful effects by the aid of superhuman beings, or of departed spirits; sorcery; enchantment. [*This art or science is now discarded.*]

Magic lantern. ☞ Webster forgets that he has already defined this phrase under LANTERN, and in a somewhat different way. Athanasius Kircher (1602?–80), the German Jesuit polymath, used a microscope to investigate the blood of plague victims; perfected the Aeolian harp; did research on magnetism; and interpreted Egyptian hieroglyphs as occult symbols, a mistaken view that survived until Champollion's decipherment of the Rosetta Stone.

Magic lantern, a dioptric machine invented by Kircher, which, by means of a lamp in a dark room, exhibits images of objects in their distinct colors and proportions, with the appearance of life itself.   *Encyc.*

MAGNANIMITY, *n*. Greatness of mind; that elevation or dignity of soul, which encounters danger and trouble with tranquillity and firmness, which raises the possessor above revenge, and makes him delight in acts of benevolence, which makes him disdain injustice and meanness, and prompts him to sacrifice personal ease, interest and safety for the accomplishment of useful and noble objects.

Animal magnetism, a sympathy supposed to exist between the magnet and the human body, by means of which the magnet is said to be able to cure diseases; or a fluid supposed to exist throughout nature, and to be the medium of influence between celestial bodies, and the earth and human bodies.

MAHOGANY, *n*. A tree of the genus Swietenia, growing in the tropical climates of America. The wood is of a reddish or brown color, very hard, and susceptible of a fine polish. Of this are made our most beautiful and durable pieces of cabinet furniture.

MAIN, *n*. 4. The continent, as distinguished from an isle. We arrived at Nantucket on Saturday, but did not reach the *main* till Monday. In this use of the word, *land* is omitted; *main* for *main land*.

MAINTAIN, *v.t.* 4. To keep up; to uphold; to support the expense of; as, to *maintain* state or equipage.
What *maintains* one vice would bring up two children.   *Franklin.*

MALADY, *n*. Any sickness or disease of the human body; any distemper, disorder or indisposition, proceeding from impaired, defective or morbid organic functions; more particularly, a lingering or deep seated disorder or indisposition. It may be applied to any animal body, but is, I believe, rarely or never applied to plants.
The *maladies* of the body may prove medicines to the mind.
Buckminster.

MAN, *n.* [. . . Man in its radical sense, agrees almost precisely with *Adam,* in the Shemitic languages.] 1. Mankind; the human race; the whole species of human beings; beings distinguished from all other animals by the powers of reason and speech, as well as by their shape and dignified aspect. "Os homini sublime dedit."

MANATI, MANATUS, *n.* The sea-cow, or fish-tailed walrus, an animal of the genus Trichechus, which grows to an enormous size; sometimes it is said, to the length of twenty three feet. Of this animal there are two varieties, the australis, or lamentin, and borealis, or whale-tailed manati. It has fore feet palmated, and furnished with claws, but the hind part ends in a tail like that of a fish. The skin is of a dark color, the eyes small, and instead of teeth, the mouth is furnished with hard bones, extending the whole length of the jaws. [There are eight grinders on each side in each jaw. *Cuvier.*] It never leaves the water, but frequents the mouths of rivers, feeding on grass that grows in the water.   *Encyc.   Dict. Nat. Hist.*

MARANON, *n.* The proper name of a river in South America, the largest in the world; most absurdly called Amazon.   *Garcilasso.*

MARCH, *v.t.* 1. To cause to move, as an army. Buonaparte *marched* an immense army to Moscow, but he did not *march* them back to France.

MARE, *n.* 2. [Sax. *mara,* D. *merrie,* the name of a spirit imagined by the nations of the north of Europe to torment persons in sleep.] A kind of torpor or stagnation which seems to press the stomach in sleep; the incubus. [It is now used only in the compound, *nightmare,* which ought to be written *nightmar.*]

MAROON, *n.* A name given to free blacks living on the mountains in the West India isles.

MARRIAGE, *n.* The act of uniting a man and woman for life; wedlock; the legal union of a man and woman for life. Marriage is a contract both civil and religious, by which the parties engage to live together in mutual affection and fidelity, till death shall separate them. Marriage was instituted by God himself for the purpose of preventing the promiscuous intercourse of the sexes, for promoting domestic felicity, and for securing the maintenance and education of children.

MARVEL, *n.* 1. A wonder; that which arrests the attention and causes a person to stand or gaze, or to pause. [This word is nearly obsolete, or at least little used in elegant writings.]

MASSACRE, *n.* 1. The murder of an individual, or the slaughter of numbers of human beings, with circumstances of cruelty; the indiscriminate killing of

MAN. The truncated Latin quote is from Ovid's *Metamorphoses.* The whole is usually translated as "God gave man an upright countenance to survey the heavens, and to look upward to the stars."

M

human beings, without authority or necessity, and without forms civil or military. It differs from *assassination,* which is a *private* killing. It differs from *carnage,* which is rather the effect of slaughter than slaughter itself, and is applied to the authorized destruction of men in battle.

Massacre is sometimes called *butchery,* from its resemblance to the killing of cattle. If a soldier kills a man in battle in his own defense, it is a lawful act; it is killing, and it is slaughter, but it is not a *massacre.* Whereas, if a soldier kills an enemy after he has surrendered it is *massacre,* a killing without necessity, often without authority, contrary to the usages of nations, and of course with cruelty. The practice of killing prisoners, even when authorized by the commander, is properly *massacre;* as the authority given proceeds from cruelty. We have all heard of the *massacre* of the protestants in France, in the reign of Charles IX. and frequent instances of barbarous *massacre* occur in the war between the Turks and Greeks.

MATCH, *n.* 1. Some very combustible substance used for catching fire from a spark, as hemp, flax, cotton, tow dipped in sulphur, or a species of dry wood, called vulgarly touchwood.

2. A rope or cord made of hempen tow, composed of three strands slightly twisted, and again covered with tow and boiled in the lees of old wine. This when lighted at one end, retains fire and burns slowly till consumed. It is used in firing artillery, &c.   *Encyc.*

MATERIALIST, *n.* One who denies the existence of spiritual substances, and maintains that the soul of man is the result of a particular organization of matter in the body.

MATTER, *n.* Matter is usually divided by philosophical writers into four kinds or classes; *solid, liquid, aeriform,* and *imponderable. Solid* substances are those whose parts firmly cohere and resist impression, as wood or stone; *liquid* have free motion among their parts, and easily yield to impression, as water and wine. *Aeriform* substances are elastic fluids, called vapors and gases, as air and oxygen gas. The *imponderable* substances are destitute of weight, as light, caloric, electricity, and magnetism.

MATURE, *a.* 1. Ripe; perfected by time or natural growth; as a man of *mature* age. We apply it to a young man who has arrived to the age when he is supposed to be competent to manage his own concerns; to a young woman who is fit to be married; and to elderly men who have much experience.

MEAD, MEADOW, *n.* [. . . The sense is extended or flat depressed land. It is supposed that this word enters into the name *Mediolanum,* now *Milan,* in Italy; that is, *mead-land.*] A tract of low land. In America, the word is applied particularly to the low ground on the banks of rivers, consisting of a rich mold or an alluvial soil, whether grass land, pasture, tillage or wood land; as the *meadows* on the banks of the Connecticut. The word with us does not necessarily imply wet land. This species of land is called, in the western states, *bottoms*, or *bottom land*. The word is also used for other low or flat lands, particularly lands appropriated to the culture of grass.

The word is said to be applied in Great Britain to land somewhat watery, but covered with grass.   *Johnson.*

Meadow means pasture or grass land, annually mown for hay; but more particularly, land too moist for cattle to graze on in winter, without spoiling the sward.   *Encyc.   Cyc.*

MEAL, *n.* 1. The substance of edible grain ground to fine particles, and not bolted or sifted. Meal primarily includes the bran as well as the flour. Since bolting has been generally practiced, the word *meal* is not generally applied to the finer part, or flour, at least in the United States, though I believe it is sometimes so used. In New England, *meal* is now usually applied to ground maiz, whether bolted or unbolted, called *Indian meal*, or *corn-meal*. The words *wheat-meal* and *rye-meal* are rarely used, though not wholly extinct; and *meal* occurs also in *oatmeal*.

MEASURE, *n.* 15. Means to an end; an act, step or proceeding towards the accomplishment of an object; *an extensive signification of the word, applicable to almost every act preparatory to a final end, and by which it is to be attained.* Thus we speak of legislative *measures*, political *measures*, public *measures*, prudent *measures*, a rash *measure*, effectual *measures*, inefficient *measures*.

MEAT, *n.* 2. The flesh of animals used as food. *This is now the more usual sense of the word.* The *meat* of carnivorous animals is tough, coarse and ill flavored. The *meat* of herbivorous animals is generally palatable.

MECHANIC, MECHANICAL, *a.* The terms *mechanical* and *chimical*, are thus distinguished: those changes which bodies undergo without altering their constitution, that is, losing their identity, such as changes of place, of figure, &c. are *mechanical;* those which alter the constitution of bodies, making them different substances, as when flour, yeast and water unite to form bread, are *chimical.* In the one case, the changes relate to *masses* of matter, as the motions of the heavenly bodies, or the action of the wind on a ship under sail; in the other case, the changes occur between the *particles* of matter, as the action of heat in melting lead, or the union of sand and lime forming mortar. Most of what are usually called the *mechanic arts*, are partly mechanical, and partly chimical.

MEDICINE, *n.* 1. Any substance, liquid or solid, that has the property of curing or mitigating disease in animals, or that is used for that purpose. Simples, plants and minerals furnish most of our *medicines*. Even poisons used with judgment and in moderation, are safe and efficacious *medicines*.

M

MEAT. Johnson quotes from Bacon's *Natural History,* which says that ducks feed on flesh but still taste good.

MEDICINE. Webster defines *simple* as "something not mixed or compounded. In the *materia medica,* the general denomination of an herb or plant, as each vegetable is supposed to possess its particular virtue, and therefore to constitute a simple remedy."

MEDIUM, *n. plu. mediums; media* not being generally, though sometimes used. In *philosophy*, the space or substance through which a body moves or passes to any point. Thus ether is supposed to be the *medium* through which the planets move; air is the *medium* through which bodies move near the earth; water the *medium* in which fishes live and move; glass a *medium* through which light passes; and we speak of a resisting *medium*, a refracting *medium*, &c.

MELANCHOLY, *n.* 1. A gloomy state of mind, often a gloomy state that is of some continuance, or habitual; depression of spirits induced by grief; dejection of spirits. This was formerly supposed to proceed from a redundance of black bile. *Melancholy*, when extreme and of long continuance, is a disease, sometimes accompanied with partial insanity. Cullen defines it, partial insanity without dyspepsy.

In *nosology*, mental alienation restrained to a single object or train of ideas, in distinction from *mania*, in which the alienation is general.

Good.

Moon-struck madness, moping *melancholy*.   *Milton.*

MELIORATE, *v.t.* To make better; to improve; as, to *meliorate* fruit by grafting, or soil by cultivation. Civilization has done much, but Christianity more, to *meliorate* the condition of men in society.

MELIORATING, *ppr.* Improving; advancing in good qualities.

The pure and benign light of revelation has had a *meliorating* influence on mankind.   *Washington.*

MELODRAME, *n.* A dramatic performance in which songs are intermixed.

Todd.

MEMORY, *n.* 1. The faculty of the mind by which it retains the knowledge of past events, or ideas which are past. A distinction is made between *memory* and *recollection. Memory* retains past ideas without any, or with little effort; *recollection* implies an effort to recall ideas that are past.

Beattie.   Reid.   Stewart.

Memory is the purveyor of reason.   *Rambler.*

2. A retaining of past ideas in the mind; remembrance. Events that excite little attention are apt to escape from *memory*.

3. Exemption from oblivion.

That ever-living man of *memory*,
Henry the fifth.   *Shak.*

4. The time within which past events can be remembered or recollected, or the time within which a person may have knowledge of what is past. The revolution in England was before my *memory;* the revolution in America was within the author's *memory*.

MENIAL, *a.* 1. Pertaining to servants, or domestic servants; low; mean.

The women attendants perform only the most *menial* offices.   *Swift.*

[Johnson observes on this passage, that Swift seems not to have known the meaning of this word. But this is the only sense in which it is now used.]
2. Belonging to the retinue or train of servants.   *Johnson.*

Two *menial* dogs before their master pressed.   *Dryden.*

[If this definition of Johnson is correct, it indicates that *menial* is from *meinez*, many, rather than from *mesnie*, family. But the sense may be *house-dogs.*]

MERITORIOUS, *a.* Deserving of reward or of notice, regard, fame or happiness, or of that which shall be a suitable return for services or excellence of any kind. We applaud the meritorious services of the laborer, the soldier and the seaman. We admire the *meritorious* labors of a Watts, a Doddridge, a Carey and a Martyn. We rely for salvation on the *meritorious* obedience and sufferings of Christ.

METAL, *n.* A simple, fixed, shining, opake body or substance, insoluble in water, fusible by heat, a good conductor of heat and electricity, capable when in the state of an oxyd, of uniting with acids and forming with them metallic salts. Many of the metals are also malleable or extensible by the hammer, and some of them extremely ductile. Metals are mostly fossil, sometimes found native or pure, but more generally combined with other matter. Some metals are more malleable than others, and this circumstance gave rise to the distinction of metals and semi-metals; a distinction little regarded at the present day. Recent discoveries have enlarged the list of the metals, and the whole number now recognized is thirty, exclusive of those which have been recently discovered, as the bases of the earths and alkalies. Twelve of these are malleable, viz. platina, gold, silver, mercury, lead, copper, tin, iron, zink, palladium, nickel, and cadmium. The following sixteen are not sufficiently tenacious to bear extension by beating, viz. arsenic, antimony, bismuth, cobalt, manganese, tellurium, titanium, columbium, molybden, tungsten, chrome, osmium, iridium, rhodium, uranium, and cerium.

                    Encyc. Nicholson. Thomson. Phillips. Ure.

To these may be added potassium, sodium, barium, strontium, calcium, and lithium.   *Henry.*

The following have not been exhibited in a separate form; magnesium, glucinum, yttrium, aluminum, thorinum, zirconium, and silicium.

METAPHYSICS, *n.* [It is said that this name was given to the science by Aristotle or his followers, who considered the science of natural bodies, physics, as the first in the order of studies, and the science of mind or intelligence to be the second.] The science of the principles and causes of all things existing; hence, the science of mind or intelligence. This science comprehends *ontology*, or the science which treats of the nature, essence, and qualities or attributes of being; *cosmology,* the science of the world, which treats of the nature and laws of matter and of motion; *anthroposophy,* which treats of the powers of man, and the motions by which life is produced; *psychology,* which treats of the intellectual soul; *pneumatology,* or the science of spirits or angels, &c. *Metaphysical theology,* called by Leibnitz and others *theodicy,* treats of the existence of God, his essence and attributes. These divisions of the science of metaphysics, which prevailed in the ancient schools, are now not much regarded. The natural division of things that exist is into body and mind, things material and immaterial. The former belong to physics, and the latter to the science of metaphysics.   *Encyc.*

METEOR, *n.* 1. In *a general sense,* a body that flies or floats in the air, and in this sense it includes rain, hail, snow, &c. But in a restricted sense, in which it is commonly understood,

2. A fiery or luminous body or appearance flying or floating in the atmosphere, or in a more elevated region. We give this name to the brilliant globes or masses of matter which are occasionally seen moving rapidly through our atmosphere, and which throw off, with loud explosions, fragments that reach the earth, and are called falling stones. We call by the same name those fire balls which are usually denominated falling stars, supposed to be owing to gelatinous matter inflated by phosphureted hydrogen gas; also, the lights which appear over moist grounds and grave yards, called *ignes fatui,* which are ascribed to the same cause.

METROPOLIS, *n.* Literally, the mother-city, that is, the chief city or capital of a kingdom, state or country, as Paris in France, Madrid in Spain, London in Great Britain. In the United States, Washington, in the District of Columbia, is the *metropolis,* as being the seat of government; but in several of the states, the largest cities are not the seats of the respective governments. Yet New York city, in the state of that name, and Philadelphia in Pennsylvania, are the chief cities, and may be called each the *metropolis* of the state in which it is situated, though neither of them is the seat of government in the state.

MIDDLE-EARTH, *n.* The world. *Obs.*   *Shak.*

MIGRATE, *v.i.* To pass or remove from one country or from one state to another, with a view to permanent residence, or residence of some continuance. The first settlers of New England *migrated* first to Holland, and afterwards to America. Some species of fowls *migrate* in autumn to a warmer climate for a temporary residence. To change residence in the same city or state is not to *migrate.*

MILE, *n.* A measure of length or distance, containing eight furlongs, 320 rods, poles or perches, 1760 yards, 5280 feet, or 80 chains. The Roman mile was a thousand paces, equal to 1600 yards English measure.

MISCHIEVOUSNESS, *n.* Hurtfulness; noxiousness.

2. Disposition to do harm, or to vex or annoy; as the *mischievousness* of youth.

Mischief denotes injury, harm or damage of less malignity and magnitude than what are usually called crimes. We never give the name of mischief to theft, robbery or murder. And it so commonly implies *intention* in committing petty offenses, that it shocks us to hear the word applied to the calamities inflicted by Providence. We say, a tempest has done great *damage*, but not *mischief.* In like manner, the adjective *mischievous* is not applied to thieves, pirates and other felons, but to persons committing petty trespasses and offenses.

MISSION, *n.* 2. Persons sent; any number of persons appointed by authority to perform any service; particularly, the persons sent to propagate religion, or evangelize the heathen. The societies for propagating the gospel have *missions* in almost every country.

  Last week a *mission* sailed for the Sandwich isles. We have domestic *missions* and foreign *missions.*

MISSION. The Sandwich Islands are now called Hawaii.

MOCCASON, *n.* A shoe or cover for the feet, made of deer-skin or other soft lether, without a sole, and ornamented on the upper side; the customary shoe worn by the native Indians.

MODEL, *n.* 6. A pattern; any thing to be imitated. Take Cicero, lord Chatham or Burke, as a *model* of eloquence; take Washington as a *model* of prudence, integrity and patriotism; above all, let Christ be the *model* of our benevolence, humility, obedience and patience.

7. A copy; representation; something made in imitation of real life; as anatomical *models,* representing the parts of the body. General Pfiffer constructed a *model* of the mountainous parts of Switzerland.

MODEL. General Pfiffer's model of the region surrounding Lucerne was twenty years in the making. It is described by William Coxe in *Travels in Switzerland,* 1789.

MODESTY, *n.* That lowly temper which accompanies a moderate estimate of one's own worth and importance. This temper when natural, springs in some measure from timidity, and in young and inexperienced persons, is allied to bashfulness and diffidence. In persons who have seen the world, and lost their natural timidity, *modesty* springs no less from principle than from feeling, and is manifested by retiring, unobtrusive manners, assuming less to itself than others are willing to yield, and conceding to others all due honor and respect, or even more than they expect or require.

2. Modesty, as an act or series of acts, consists in humble, unobtrusive deportment, as opposed to extreme boldness, forwardness, arrogance, presumption, audacity or impudence. Thus we say, the petitioner urged his claims with *modesty;* the speaker addressed the audience with *modesty.*

4. In *females,* modesty has the like character as in males; but the word is used also as synonymous with chastity, or purity of manners. In this sense,

modesty results from purity of mind, or from the fear of disgrace and ignominy fortified by education and principle. Unaffected *modesty* is the sweetest charm of female excellence, the richest gem in the diadem of their honor.

MOHAWK, MOHOCK, *n.* The appellation given to certain ruffians who infested the streets of London; so called from the nation of Indians of that name in America.   *Prior.*

MOLASSES, an incorrect orthography of *melasses.*

MOLECULE, *n.* A very minute particle of matter. Molecules are elementary, constituent, or integrant. The latter result from the union of the elementary.
                                        Dict. Nat. Hist.   Fourcroy.   Kirwan.

MONOPOLY, *n.* The sole power of vending any species of goods, obtained either by engrossing the articles in market by purchase, or by a license from the government confirming this privilege. Thus the East India Company in Great Britain has a *monopoly* of the trade to the East Indies, granted to them by charter. *Monopolies* by individuals obtained by engrossing, are an offense prohibited by law. But a man has by natural right the exclusive power of vending his own produce or manufactures, and to retain that exclusive right is not a *monopoly* within the meaning of law.

MONOTONY, *n.* 2. Uniformity; sameness.
        At sea, every thing that breaks the *monotony* of the surrounding expanse attracts attention.   *Irving.*

MONUMENT, *n.* Any thing by which the memory of a person or an event is preserved or perpetuated; a building, stone or other thing placed or erected to remind men of the person who raised it, or of a person deceased, or of any remarkable event; as a mausoleum, a pillar, a pyramid, a triumphal arch, a tombstone and the like. A pillar of 200 feet in highth, composed of Portland stone, was erected in London as a *monument* to preserve the memory of the great conflagration in 1666. A *monument* is erected on Bunker Hill to commemorate the battle of June 17, 1775.

MOON, *n.* The heavenly orb which revolves round the earth; a secondary planet or satellite of the earth, whose borrowed light is reflected to the earth and serves to dispel the darkness of night. Its mean distance from the earth is $60\frac{1}{2}$ semidiameters of the earth, or 240,000 miles. Its revolution round the earth in 27 days, 7 hours, 43 minutes, constitutes the lunar month.

MOOR, *n.* A native of the northern coast of Africa, called by the Romans from the color of the people, *Mauritania*, the country of dark-complexioned people. The same country is now called Morocco, Tunis, Algiers, &c.

MOOSE, *n.* [a native Indian name.] An animal of the genus Cervus, and the largest of the deer kind, growing sometimes to the highth of 17 hands, and weighing 1200 pounds. This animal has palmated horns, with a short thick neck, and an upright mane of a light brown color. The eyes are small, the ears a foot long, very broad and slouching; the upper lip is square, hangs over the lower one, and has a deep sulcus in the middle so as to appear bifid. This animal inhabits cold northern climates, being found in the American forests of Canada and New England, and in the corresponding latitudes of Europe and Asia. It is the elk of Europe.   *Encyc.*

MORAL, *a.* 7. In general, *moral* denotes something which respects the conduct of men and their relations as social beings whose actions have a bearing on each other's rights and happiness, and are therefore right or wrong, virtuous or vicious; as *moral* character, *moral* views; *moral* knowledge; *moral* sentiments; *moral* maxims; *moral* approbation; *moral* doubts; *moral* justice; *moral* virtue; *moral* obligations, &c. Or *moral* denotes something which respects the intellectual powers of man, as distinct from his physical powers. Thus we speak of *moral* evidence, *moral* arguments, *moral* persuasion, *moral* certainty, *moral* force; which operate on the mind.

Moral philosophy, the science of manners and duty; the science which treats of the nature and condition of man as a social being, of the duties which result from his social relations, and the reasons on which they are founded.

Moral sense, an innate or natural sense of right and wrong; an instinctive perception of what is right or wrong in moral conduct, which approves some actions and disapproves others, independent of education or the knowledge of any positive rule or law. But the existence of any such moral sense is very much doubted.   *Paley. Encyc.*

MORNING, *n.* 1. The first part of the day, beginning at twelve o'clock at night and extending to twelve at noon. Thus we say, a star rises at one o'clock in the *morning.* In a more limited sense, *morning* is the time beginning an hour or two before sunrise, or at break of day, and extending to the hour of breakfast and of beginning the labors of the day. Among men of business in large cities, the *morning* extends to the hour of dining.

MORRICE, MORRIS, MORRIS-DANCE, *n.* A moorish dance; a dance in imitation of the Moors, as sarabands, chacons, &c. usually performed with castanets, tambours, &c. by young men in their shirts, with bells at their feet and ribins of various colors tied round their arms and flung across their shoulders.   *Encyc.*

MOSK, *n.* A Mohammedan temple or place of religious worship. Mosks are square buildings, generally constructed of stone. Before the chief gate is a

M

square court paved with white marble, and surrounded with a low gallery
whose roof is supported by pillars of marble. In this gallery the worshipers
wash themselves before they enter the mosk.   *Encyc.*

MOTHER, *n.* [. . . We observe that in some other languages, as well as in
English, the same word signifies a female parent, and the thick slime formed
in vinegar; and in all the languages of Europe here cited, the orthography is
nearly the same as that of *mud* and *matter.* The question then occurs whether
the name of a female parent originated in a word expressing *matter,* mold;
either the soil of the earth, as the producer, or the like substance, when
shaped and fitted as a mold for castings; or whether the name is connected
with the opinion that the earth is the *mother* of all productions; whence the
word *mother-earth.* We are informed by a fragment of Sanchoniathon, that the
ancient Phenicians considered *mud,* *μωτ* to be the substance from which all
things were formed. See *Mud.* The word *matter* is evidently from the Ar.
ﺩﻣ *madda,* to secrete, eject or discharge a purulent substance; and I think
cannot have any direct connection with *mud.* But in the Italian, Spanish and
Portuguese, the same word *madre* signifies mother, and a mold for castings;
and the northern languages, particularly the German and Danish, seem to
establish the fact that the proper sense of *mother* is matrix. Hence *mother* of
pearl, the matrix of pearl. If this word had its origin in the name of the earth
used for the forms of castings, it would not be a singular fact; for our word
mold, in this sense, I suppose to be so named from *mold,* fine earth. The
question remains *sub judice.*]

MOTION, *n.* The act or process of changing place; change of local position;
the passing of a body from one place to another; change of distance between
bodies; opposed to *rest.*
    Animal motion is that which is performed by animals in consequence of
volition or an act of the will; but how the will operates on the body in producing motion, we cannot explain. *Mechanical motion* is effected by the force or
power of one body acting on another. *Perpetual motion* is that which is
effected or supplied by itself, without the impulse or intervention of any
external cause. Hitherto it has been found impossible to invent a machine
that has this principle.
    9. The effect of impulse; action proceeding from any cause, external or
internal. In the growth of plants and animals, there must be a *motion* of the
component parts, though invisible. Attraction or chemical affinity produces
sensible *motion* of the parts of bodies. *Motions* of the mind ascribed to the
invisible agency of the Supreme Being, are called good *motions.*

MOUNT, *n.* 1. A mass of earth, or earth and rock, rising considerably above
the common surface of the surrounding land. *Mount* is used for an eminence
or elevation of earth, indefinite in highth or size, and may be a hillock, hill or

mountain. We apply it to *Mount* Blanc, in Switzerland, to *Mount* Tom and *Mount* Holyoke, in Massachusetts, and it is applied in Scripture to the small hillocks on which sacrifice was offered, as well as to *Mount* Sinai.

MOUNTAIN, *n.* A large mass of earth and rock, rising above the common level of the earth or adjacent land, but of no definite altitude. We apply *mountain* to the largest eminences on the globe; but sometimes the word is used for a large hill. In general, *mountain* denotes an elevation higher and larger than a hill; as the Altaic *mountains* in Asia, the Alps in Switzerland, the Andes in South America, the Alleghany *mountains* in Virginia, the Kaatskill in New York, the White *mountains* in New Hampshire, and the Green *mountains* in Vermont. The word is applied to a single elevation, or to an extended range.

MOUNTEBANK, *n.* 1. One who mounts a bench or stage in the market or other public place, boasts of his skill in curing diseases, vends medicines which he pretends are infallible remedies, and thus deludes the ignorant multitude. Persons of this character may be indicted and punished.

 2. Any boastful and false pretender.

   Nothing so impossible in nature, but *mountebanks* will undertake.

                                                                                    Arbuthnot.

MUD, *n.* [. . . This is said to be a fragment of Sanchoniathon's Phenician history, translated by Philo and preserved by Eusebius. This Phenician word *mod*, . . . is precisely the English *mud*, the matter, material or substance of which, according to the ancients, all things were formed. See Castel. Col. 2010, and the word *mother*. Plutarch, de Iside, says the Egyptians called Isis *muth*, that is, mother. This is a remarkable fact, and proves beyond controversy the common origin of the Phenician, Celtic and Teutonic nations. *Mud* may perhaps be named from wetness, and be connected with L. *madeo*, . . . to wet.]

MUG, *n.* [I know not whence derived.] A kind of cup from which liquors are drank. In America, the word is applied chiefly or solely to an earthen cup.

MUGGISH, MUGGY, *a.* 2. Moist; damp; close; warm and unelastic; as *muggy* air. [*This is the principal use of the word in America.*]

MUMMERY, *n.* 1. Masking; sport; diversion; frolicking in masks; low contemptible amusement; buffoonery.

 2. Farcical show; hypocritical disguise and parade to delude vulgar minds.

MUMMY, *n.* 1. A dead human body embalmed and dried after the Egyptian manner; a name perhaps given to it from the substance used in preserving it.

There are two kinds of mummies. The first are bodies dried by the heat of the sun. Such are found in the sands of Libya. The other kind is taken from the catacombs in Egypt.   *Encyc.*

3. There are found in Poland natural mummies lying in caverns, supposed to be the remains of persons who in time of war took refuge in caves, but being discovered were suffocated by their enemies. These bodies are dried, with the flesh and skin shrunk almost close to the bones, and are of a blackish color.   *Encyc.*

MUSCLE, *n.* 1. In *anatomy,* the muscles are the organs of motion, consisting of fibers or bundles of fibers inclosed in a thin cellular membrane. The muscles are susceptible of contraction and relaxation, and in a healthy state the proper muscles are subject to the will, and are called *voluntary* muscles. But other parts of the body, as the heart, the urinary bladder, the stomach, &c. are of a muscular texture, and susceptible of contraction and dilatation, but are not subject to the will, and are therefore called *involuntary* muscles. The red color of the muscles is owing to the blood vessels which they contain. The ends of the muscles are fastened to the bones which they move, and when they act in opposition to each other, they are called *antagonists.*
                                                                        Encyc.

MUSEUM, *n.* A house or apartment appropriated as a repository of things that have an immediate relation to the arts; a cabinet of curiosities.

MUSKRAT, MUSQUASH, *n.* An American animal of the murine genus, the *Mus zibethicus.* It has a compressed, lanceolated tail, with toes separate. It has the smell of musk in summer, but loses it in winter. The fur is used by hatters. Its popular name in America is *musquash.*   *Belknap.*

MUTINY, *n.* [*Note.* In good authors who lived a century ago, *mutiny* and *mutinous* were applied to insurrection and sedition in civil society. But I believe these words are now applied exclusively to soldiers and seamen.]

MYSTERIOUS, *a.* Obscure; hid from the understanding; not clearly understood. The birth and connections of the man with the iron mask in France are *mysterious,* and have never been explained.

2. In religion, obscure; secret; not revealed or explained; hidden from human understanding, or unintelligible; beyond human comprehension. Applied to the divine counsels and government, the word often implies something awfully obscure; as, the ways of God are often *mysterious.*

N

Natural history, in its most extensive sense, is the description of whatever is created, or of the whole universe, including the heavens and the earth, and all the productions of the earth. But more generally, natural history is limited to a description of the earth and its productions, including zoology, botany, geology, mineralogy, meteorology, &c.

Natural philosophy, the science of material natural bodies, of their properties, powers and motions. It is distinguished from intellectual and moral philosophy, which respect the mind or understanding of man and the qualities of actions. Natural philosophy comprehends mechanics, hydrostatics, optics, astronomy, chimistry, magnetism, electricity, galvanism, &c.

NATURE, *n.* 2. By a metonymy of the effect for the cause, *nature* is used for the agent, creator, author, producer of things, or for the powers that produce them. By the expression, "trees and fossils are produced by *nature*," we mean, they are formed or produced by certain inherent powers in matter, or we mean that they are produced by God, the Creator, the Author of whatever is made or produced. The opinion that things are produced by inherent powers of matter, independent of a supreme intelligent author, is atheism. But generally men mean by *nature*, thus used, the Author of created things, or the operation of his power.

NECESSARY, *a.* That must be; that cannot be otherwise; indispensably requisite. It is *necessary* that every effect should have a cause. 2. Indispensable; requisite; essential; that cannot be otherwise without preventing the purpose intended. Air is *necessary* to support animal life; food is *necessary* to nourish the body; holiness is a *necessary* qualification for happiness; health is *necessary* to the enjoyment of pleasure; subjection to law is *necessary* to the safety of persons and property. 4. Acting from necessity or compulsion; opposed to *free.* Whether man is a *necessary* or a free agent is a question much discussed.

NECESSARY, *n.* A privy.

NECK, *n.* 2. A long narrow tract of land projecting from the main body, or a narrow tract connecting two larger tracts; as the *neck* of land between Boston and Roxbury.

NECROMANCY, *n.* 1. The art of revealing future events by means of a pretended communication with the dead. This imposture is prohibited.

Negative electricity, according to Dr. Franklin, is a deficiency of the fluid in a substance, or less than the substance naturally contains.

NEGLIGENCE, *n.* Habitual omission of that which ought to be done, or a habit of omitting to do things, either from carelessness or design. *Negligence* is usually the child of sloth or laziness, and the parent of disorders in business, often of poverty.

NEGRO, *n.* [It. Sp. *negro,* black, from L. *niger.* It is remarkable that our common people retain the exact Latin pronunciation of this word, *neger.*] A native or descendant of the black race of men in Africa. The word is never applied to the tawny or olive colored inhabitants of the northern coast of Africa, but to the more southern race of men who are quite black.

NEIGHBOR, NEHBOOR, *n.* [. . . The true orthography, as this word is now pronounced, is *nehboor.*] 1. One who lives near another. In large towns, a *neighbor* is one who lives within a few doors. In the country, a *neighbor* may live at a greater distance; and in new settlements, where the people are thinly scattered over the country, a *neighbor* may be distant several miles. Such is the use of the word in the United States.

NEOLOGIST, *n.* One who introduces new words into a language. Lavoisier has been a successful *neologist.*   *Med. Repos.*

NEPTUNIAN, NEPTUNIST, *n.* One who adopts the theory that the whole earth was once covered with water, or rather that the substances of the globe were formed from aqueous solution; opposed to the *Plutonic theory.*
                                                        Pinkerton.   Good.

NEST, *n.* 2. Any place where irrational animals are produced.   *Bentley.*

NEUROTIC, *n.* A medicine useful in disorders of the nerves.   *Encyc.*

NEUTER, *a.* 1. Not adhering to either party; taking no part with either side, either when persons are contending, or questions are discussed. It may be synonymous with *indifferent,* or it may not. The United States remained *neuter* during the French Revolution, but very few of the people were *indifferent* as to the success of the parties engaged. . . .

NICOTIAN, *a.* Pertaining to or denoting tobacco; and as a noun, tobacco; so called from Nicot, who first introduced it into France, A. D. 1560.

NIGHTMAR, *n.* Incubus; a sensation in sleep resembling the pressure of a weight on the breast or about the præcordia. It is usually the effect of indigestion or of a loaded stomach.

NIGHT-WALKER, *n.* One that walks in his sleep; a somnambulist.

2. One that roves about in the night for evil purposes. *Night-walkers* are punishable by law.

NOMAD, *n.* One who leads a wandering life, and subsists by tending herds of cattle which graze on herbage of spontaneous growth. Such is the practice at this day in the central and northern parts of Asia, and the Numidians in Africa are supposed to have been so called from this practice.
Tooke. Encyc.

NON-RESIDENT, *n.* One who does not reside on one's own lands, or in the place where official duties require. In the United States, lands in one state or township belonging to a person residing in another state or township, are called the lands of *non-residents.*

NOSE, *n.* 1. . . . In man, the nose is situated near the middle of the face; but in quadrupeds, the nose is at or near the lower extremity of the head.

NOSTRUM, *n.* A medicine, the ingredients of which are kept secret for the purpose of restricting the profits of sale to the inventor or proprietor. *Pope.*

NOTCH, *n.* 2. An opening or narrow passage through a mountain or hill. We say, the *notch* of a mountain. *U. States.*

NOTHING, *n.* Not any thing; not any being or existence; a word that denies the existence of any thing; non-entity; opposed to *something.* The world was created from *nothing.*

NOTIFY, *v.t.* 3. To give notice to; to inform by words or writing, in person or by message, or by any signs which are understood. The constable has *notified* the citizens to meet at the City Hall. The bell *notifies* us of the time of meeting.

The President of the United States has *notified* the House of Representatives, that he has approved and signed the act. *Journals of the Senate.*

[*Note.* This application of *notify* has been condemned, but it is in constant good use in the U. States, and in perfect accordance with the use of *certify.*]

NOTORIOUS, *a.* 1. Publicly known; manifest to the world; evident; usually, known to disadvantage; hence almost always used in an ill sense; as a *noto-*

rious thief; a *notorious* crime or vice; a man *notorious* for lewdness or gaming.

NUMERAL, *a.* 3. Expressing numbers; as numeral characters. The figures we now use to express numbers are 1. 2. 3. 4. 5. 6. 7. 8. 9. 0. They are said to be of Arabian origin; but the Arabians might have received them from India. This is a controverted question.

NYCTALOPY, *n.* The faculty of seeing best in darkness, or the disorder from which this faculty proceeds.   *Todd.*

2. In present usage, the disorder in which the patient loses his sight as night approaches, and remains blind till morning.

O

OAK, *n.* [. . . Dan. *eegetræe*, oak-tree. It is probable that the first syllable, *oak*, was originally an adjective expressing some quality, as hard or strong, and by the disuse of *tree*, *oak* became the name of the tree.] A tree of the genus Quercus, or rather the popular name of the genus itself, of which there are several species. The white oak grows to a great size, and furnishes a most valuable timber; but the live oak of the United States is the most durable timber for ships. In Hartford still stands the venerable *oak*, in the hollow stem of which was concealed and preserved the colonial charter of Connecticut, when Sir E. Andros, by authority of a writ of quo warranto from the British crown, attempted to obtain possession of it, in 1687. As it was then a large tree, it must now be nearly three hundred years old.

OBBLIGATO, *a.* A term in music, signifying on purpose for the instrument named.
                                                                    Cyc.

OBLIGATION, *n.* The binding power of a vow, promise, oath or contract, or of law, civil, political or moral, independent of a promise; that which constitutes legal or moral duty, and which renders a person liable to coercion and punishment for neglecting it. The laws and commands of God impose on us an *obligation* to love him supremely, and our neighbor as ourselves. Every citizen is under an *obligation* to obey the laws of the state. Moral *obligation* binds men without promise or contract.

2. The binding force of civility, kindness or gratitude, when the performance of a duty cannot be enforced by law. Favors conferred impose on men an *obligation* to make suitable returns.

OBSCENE, *a.* Offensive to chastity and delicacy; impure; expressing or presenting to the mind or view something which delicacy, purity and decency forbid to be exposed; as *obscene* language; *obscene* pictures.

OBTAIN, *v.t.* 1. To get; to gain; to procure; in *a general sense*, to gain possession of a thing, whether temporary or permanent; to acquire. This word usually implies exertion to get possession, and in this it differs from *receive*, which may or may not imply exertion. It differs from *acquire*, as genus from

OBBLIGATO. Webster, unlike *Cyc.*, fails to make clear what this musical instruction actually calls for.

201

species; *acquire* being properly applied only to things permanently possessed; but *obtain* is applied both to things of temporary and of permanent possession. We *obtain* loans of money on application; we *obtain* answers to letters; we *obtain* spirit from liquors by distillation and salts by evaporation. We *obtain* by seeking; we often *receive* without seeking. We *acquire* or *obtain* a good title to lands by deed, or by a judgment of court; but we do not *acquire* spirit by distillation; nor do we *acquire* an answer to a letter or an application.

OCEAN, *n.* 1. The vast body of water which covers more than three fifths of the surface of the globe, called also the sea, or great sea. It is customary to speak of the ocean as if divided into three parts, the Atlantic ocean, the Pacific ocean, and the Indian ocean; but the ocean is *one* mass or body, partially separated by the continents of Europe, Asia and Africa on one side, and by America on the other.

OFFENSIVE, *a.* 1. Causing displeasure or some degree of anger; displeasing. All sin is *offensive* to God. Rude behavior is *offensive* to men. Good breeding forbids us to use *offensive* words.

OFFERING, *n.* That which is presented in divine service; an animal or a portion of bread or corn, or of gold and silver, or other valuable articles, presented to God as an atonement for sin, or as a return of thanks for his favors, or for other religious purpose; a sacrifice; an oblation. In the Mosaic economy, there were burnt-*offerings*, sin-*offerings*, peace-*offerings*, trespass-*offerings*, thank-*offerings*, wave-*offerings*, and wood-*offerings*. Pagan nations also present *offerings* to their deities. Christ by the *offering* of himself has superseded the use of all other *offerings*, having made atonement for all men.

OFFING, *n.* That part of the sea which is at a good distance from the shore, or at a competent distance, where there is deep water and no need of a pilot. We saw a ship in the *offing*.   *Mar. Dict.   Encyc.*

OILER, *n.* One who deals in oils and pickles.

OLD, *a.* 10. That has been long cultivated; as *old* land; an *old* farm; opposed to *new* land, land lately cleared and cultivated.   *America.*
    We apply *old* chiefly to things subject to decay. We never say, the *old* sun, or an *old* mountain.

OMEN, *n.* A sign or indication of some future event; a prognostic. Superstition and ignorance multiply *omens;* philosophy and truth reject all *omens*, except such as may be called *causes* of the events. Without a miracle, how can one event be the *omen* of another with which it has no connection?

ONANISM, *n.* The crime of self-pollution.

OPERA, *n.* A dramatic composition set to music and sung on the stage, accompanied with musical instruments and enriched with magnificent dresses, machines, dancing, &c. *Encyc.*

OPIUM, *n.* Opium is the inspissated juice of the capsules of the papaver somniferum, or somniferous white poppy with which the fields in Asia Minor are sown, as ours are with wheat and rye. It flows from incisions made in the heads of the plant, and the best flows from the first incision. It is imported into Europe and America from the Levant and the East Indies. It is brought in cakes or masses weighing from eight ounces to a pound. It is heavy, of a dense texture, of a brownish yellow color, not perfectly dry, but easily receiving an impression from the finger; it has a dead and faint smell, and its taste is bitter and acrid. Opium is of great use as a medicine. *Hill. Encyc.*

OPPOSITE, *a.* Standing or situated in front; facing; as an edifice *opposite* to the Exchange. Brooklyn lies *opposite* to New York, or on the *opposite* side of the river.

OPTIMISM, *n.* The opinion or doctrine that every thing in nature is ordered for the best; or the order of things in the universe that is adapted to produce the most good.

ORANG-OUTANG, *n.* The satyr or great ape (*Simia satyrus,*) an animal with a flat face and deformed resemblance of the human form. These animals walk erect like man, feed on fruits, sleep on trees, and make a shelter against inclemencies of the weather. They grow to the highth of six feet, are remarkably strong, and wield weapons with the hand. They are solitary animals, inhabiting the interior of Africa and the isles of Sumatra, Borneo and Java. *Encyc.*
    The orang-outang is found only in S. Eastern Asia. The African animal resembling it, is the chimpanzee (*Simia troglodytes.*) *Cuvier.*

ORANG-OUTANG. Baron Georges Cuvier (1769–1832), the French naturalist and paleontologist, had found evidence to invalidate Webster's original definition, but it is retained along with the correction. See also CHIMPANZEE and PONGO.

ORIENTAL, *n.* A native or inhabitant of some eastern part of the world. We give the appellation to the inhabitants of Asia from the Hellespont and Mediterranean to Japan.

ORRERY, *n.* A machine so constructed as to represent by the movements of its parts, the motions and phases of the planets in their orbits. This machine was invented by George Graham, but Rowley, a workman, borrowed one from him and made a copy for the earl of Orrery, after whom it was named by Sir Richard Steele. Similar machines are called also planetariums. *Cyc.*

ORTHOLOGY, *n.* The right description of things.   *Fotherby.*

ORTOLAN, *n.* A bird of the genus Emberiza, about the size of the lark, with black wings. It is found in France and Italy, feeds on panic grass, and is delicious food.   *Encyc.*

OSTRICH, *n.* A fowl now considered as constituting a distinct genus, the Struthio. This is the largest of all fowls, being four feet high from the ground to the top of the back, and seven, eight, and it is said even ten to the top of the head, when standing erect. Its thighs and the sides of the body are naked, and the wings are so short as to be unfit for flying. The plumage is elegant, and much used in ornamental and showy dress. The speed of this fowl in running exceeds that of the fleetest horse.   *Encyc.*

OUTGROW, *v.t.* 2. To grow too great or too old for any thing. Children *outgrow* their garments, and men *outgrow* their usefulness.

OUTHOUSE, *n.* A small house or building at a little distance from the main house.

OUTLAW, *n.* A person excluded from the benefit of the law, or deprived of its protection. Formerly any person might kill an outlaw; but it is now held unlawful for any person to put to death an outlaw, except the sheriff, who has a warrant for that purpose.   *Blackstone.*

OVERSEER, *n.* 2. An officer who has the care of the poor or of an idiot, &c.

OX, *n.* The male of the bovine genus of quadrupeds, castrated and grown to his size or nearly so. The young male is called in America a *steer.* The same animal not castrated is called a *bull.*

OXYGEN, *n.* In *chimistry,* oxygen or oxygen gas is an element or substance so named from its property of generating acids; it is the respirable part of air, vital air, or the basis of it; it is called the acidifying principle, and the principle or support of combustion. Modern experiments, however, prove that it is not necessary in all cases to combustion or to acidity. Oxygen is a permanently elastic fluid, invisible, inodorous, and a little heavier than atmospheric air. In union with azote or nitrogen, it forms atmospheric air, of which it constitutes about a fifth part. Water contains about 85 per cent. of it, and it exists in most vegetable and animal products, acids, salts and oxyds. It forms 50 per cent. of silex, 47 of alumin, 28 of lime, 40 of magnesia, 17 of potash, and 25 of soda.   *Dict. Nat. Hist.   Cyc.   Ure.   Phillips.*

P

PACCAN, *n.* An American tree and its nut.

PACE, *n.* 2. The space between the two feet in walking, estimated at two feet and a half. But the geometrical pace is five feet, or the whole space passed over by the same foot from one step to another. Sixty thousand such paces make one degree on the equator. *Encyc.*

PAGAN, *n.* A heathen; a Gentile; an idolater; one who worships false gods. This word was originally applied to the inhabitants of the country, who on the first propagation of the christian religion adhered to the worship of false gods, or refused to receive Christianity, after it had been received by the inhabitants of the cities. In like manner, *heathen* signifies an inhabitant of the *heath* or woods, and *caffer*, in Arabic, signifies the inhabitant of a hut or cottage, and one that does not receive the religion of Mohammed. Pagan is used to distinguish one from a Christian and a Mohammedan.

PAGE, *n.* 1. A boy attending on a great person, rather for formality or show, than for servitude.

He had two *pages* of honor, on either hand one. *Bacon.*

2. A boy or man that attends on a legislative body. In Massachusetts, the page is a boy that conveys papers from the members of the house of representatives to the speaker, and from the speaker or clerk to the members.

PAGODA, *n.* 1. A temple in the East Indies in which idols are worshiped. *Pope.*

P. This letter is found in the oriental languages, from which it was received into the Greek and Latin; except however the Arabic, which has not this letter, and the Arabians cannot easily pronounce it.

PAINTING, *n.* The art of forming figures, or resembling objects in colors on canvas or other material, or the art of representing to the eye by means of figures and colors, any object of sight, and sometimes the emotions of the mind.   *Encyc.*

PALATE, *n.* 2. Taste.
> Hard task to hit the *palates* of such guests.   *Pope.*

[This signification of the word originated in the opinion that the palate is the instrument of taste. This is a mistake. In itself it has no power of taste.]
> 3. Mental relish; intellectual taste.
>> Men of nice *palates* could not relish Aristotle, as dressed up by the schoolmen.   *Baker.*

PALAVER, *n.* 1. Idle talk.
> 2. Flattery; adulation. [*This is used with us in the vulgar dialect.*]
> 3. Talk; conversation; conference; *a sense used in Africa, as appears by the relations of missionaries.*

PALMISTRY, *n.* The art or practice of divining or telling fortunes by the lines and marks in the palm of the hand; a trick of imposture, much practiced by gipseys.

PALM-TREE, *n.* The date tree, or *Phœnix Lactylifera,* a native of Asia and Africa, which grows to the highth of 60 and even of 100 feet, with an upright stem, crowned with a cluster of leaves or branches eight or nine feet long, extending all around like an umbrella. The fruit is in shape somewhat like an acorn. This tree transplanted will grow in Europe, but the fruit never ripens.
Encyc.

PANCAKE, *n.* A thin cake fried in a pan.
> Some folks think it will never be good times, till houses are tiled with *pancakes.*   *Franklin.*

PANORAMA, *n.* Complete or entire view; a circular painting having apparently no beginning or end, from the center of which the spectator may have a complete view of the objects presented.

PARACHUTE. The ☞ first successful parachute descent from a great height was made in 1797 by the French AERONAUT Jacques Garnerin, who dropped three thousand feet from a balloon.

PARACHUTE, *n.* In *aerostation,* an instrument to prevent the rapidity of descent.

PARAPHERNALIA, *n.* The goods which a wife brings with her at her marriage, or which she possesses beyond her dower or jointure, and which remain at her disposal after her husband's death. Such are her apparel and her ornaments, over which the executors have no control, unless when the assets are insufficient to pay the debts.   *Blackstone.*

PARASOL, *n.* A small umbrella used by ladies to defend themselves from rain, or their faces from the sun's rays.

PARCHMENT, *n.* The skin of a sheep or goat dressed or prepared and rendered fit for writing on. This is done by separating all the flesh and hair, rubbing the skin with pumice stone, and reducing its thickness with a sharp instrument. Vellum is made of the skins of abortive or very young calves.
Encyc.

PARENT, *n.* 1. A father or mother; he or she that produces young. The duties of *parents* to their children are to maintain, protect and educate them.
When *parents* are wanting in authority, children are wanting in duty. *Ames.*

PARLOR, *n.* Primarily, the apartment in a nunnery where the nuns are permitted to meet and converse with each other; hence with us, the room in a house which the family usually occupy when they have no company, as distinguished from a drawing room intended for the reception of company, or from a dining room, when a distinct apartment is allotted for that purpose. In most houses, the parlor is also the dining room.

PARODY, *n.* 1. A kind of writing in which the words of an author or his thoughts are, by some slight alterations, adapted to a different purpose; a kind of poetical pleasantry, in which verses written on one subject, are altered and applied to another by way of burlesque. *Johnson. Encyc.*

PARROT, *n.* 1. The name of fowls of the genus Psittacus, of numerous species. The bill is hooked and the upper mandible movable. The hooked bill of the parrot is used in climbing. These fowls are found almost everywhere in tropical climates. They breed in hollow trees and subsist on fruits and seeds. They are also remarkable for the faculty of making indistinct articulations of words in imitation of the human voice.

PARTRIDGE, *n.* A wild fowl of the genus Tetrao. (Linn.) Latham arranges the partridge and quail in a genus under the name of *Perdix*, and assigns the grous to the genus *Tetrao*. The partridge is esteemed a great delicacy at the table.
The term *partridge* is applied in Pennsylvania to the bird called quail in New England, a peculiar species of Perdix; in New England it is applied to the ruffed grous, a species of Tetrao.

PATIENCE, *n.* The suffering of afflictions, pain, toil, calamity, provocation or other evil, with a calm, unruffled temper; endurance without murmuring or fretfulness. *Patience* may spring from constitutional fortitude, from a kind of heroic pride, or from christian submission to the divine will.
2. A calm temper which bears evils without murmuring or discontent.

P

3. The act or quality of waiting long for justice or expected good without discontent.

PATRIOTISM, *n.* Love of one's country; the passion which aims to serve one's country, either in defending it from invasion, or protecting its rights and maintaining its laws and institutions in vigor and purity. *Patriotism* is the characteristic of a good citizen, the noblest passion that animates a man in the character of a citizen.

PAUPERISM, *n.* The state of being poor or destitute of the means of support; the state of indigent persons requiring support from the community. The increase of *pauperism* is an alarming evil.

PAVAN. Actually, a ☞ dance from Padua.

PAVAN, *n.* A grave dance among the Spaniards. In this dance, the performers make a kind of wheel before each other, the gentlemen dancing with cap and sword, princes with long robes, and the ladies with long trails; the motions resembling the stately steps of the peacock.
Encyc. Sp. Dict. Shak.

PEACH, *n.* A tree and its fruit, of the genus Amygdalus, of many varieties. This is a delicious fruit, the produce of warm or temperate climates. In America, the *peach* thrives and comes to perfection in the neighborhood of Boston, northward of which it usually fails.

PEDERASTY, *n.* Sodomy; the crime against nature.

PEDESTRIAN, *n.* One that walks or journeys on foot.
2. One that walks for a wager; a remarkable walker.

PELICAN, *n.* A fowl of the genus Pelicanus. It is larger than the swan, and remarkable for its enormous bill, to the lower edges of the under chop of which is attached a pouch or bag, capable of being distended so as to hold many quarts of water. In this bag the fowl deposits the fish it takes for food.
Encyc.

PENCIL, *n.* 1. A small brush used by painters for laying on colors. The proper pencils are made of fine hair or bristles, as of camels, badgers or squirrels, or of the down of swans, inclosed in a quill. The larger pencils, made of swine's bristles, are called *brushes.*   *Encyc.*
2. A pen formed of carburet of iron or plumbago, black lead or red chalk, with a point at one end, used for writing and drawing.   *Encyc.*
3. Any instrument of writing without ink.   *Johnson.*

PENGUIN, *n.* A genus of fowls of the order of Palmipeds. The penguin is an aquatic fowl with very short legs, with four toes, three of which are webbed;

the body is clothed with short fethers, set as compactly as the scales of a fish; the wings are small like fins, and covered with short scale-like fethers, so that they are useless in flight. Penguins seldom go on shore, except in the season of breeding, when they burrow like rabbits. On land they stand erect; they are tame and may be driven like a flock of sheep. In water they swim with rapidity, being assisted by their wings. These fowls are found only in the southern latitudes.   *Encyc.*

PENNYPOST, *n.* One that carries letters from the post office and delivers them to the proper persons for a penny or other small compensation.

PEON, *n.* In Hindoostan, a foot soldier, or a footman armed with sword and target; said to be corrupted from *piadah.* Hence,
    2. In *France,* a common man in chess; usually written and called *pawn.*

PEOPLE, *n.* 2. The vulgar; the mass of illiterate persons.

PERAMBULATE, *v.t.* To walk through or over; properly and technically, to pass through or over for the purpose of surveying or examining something; to visit as overseers; as, to *perambulate* a parish. So in New England, the laws require the selectmen of towns to *perambulate* the borders or bounds of the township, and renew the boundaries, or see that the old ones are in a good state.

PERCH, *n.* 1. A pole; hence, a roost for fowls, which is often a pole; also, any thing on which they light. 2. A measure of length containing five yards and a half; a rod. In the popular language of America, *rod* is chiefly used; but *rod, pole* and *perch,* all signifying the same thing, may be used indifferently.

PERIWIG, *n.* A small wig; a kind of close cap formed by an intertexture of false hair, worn by men for ornament or to conceal baldness. *Periwigs* were in fashion in the days of Addison.

PERMUTATION, *n.* 3. In *algebra,* change or different combination of any number of quantities.   *Wallis.*

PERORATION, *n.* The concluding part of an oration, in which the speaker recapitulates the principal points of his discourse or argument, and urges them with greater earnestness and force, with a view to make a deep impression on his hearers.   *Encyc.*

Perpetual motion, motion that generates a power of continuing itself forever or indefinitely, by means of mechanism or some application of the force of gravity; not yet discovered, and probably impossible.

PERSECUTION, *n.* The act or practice of persecuting; the infliction of pain, punishment or death upon others unjustly, particularly for adhering to a religious creed or mode of worship, either by way of penalty or for compelling them to renounce their principles. Historians enumerate ten *persecutions* suffered by the Christians, beginning with that of Nero, A. D. 31, and ending with that of Diocletian, A. D. 303 to 313.

PEST, *n.* 2. Any thing very noxious, mischievous or destructive. The tale-bearer, the gambler, the libertine, the drunkard, are *pests* to society.

PETROLEUM, *n.* Rock oil, a liquid inflammable substance or bitumen exsuding from the earth and collected on the surface of the water in wells, in various parts of the world, or oozing from cavities in rocks. This is essentially composed of carbon and hydrogen. *Fourcroy. Kirwan. Cyc.*

PHRENOLOGY. An exact contemporary of Webster, Francis Joseph Gall (1758–1828) had defensible ideas about the localization of brain function which were (temporarily) cast aside by scientists when phrenology was discredited as a method and, as Webster liked to say about earlier pseudoscience, "held in contempt." ☞

PHAETON, *n.* In *mythology,* the son of Phoebus and Clymene, or of Cephalus and Aurora, that is, the son of light or of the sun. This aspiring youth begged of Phoebus that he would permit him to guide the chariot of the sun, in doing which he manifested want of skill, and being struck with a thunderbolt by Jupiter, he was hurled headlong into the river Po. This fable probably originated in the appearance of a comet with a splendid train, which passed from the sight in the northwest of Italy and Greece.

2. An open carriage like a chaise, on four wheels, and drawn by two horses.

PHEASANT, *n.* A fowl of the genus Phasianus, of beautiful plumage, and its flesh delicate food.

PHRENOLOGY, *n.* The science of the human mind and its various properties. *Ch. Obs.*

Phrenology is now applied to the science of the mind as connected with the supposed organs of thought and passion in the brain, broached by Gall.

PHYSICS, *n.* In *its most extensive sense,* the science of nature or of natural objects, comprehending the study or knowledge of whatever exists.

2. In *the usual and more limited sense,* the science of the material system, including natural history and philosophy. This science is of vast extent, comprehending whatever can be discovered of the nature and properties of bodies, their causes, effects, affections, operations, phenomena and laws.

PHYSIOGNOMY. A contemporary of Webster, Johann Kaspar Lavater (1741–1801), was a popular Swiss theologian and mystic. ☞

PHYSIOGNOMY, *n.* 1. The art or science of discerning the character of the mind from the features of the face; or the art of discovering the predominant temper or other characteristic qualities of the mind by the form of the body, but especially by the external signs of the countenance, or the combination of the features. *Bacon. Lavater.*

PHYSIOLOGY, *n.* 1. According to the Greek, this word signifies a discourse or treatise of nature, but the moderns use the word in a more limited sense, for the science of the properties and functions of animals and plants, comprehending what is common to all animals and plants, and what is peculiar to individuals and species.

2. The science of the mind, of its various phenomena, affections and powers.   *Brown.*

PIANO-FORTE, *n.* A keyed musical instrument of German origin and of the harpsichord kind, but smaller; so called from its softer notes or expressions. Its tones are produced by hammers instead of quills, like the virginal and spinet.   *Encyc.   Cyc.*

PICKNICK, *n.* An assembly where each person contributes to the entertainment.   *Todd.*

PICKTOOTH, *n.* An instrument for picking or cleaning the teeth. [But *toothpick* is more generally used.]

PINEAL, *a.* The *pineal* gland is a part of the brain, about the bigness of a pea, situated in the third ventricle; so called from its shape. It was considered by Descartes as the seat of the soul.

PIPPIN, *n.* A kind of apple; a tart apple. This name in America is given to several kinds of apples, as to the Newtown pippin, an excellent winter apple, and the summer pippin, a large apple, but more perishable than the Newtown pippin.

> PIPPIN. The Newtown pippin, grown in Virginia, was Jefferson's favorite apple. Had Webster known this, he might not have bothered to define it.

P

PISS, *v.t.* To discharge the liquor secreted by the kidneys and lodged in the urinary bladder.

PITFALL, *n.* A pit slightly covered for concealment, and intended to catch wild beasts or men.

PLACARD, *n.* Properly, a written or printed paper posted in a public place. It seems to have been formerly the name of an edict, proclamation or manifesto issued by authority, but this sense is, I believe, seldom or never annexed to the word. A *placard* now is an advertisement, or a libel, or a paper intended to censure public or private characters or public measures, posted in a public place. In the case of libels or papers intended to censure public or private characters, or the measures of government, these papers are usually pasted up at night for secrecy.

PLAGIARIST, *n.* One that purloins the writings of another and puts them off as his own.

PLAGUE, *n.* 2. A pestilential disease; an acute, malignant and contagious disease that often prevails in Egypt, Syria and Turkey, and has at times infected the large cities of Europe with frightful mortality.

PLANET, *n.* A celestial body which revolves about the sun or other center, or a body revolving about another planet as its center. The planets which revolve about the sun as their center, are called *primary* planets; those which revolve about other planets as their center, and with them revolve about the sun, are called *secondary* planets, satellites or moons. The primary planets are named Mercury, Venus, Earth, Mars, Jupiter, Saturn and Herschell. Four smaller planets, denominated by some, *asteroids,* namely, Ceres, Pallas, Juno and Vesta, have recently been discovered between the orbits of Mars and Jupiter. Mars, Jupiter, Saturn and Herschell, being without the earth's orbit, are sometimes called the *superior* planets; Venus and Mercury, being within the earth's orbit, are called *inferior* planets. The planets are opake bodies which receive their light from the sun. They are so named from their *motion* or *revolution,* in distinction from the *fixed* stars, and are distinguished from the latter by their not twinkling.

PLANK, *n.* A broad piece of sawed timber, differing from a board only in being thicker. In America, broad pieces of sawed timber which are not more than an inch or an inch and a quarter thick, are called *boards;* like pieces from an inch and a half to three or four inches thick, are called *planks.* Sometimes pieces more than four inches thick are called *planks.*

PLANTATION, *n.* 3. In *the United States* and *the West Indies,* a cultivated estate; a farm. In *the United States,* this word is applied to an estate, a tract of land occupied and cultivated, in those states only where the labor is performed by slaves, and where the land is more or less appropriated to the culture of tobacco, rice, indigo and cotton, that is, from Maryland to Georgia inclusive, on the Atlantic, and in the western states where the land is appropriated to the same articles or to the culture of the sugar cane. From Maryland, northward and eastward, estates in land are called *farms.*

PLATYPUS, *n.* A quadruped of New Holland, whose jaws are elongated into the shape of a duck's bill. The body is covered with thick hair and the feet are webbed.

PLEASURE, *n.* 1. The gratification of the senses or of the mind; agreeable sensations or emotions; the excitement, relish or happiness produced by enjoyment or the expectation of good; opposed to *pain.* We receive *pleasure* from the indulgence of appetite; from the view of a beautiful landscape; from the harmony of sounds; from agreeable society; from the expectation of seeing an absent friend; from the prospect of gain or success of any kind.

Pleasure, bodily and mental, carnal and spiritual, constitutes the whole of positive happiness, as *pain* constitutes the whole of misery.

Pleasure is properly positive excitement of the passions or the mind; but we give the name also to the absence of excitement, when that excitement is painful; as when we cease to labor, or repose after fatigue, or when the mind is tranquilized after anxiety or agitation.

Pleasure is susceptible of increase to any degree; but the word when unqualified, expresses less excitement or happiness than *delight* or *joy*.

PLEDGE, *v.t.* 4. To invite to drink by accepting the cup or health after another.   *Johnson.*

Or to warrant or be surety for a person that he shall receive no harm while drinking, or from the draught; a practice which originated among our ancestors in their rude state, and which was intended to secure the person from being stabbed while drinking, or from being poisoned by the liquor. In the first case, a by-stander *pledges* the person drinking; in the latter, the person drinking *pledges* his guest by drinking first, and then handing the cup to his guest. The latter practice is frequent among the common people in America to this day; the owner of the liquor taking the cup says to his friend, *I pledge you*, and drinks, then hands the cup to his guest; a remarkable instance of the power of habit, as the reason of the custom has long since ceased.

PLOW, *n.* 1. In *agriculture*, an instrument for turning up, breaking and preparing the ground for receiving the seed. It is drawn by oxen or horses and saves the labor of digging; it is therefore the most useful instrument in agriculture.

PLUTONIAN, *n.* One who maintains the origin of mountains, &c. to be from fire.   *Journ. of Science.*

The *Plutonian* theory of the formation of rocks and mountains is opposed to the *Neptunian*.

POET, *n.* 1. The author of a poem; the inventor or maker of a metrical composition.

A *poet* is a maker, as the word signifies; and he who cannot make, that is, invent, hath his name for nothing.   *Dryden.*

2. One skilled in making poetry, or who has a particular genius for metrical composition; one distinguished for poetic talents. Many write verses who cannot be called *poets*.

POISON, *v.t.* 4. To corrupt. Our youth are *poisoned* with false notions of honor, or with pernicious maxims of government.

To suffer the thoughts to be vitiated, is to *poison* the fountains of morality.
                                                                    Rambler.

P

POKER, *n.* Any frightful object, especially in the dark; a bugbear; a word in common popular use in America.

Polarization of light, a change produced upon light by the action of certain media, by which it exhibits the appearance of having *polarity,* or poles possessing different properties. This property of light was first discovered by Huygens in his investigation of the cause of double refraction, as seen in the Iceland crystal. The attention of opticians was more particularly directed towards it by the discoveries of Malus, in 1810. The knowledge of this singular property of light, has afforded an explanation of several very intricate phenomena in optics.

POLEMOSCOPE, *n.* An oblique perspective glass contrived for seeing objects that do not lie directly before the eye. It consists of a concave glass placed near a plane mirror in the end of a short round tube, and a convex glass in a hole in the side of the tube. It is called *opera-glass,* or *diagonal opera-glass.*   *Encyc.*

POLICE, *n.* 1. The government of a city or town; the administration of the laws and regulations of a city or incorporated town or borough; as the *police* of London, of New York or Boston. The word is applied also to the government of all towns in New England which are made corporations by a general statute, for certain purposes.

POLICY, *n.* 2. Art, prudence, wisdom or dexterity in the management of public affairs; *applied to persons governing.* It has been the *policy* of France to preclude females from the throne. It has been the *policy* of Great Britain to encourage her navy, by keeping her carrying trade in her own hands. In this she manifests sound *policy.* Formerly, England permitted wool to be exported and manufactured in the Low Countries, which was very bad *policy.*

POLITICS, *n.* The science of government; that part of ethics which consists in the regulation and government of a nation or state, for the preservation of its safety, peace and prosperity; comprehending the defense of its existence and rights against foreign control or conquest, the augmentation of its strength and resources, and the protection of its citizens in their rights, with the preservation and improvement of their morals. *Politics,* as a science or an art, is a subject of vast extent and importance.

POLYGAMY, *n.* A plurality of wives or husbands at the same time; or the having of such plurality. When a man has more wives than one, or a woman more husbands than one, at the same time, the offender is punishable for *polygamy.* Such is the fact in christian countries. But *polygamy* is allowed in some countries, as in Turkey.

POLYNESIA, *n.* A new term in geography, used to designate a great number of isles in the Pacific ocean, as the Pelew isles, the Ladrones, the Carolines, the Sandwich isles, the Marquesas, the Society isles and the Friendly isles.
De Brosses.   Pinkerton.

POLYPHONY, *n.* Multiplicity of sounds, as in the reverberations of an echo.
Derham.

POND, *n.* 1. A body of stagnant water without an outlet, larger than a puddle, and smaller than a lake; or a like body of water with a small outlet. In the United States, we give this name to collections of water in the interior country, which are fed by springs, and from which issues a small stream. These ponds are often a mile or two or even more in length, and the current issuing from them is used to drive the wheels of mills and furnaces.

PONGO, *n.* A name of the orang outang.   *Dict. Nat. Hist.*
The name *pongo* was applied by Buffon to a large species of orang outang, which is now ascertained to have been an imaginary animal. It is applied by Cuvier to the largest species of ape known, which inhabits Borneo, and resembles the true orang outang in its general form and erect position, but has the cheek pouches and lengthened muzzle of the baboon. It has also been applied (*Ed. Encyc.*) to the *Simia troglodytes* or chimpanzee of Cuvier, a native of W. Africa.   *Cuvier.   Ed. Encyc.*

POOL, *n.* A small collection of water in a hollow place, supplied by a spring, and discharging its surplus water by an outlet. It is smaller than a lake, and in New England is never confounded with *pond* or *lake*. It signifies with us, a spring with a small bason or reservoir on the surface of the earth. It is used by writers with more latitude, and sometimes signifies a body of stagnant water.   *Milton.   Encyc.   Bacon.*

POPULAR, *a.* [Note. *Popular*, at least in the United States, is not synonymous with *vulgar*; the latter being applied to the lower classes of people, the illiterate and low bred; the former is applied to all classes, or to the body of the people, including a great portion at least of well educated citizens.]

POPULARITY, *n.* Favor of the people; the state of possessing the affections and confidence of the people in general; as the *popularity* of the ministry; the *popularity* of a public officer or of a preacher. It is applied also to things; as the *popularity* of a law or public measure; the *popularity* of a book or poem. The most valuable trait in a patriot's character is to forbear all improper compliances for gaining *popularity*.
I have long since learned the little value which is to be placed in *popularity*, acquired by any other way than virtue; I have also learned that it is often obtained by other means.   *P. Henry, Wirt's Sketches.*

The man whose ruling principle is duty—is never perplexed with anxious corroding calculations of interest and *popularity*.   *J. Howes.*

PORTAGE, *n.* 4. A carrying place over land between navigable waters.
Jefferson.   Gallatin.

Posse comitatus, in law, the power of the country, or the citizens, who are summoned to assist an officer in suppressing a riot, or executing any legal precept which is forcibly opposed. The word *comitatus* is often omitted, and *posse* alone is used in the same sense.   *Blackstone.*

POSSIBILITY, *n.* The power of being or existing; the power of happening; the state of being possible. It often implies improbability or great uncertainty. There is a *possibility* that a new star may appear this night. There is a *possibility* of a hard frost in July in our latitude. It is not expedient to hazard much on the bare *possibility* of success. It is prudent to reduce contracts to writing, and to render them so explicit as to preclude the *possibility* of mistake or controversy.

POSSIBLE, *a.* That may be or exist; that may be now, or may happen or come to pass; that may be done; not contrary to the nature of things. It is *possible* that the Greeks and Turks may now be engaged in battle. It is *possible* the peace of Europe may continue a century. It is not physically *possible* that a stream should ascend a mountain, but it is *possible* that the Supreme Being may suspend a law of nature, that is, his usual course of proceeding. It is not *possible* that 2 and 3 should be 7, or that the same action should be morally right and morally wrong.

This word when pronounced with a certain emphasis, implies improbability. A thing is *possible,* but very improbable.

POTASSIUM, *n.* A name given to the metallic basis of vegetable alkali. According to Dr. Davy, 100 parts of potash consist of 86.1 parts of the basis, and 13.9 of oxygen.   *Med. Repos.*

Potassium has the most powerful affinity for oxygen of all substances known; it takes it from every other compound, and hence is a most important agent in chimical analysis.

POTATO, *n.* A plant and esculent root of the genus Solanum, a native of America. The root of this plant, which is usually called *potatoe*, constitutes one of the cheapest and most nourishing species of vegetable food; it is the principal food of the poor in some countries, and has often contributed to prevent famine. It was introduced into the British dominions by Sir Walter Raleigh or other adventurers in the 16th century; but it came slowly into use, and at this day is not much cultivated and used in some countries of Europe. In the British dominions and in the United

States, it has proved one of the greatest blessings bestowed on man by the Creator.

PRAGMATIST, *n.* One who is impertinently busy or meddling.   *Reynolds.*

PRAIRY, *n.* An extensive tract of land, mostly level, destitute of trees, and covered with tall coarse grass. These *prairies* are numerous in the United States, west of the Alleghany mountains, especially between the Ohio, Mississippi and the great lakes.

PRECLUDE, *v.t.* 1. To prevent from entering by previously shutting the passage, or by any previous measures; hence, to hinder from access, possession or enjoyment. Sin, by its very nature, *precludes* the sinner from heaven; it *precludes* the enjoyment of God's favor; or it *precludes* the favor of God.

The valves *preclude* the blood from entering the veins.   *Darwin.*

PRE-EMPTION, *n.* 2. The right of purchasing before others. Prior discovery of unoccupied land gives the discoverer the prior right of occupancy. Prior discovery of land inhabited by savages is held to give the discoverer the *pre-emption,* or right of purchase before others.

PREJUDICE, *n.* 1. Prejudgment; an opinion or decision of mind, formed without due examination of the facts or arguments which are necessary to a just and impartial determination. It is used in a good or bad sense. Innumerable are the *prejudices* of education; we are accustomed to believe what we are taught, and to receive opinions from others without examining the grounds by which they can be supported. A man has strong *prejudices* in favor of his country or his party, or the church in which he has been educated; and often our *prejudices* are unreasonable. A judge should disabuse himself of *prejudice* in favor of either party in a suit.

PREPOSTEROUS, *a.* 2. Perverted; wrong; absurd; contrary to nature or reason; not adapted to the end; as, a republican government in the hands of females, is *preposterous.*

PRESAGE, *v.t.* To forebode; to foreshow; to indicate by some present fact what is to follow or come to pass. A fog rising from a river in an autumnal morning *presages* a pleasant day. A physical phenomenon cannot be considered as *presaging* an event, unless it has some connection with it in cause. Hence the error of vulgar superstition, which *presages* good or evil from facts which can have no relation to the future event.

PRESERVATIVE, *n.* . . . . Persons formerly wore tablets of arsenic, as *preservatives* against the plague. . . . Temperance and exercise are the best *preservatives* of health.

PREPOSTEROUS. Webster comes from a long line of misogynists. Johnson quotes from Bacon, probably approvingly: "Put a case of a land of Amazons, where the whole government, publick and private, is in the hands of women: is not such a preposterous government against the first order of nature, for women to rule over men, and in itself void?" (To "put the case" is, as Webster defines it, to suppose an event to be real true.)

P

PRESTIGIOUS, *a.* Practicing tricks; juggling.   *Bale.*

PRETENSE, *n.* 1. A holding out or offering to others something false or feigned. . . . Under *pretense* of giving liberty to nations, the prince conquered and enslaved them. Under *pretense* of patriotism, ambitious men serve their own selfish purposes.

PRETTY, *adv.* In some degree; tolerably; moderately; as a farm *pretty* well stocked; the colors became *pretty* vivid; I am *pretty* sure of the fact; the wind is *pretty* fair. The English farthing is *pretty* near the value of the American cent. In these and similar phrases, *pretty* expresses less than *very.*

PRIDE, *n.* 1. Inordinate self-esteem; an unreasonable conceit of one's own superiority in talents, beauty, wealth, accomplishments, rank or elevation in office, which manifests itself in lofty airs, distance, reserve, and often in contempt of others.
　　　Pride that dines on vanity, sups on contempt.   *Franklin.*

PRIMOGENITURE, *n.* . . . Before the revolution, *primogeniture,* in some of the American colonies, entitled the eldest son to a double portion of his father's estate, but this right has been abolished.

PRINCIPLE, *n.* 8. A *principle of human nature,* is a law of action in human beings; a constitutional propensity common to the human species. Thus it is a *principle of human nature* to resent injuries and repel insults.

PRIVATEER, *n.* A ship or vessel of war owned and equipped by a private man or by individuals, at their own expense, to seize or plunder the ships of an enemy in war. Such a ship must be licensed or commissioned by government, or it is a pirate.

PROFANE, *v.t.* To violate any thing sacred, or treat it with abuse, irreverence, obloquy or contempt; as, to *profane* the name of God; to *profane* the sabbath; to *profane* the Scriptures or the ordinances of God.   *Dwight.*

PROFUSE, *a.* Lavish; liberal to excess; prodigal; as a *profuse* government; a *profuse* administration. Henry the eighth, a *profuse* king, dissipated the treasures which the parsimony of his father had amassed. A man's friends are generally too *profuse* of praise, and his enemies too sparing.

PROMISE, *n.* 1. In *a general sense,* a declaration, written or verbal, made by one person to another, which binds the person who makes it, either in honor, conscience or law, to do or forbear a certain act specified; a declaration which gives to the person to whom it is made, a right to expect or to claim the performance or forbearance of the act. The promise of a visit to my neighbor, gives him a right to expect it, and I am bound in honor and civility to perform the *promise*. Of such a *promise* human laws have no cognizance; but the fulfillment of it is one of the minor moralities, which civility, kindness and strict integrity require to be observed.

4. Hopes; expectation, or that which affords expectation of future distinction; as a youth of great *promise*.

My native country was full of youthful *promise*.   *Irving.*

PROPER, *a.* Peculiar; naturally or essentially belonging to a person or thing; not common. That is not *proper*, which is common to many. Every animal has his *proper* instincts and inclinations, appetites and habits. Every muscle and vessel of the body has its *proper* office. Every art has its *proper* rules. Creation is the *proper* work of an Almighty Being.

PROPERTY, *n.* 4. The exclusive right of possessing, enjoying and disposing of a thing; ownership. In the beginning of the world, the Creator gave to man dominion over the earth, over the fish of the sea and the fowls of the air, and over every living thing. This is the foundation of man's *property* in earth and in all its productions. Prior occupancy of land and of wild animals gives to the possessor the *property* of them. The labor of inventing, making or producing any thing constitutes one of the highest and most indefeasible titles to *property*. *Property* is also acquired by inheritance, by gift or by purchase. *Property* is sometimes held in common, yet each man's right to his share in common land or stock is exclusively his own. One man may have the *property* of the soil, and another the right or use, by prescription or by purchase.

Literary property, the exclusive right of printing, publishing and making profit by one's own writings. No right or title to a thing can be so perfect as that which is created by a man's own labor and invention. The exclusive right of a man to his literary productions, and to the use of them for his own profit, is entire and perfect, as the faculties employed and labor bestowed are entirely and perfectly his own. On what principle then can a legislature or a court determine that an author can enjoy only a *temporary property* in his own productions? If a man's right to his own *productions in writing* is as perfect as to the *productions* of his farm or his shop, how can the former be abridged or limited, while the latter is held without limitation? Why do the *productions* of *manual labor* rank higher in the scale of rights or *property*, than the *productions* of the *intellect?*

PROPHECY, *n.* 1. A foretelling; prediction; a declaration of something to come. As God only knows future events with certainty, no being but God or some person informed by him, can utter a real *prophecy*. The *prophecies* recorded in Scripture, when fulfilled, afford most convincing evidence of the divine original of the Scriptures, as those who uttered the *prophecies* could not have foreknown the events predicted without supernatural instruction.

PROPRIETOR, *n.* An owner; the person who has the legal right or exclusive title to any thing whether in possession or not; as the *proprietor* of a farm or of a mill. By the gift of God, man is constituted the *proprietor* of the earth.

PROSPECT, *n.* 3. That which is presented to the eye; the place and the objects seen. There is a noble *prospect* from the dome of the state house in Boston, a *prospect* diversified with land and water, and every thing that can please the eye.

PROVE, *v.t.* 3. To evince truth by argument, induction or reasoning; to deduce certain conclusions from propositions that are true or admitted. If it is admitted that every immoral act is dishonorable to a rational being, and that dueling is an immoral act; then it is *proved* by necessary inference, that dueling is dishonorable to a rational being.

PROVINCE, *n.* [Fr. from L. *provincia;* usually supposed to be formed from *pro* and *vinco,* to conquer. This is very doubtful, as *provinco* was not used by the Romans.]
2. Among *the moderns,* a country belonging to a kingdom or state, either by conquest or colonization, usually situated at a distance from the kingdom or state, but more or less dependent on it or subject to it. Thus formerly, the English colonies in North America were *provinces* of Great Britain, as Nova Scotia and Canada still are. The *provinces* of the Netherlands formerly belonged to the house of Austria and to Spain.

PSYCHOLOGY, *n.* A discourse or treatise on the human soul; or the doctrine of the nature and properties of the soul.   *Campbell.*

PUBERTY. John- ☞
son's definition is per-
haps more to the point:
"the time of life in
which the two sexes
begin first to be
acquainted."

PUBERTY, *n.* The age at which persons are capable of procreating and bearing children. This age is different in different climates, but is with us considered to be at fourteen years in males, and twelve in females.

PUDDING-TIME, *n.* The time of dinner, pudding being formerly the first dish set on the table, or rather first eaten; a practice not yet obsolete among the common people of New England.

PUDENDA, *n. plu.* The parts of generation.

PUN, *n.* An expression in which a word has at once different meanings; an expression in which two different applications of a word present an odd or ludicrous idea; a kind of quibble or equivocation; *a low species of wit.* Thus a man who had a tall wife named *Experience,* observed that he had, by *long experience,* proved the blessings of a married life.

> A *pun* can be no more engraven, than it can be translated.   *Addison.*

PUNISHMENT, *n.* Any pain or suffering inflicted on a person for a crime or offense, by the authority to which the offender is subject, either by the constitution of God or of civil society. The *punishment* of the faults and offenses of children by the parent, is by virtue of the right of government with which the parent is invested by God himself. This species of punishment is *chastisement* or *correction.* The *punishment* of crimes against the laws is inflicted by the supreme power of the state in virtue of the right of government, vested in the prince or legislature. The right of *punishment* belongs only to persons clothed with authority. Pain, loss or evil willfully inflicted on another for his crimes or offenses by a private unauthorized person, is *revenge* rather than *punishment.*

Some *punishments* consist in exile or transportation, others in loss of liberty by imprisonment; some extend to confiscation by forfeiture of lands and goods, others induce a disability of holding offices, of being heirs and the like.   *Blackstone*

Divine *punishments* are doubtless designed to secure obedience to divine laws, and uphold the moral order of created intelligent beings.

> The rewards and *punishments* of another life, which the Almighty has established as the enforcements of his law, are of weight enough to determine the choice against whatever pleasure or pain this life can show.   *Locke.*

PURCHASE, *n.* 3. In *common usage,* the acquisition of the title or property of any thing by rendering an equivalent of money.

> It is foolish to lay out money in the *purchase* of repentance.   *Franklin.*

PURITAN, *n.* A dissenter from the church of England. The *puritans* were so called in derision, on account of their professing to follow the *pure* word of God, in opposition to all traditions and human constitutions.   *Encyc.*

Hume gives this name to three parties; the *political puritans,* who maintained the highest principles of civil liberty; the *puritans in discipline,* who were averse to the ceremonies and government of the episcopal church; and the *doctrinal puritans,* who rigidly defended the speculative system of the first reformers.

PURPOSE, *n.* That which a person sets before himself as an object to be reached or accomplished ; the end or aim to which the view is directed in any plan, measure or exertion. We believe the Supreme Being created intelligent beings for some benevolent and glorious *purpose,* and if so, how glorious and benevolent must be his *purpose* in the plan of redemption! The ambition of men is generally directed to one of two *purposes,* or to both; the acquisition of wealth or of power. We build houses for the *purpose* of shelter; we labor for the *purpose* of subsistence.

Of purpose, on purpose, with previous design; with the mind directed to that object. *On purpose* is more generally used, but the true phrase is *of purpose.*

PURVIEW, *n.* 3. In *modern usage,* the limit or scope of a statute; the whole extent of its intention or provisions.   *Marshall.*
  5. Limit or sphere intended; scope; extent.
    In determining the extent of information required in the exercise of a particular authority, recourse must be had to the objects within the *purview* of that authority.   *Federalist, Madison.*

PYROMETER, *n.* 1. An instrument for measuring the expansion of bodies by heat.
  2. An instrument for measuring degrees of heat above those indicated by the mercurial thermometer; as the *pyrometer* of Wedgewood.

Q

QUAHAUG, *n.* In New England, the popular name of a large species of clams or bivalvular shells. [*This name is probably derived from the natives.*]

QUAIL-PIPE, *n.* A pipe or call for alluring quails into a net; a kind of lethern purse in the shape of a pear, partly filled with horse hair, with a whistle at the end.   *Encyc.*

QUAKER, *n.* One that quakes; but usually, one of the religious sect called *friends.* This name, *quakers,* is said to have been given to the sect in reproach, on account of some agitations which distinguished them; but it is no longer appropriated to them by way of reproach.

QUALIFY, *v.t.* To fit for any place, office, occupation or character; to furnish with the knowledge, skill or other accomplishment necessary for a purpose; as, to *qualify* a man for a judge, for a minister of state or of the gospel, for a general or admiral. Holiness alone can *qualify* men for the society of holy beings.

QUARREL, *v.i.* 1. To dispute violently or with loud and angry words; to wrangle; to scold. How odious to see husband and wife *quarrel!*

2. To fight; to scuffle; to contend; to squabble; used of two persons or of a small number. It is never used of armies and navies in combat. Children and servants often *quarrel* about trifles. Tavern-haunters sometimes *quarrel* over their cups.

QUARTER, *n.* 10. In *military affairs,* the remission or sparing of the life of a captive or an enemy when in one's power; mercy granted by a conqueror to

---

Q. This letter is superfluous; for *ku* or *koo,* in English, has precisely the same pronunciation as *qu.*

---

his enemy, when no longer able to defend himself. In desperate encounters, men will sometimes neither ask nor give *quarter*. The barbarous practice of giving no *quarter* to soldiers in a fortress taken by assault, is nearly obsolete. 16. In *seminaries of learning*, a fourth part of the year, or three months. Tuition and board at twenty five dollars the *quarter*. This is a moderate *quarter* bill.

QUEACHY, *a.* Shaking; moving, yielding or trembling under the feet, as moist or boggy ground. [This word is still in use in New England, and if the word is from the root of *quick*, we recognize the application of it in *quicksand.*]

QUIDDITY, *n.* A barbarous term used in school philosophy for *essence*, that unknown and undefinable something which constitutes its peculiar nature, or answers the question, *quid est?* The essence of a thing constitutes it *tale quid*, such a thing as it is, and not another.   *Encyc.*

QUILTING, *n.* 2. In *New England*, the act of quilting by a collection of females who bestow their labor gratuitously to aid a female friend, and conclude with an entertainment.

QUINTESSENCE, *n.* 1. In alchimy, the fifth or last and highest essence of power in a natural body. Hence,
2. An extract from any thing, containing its virtues or most essential part in a small quantity. [I have followed Bailey and Ash and our general usage in the accentuation of this word. Jameson has done the same. The accent on the first syllable is very unnatural.]

R

RABBIT, *n.* A small quadruped of the genus Lepus, which feeds on grass or other herbage, and burrows in the earth. The rabbit is said to be less sagacious than the hare. It is a very prolific animal, and is kept in warrens for the sake of its flesh.

RABDOLOGY, *n.* A method of performing mathematical operations by little square rods.   *Ash.*

RACE, *n.* 1. The lineage of a family, or continued series of descendants from a parent who is called the stock. A race is the series of descendants indefinitely. Thus all mankind are called the *race* of Adam; the Israelites are of the *race* of Abraham and Jacob. Thus we speak of a *race* of kings, the *race* of Clovis or Charlemagne; a *race* of nobles, &c.

RACK, *n.* 1. An engine of torture, used for extorting confessions from criminals or suspected persons. The *rack* is entirely unknown in free countries.

RACKET, *n.* A confused, clattering noise, less loud than *uproar;* applied to the confused sounds of animal voices, or such voices mixed with other sound. We say, the children make a *racket*; the *racket* of a flock of fowls.

RACOON, *n.* An American quadruped of the genus Ursus. It is somewhat larger than a fox, and its fur is deemed valuable, next to that of the beaver. This animal lodges in a hollow tree, feeds on vegetables, and its flesh is palatable food. It inhabits North America from Canada to the tropics.
                                                        Belknap.   Dict. Nat. Hist.

RAFFLE, *v.i.* To cast dice for a prize, for which each person concerned in the game lays down a stake, or hazards a part of the value; as, to *raffle* for a watch.

RAIN, *n.* The descent of water in drops from the clouds; or the water thus falling. *Rain* is distinguished from *mist*, by the size of the drops, which are distinctly visible. When water falls in very small drops or particles, we call it

RABDOLOGY. The use of John Napier's ingenious rods, often made of bone, allowed seventeenth-century folks with the meagerest of arithmetical skills to determine products and quotients while remaining ignorant of how Napier's methods worked. Napier's rods were used in British primary schools at least into the 1960s.

RACOON. Linnaeus classified the raccoon in the *Ursus* genus (as he did for BADGER, now classified as *Taxidea taxus*). Not very bearlike, the raccoon now belongs to *Procyon*, Greek for "pre-dog." Raccoon derives from an Algonquian word meaning "he who scratches with his hands," but Webster seems unaware of this.

mist, and *fog* is composed of particles so fine as to be not only indistinguishable, but to float or be suspended in the air.

RAMAGE, *n.* The warbling of birds sitting on boughs.

RANCOR, *n.* The deepest malignity or spite; deep seated and implacable malice; inveterate enmity. [*This is the strongest term for enmity which the English language supplies.*]

RANEDEER, *n.* A species of deer found in the northern parts of Europe and Asia. He has large branched palmated horns, and travels with great speed. Among the Laplanders, he is a substitute for the horse, the cow, the goat and the sheep, as he furnishes food, clothing and the means of conveyance. This animal will draw a sled on the snow more than a hundred miles in a day.
Encyc.

RANK, *n.* 5. Degree of elevation in civil life or station; the order of elevation or of subordination. We say, all *ranks* and orders of men; every man's dress and behavior should correspond with his *rank;* the highest and the lowest *ranks* of men or of other intelligent beings.

6. Class; order; division; any portion or number of things to which place, degree or order is assigned. Profligate men, by their vices, sometimes degrade themselves to the *rank* of brutes.

RANT, *v.i.* To rave in violent, high sounding or extravagant language, without correspondent dignity of thought; to be noisy and boisterous in words or declamation; as a *ranting* preacher.

RAPACITY. One of ☞ several excuses for Webster to show his antipathy toward the Turks.

RAPACITY, *n.* Addictedness to plunder; the exercise of plunder; the act or practice of seizing by force; as the *rapacity* of a conquering army; the *rapacity* of pirates; the *rapacity* of a Turkish pashaw; the *rapacity* of extortioners.

RASCAL, *n.* A mean fellow; a scoundrel; in *modern usage,* a trickish dishonest fellow; a rogue; particularly applied to men and boys guilty of the lesser crimes, and indicating less enormity or guilt than *villain.*

REASON, *n.* 5. A faculty of the mind by which it distinguishes truth from falsehood, and good from evil, and which enables the possessor to deduce inferences from facts or from propositions.
Encyc.

REBUS, *n.* 1. An enigmatical representation of some name, &c. by using figures or pictures instead of words. A gallant in love with a woman named *Rose Hill,* painted on the border of his gown, a rose, a hill, an eye, a loaf and a well, which reads, *Rose Hill I love well.*
Encyc.

RECKON, *v.i.* *To reckon with*, to state an account with another, compare it with his account, ascertaining the amount of each and the balance which one owes the other. In this manner the countrymen of New England who have mutual dealings, *reckon with* each other at the end of the year, or as often as they think fit.

RECOGNIZE, *v.t.* [. . . The *g* in these words has properly no sound in English. It is not a part of the root of the word, being written merely to give to *con* the French sound of *gn*, or that of the Spanish *ñ*, and this sound does not properly belong to our language.]

RECOLLECTION, *n.* The act of recalling to the memory, as ideas that have escaped; or the operation by which ideas are recalled to the memory or revived in the mind. *Recollection* differs from *remembrance*, as it is the consequence of volition, or an effort of the mind to revive ideas; whereas *remembrance* implies no such volition. We often *remember* things without any voluntary effort. *Recollection* is called also *reminiscence*.

RED-BIRD, *n.* The popular name of several birds in the U. States, as the *Tanagra æstiva* or summer red-bird, the *Tanagra rubra*, and the Baltimore oriole or hang-nest.

REDEEMABLE, *a.* 2. That may be purchased or paid for in gold or silver, and brought into the possession of government or the original promiser.

> The capital of the debt of the United States may be considered in the light of an annuity *redeemable* at the pleasure of the government.   *Hamilton.*

REFEREE, *n.* One to whom a thing is referred; particularly, a person appointed by a court to hear, examine and decide a cause between parties, pending before the court, and make report to the court. In New England, a *referee* differs from an *arbitrator*, in being appointed by the court to decide in a cause which is depending before that court. An *arbitrator* is chosen by parties to decide a cause between them.

REFINEMENT, *n.* 4. Polish of manners; elegance; nice observance of the civilities of social intercourse and of graceful decorum. *Refinement* of manners is often found in persons of corrupt morals.

REFORM, *v.i.* To abandon that which is evil or corrupt, and return to a good state; to be amended or corrected. A man of settled habits of vice will seldom *reform*.

REFORMER, *n.* 2. One of those who commenced the reformation of religion from popish corruption; as Luther, Melancthon, Zuinglius and Calvin.

REFRACTORY, *a.* 1. Sullen or perverse in opposition or disobedience; obstinate in non-compliance; as a *refractory* child; a *refractory* servant.

2. Unmanageable; obstinately unyielding, as a *refractory* beast.

REFUGEE, *n.* 2. One who, in times of persecution or political commotion, flees to a foreign country for safety; as the French *refugees*, who left France after the revocation of the edict of Nantz, and settled in Flanders and America; the *refugees* from Hispaniola, in 1792; and the American *refugees*, who left their country at the revolution.

REGENT, *n.* 5. In *the state of New York*, the member of a corporate body which is invested with the superintendence of all the colleges, academies and schools in the state. This board consists of twenty one members, who are called "the regents of the university of the state of New York." They are appointed and removable by the legislature. They have power to grant acts of incorporation for colleges, to visit and inspect all colleges, academies and schools, and to make regulations for governing the same.   *Stat. N. York.*

RELIEF, *n.* The removal, in whole or in part, of any evil that afflicts the body or mind; the removal or alleviation of pain, grief, want, care, anxiety, toil or distress, or of any thing oppressive or burdensome, by which some ease is obtained. Rest gives *relief* to the body when weary; an anodyne gives *relief* from pain; the sympathy of friends affords some *relief* to the distressed; a loan of money to a man embarrassed may afford him a temporary *relief;* medicines which will not cure a disease, sometimes give a partial *relief.* A complete *relief* from the troubles of life is never to be expected.

RELIGION, *n.* 3. *Religion*, as distinct from *virtue*, or *morality*, consists in the performance of the duties we owe directly to God, from a principle of obedience to his will. Hence we often speak of *religion* and *virtue*, as different branches of one system, or the duties of the first and second tables of the law.

    Let us with caution indulge the supposition, that morality can be maintained without *religion.*   *Washington.*

RELY, *v.i.* To rest on something, as the mind when satisfied of the veracity, integrity or ability of persons, or of the certainty of facts or of evidence; to have confidence in; to trust in; to depend; with *on.* We *rely on* the promise of a man who is known to be upright; we *rely on* the veracity or fidelity of a tried friend; a prince *relies on* the affections of his subjects for support, and *on* the strength of his army for success in war; above all things, we *rely on* the mercy and promises of God. That which is the ground of confidence, is a certainty or full conviction that satisfies the mind and leaves it at rest, or undisturbed by doubt.

REMARKABLE, *a.* 2. Extraordinary; unusual; that deserves particular notice, or that may excite admiration or wonder; as the *remarkable* preservation of live in shipwreck. The dark day in May, 1790, was a *remarkable* phenomenon.

REMARKABLY, *adv.* In a manner or degree worthy of notice; as, the winters of 1825, 1826 and 1828 were *remarkably* free from snow. The winter of 1827 was *remarkable* for a great quantity of snow.

REMEDY, *n.* 1. That which cures a disease; any medicine or application which puts an end to disease and restores health; with *for;* as a *remedy for* the gout.
2. That which counteracts an evil of any kind; with *for, to* or *against;* usually with *for.* Civil government is the *remedy for* the evils of natural liberty. What *remedy* can be provided *for* extravagance in dress? The man who shall invent an effectual *remedy for* intemperance, will deserve every thing from his fellow men. 3. That which cures uneasiness.

RENDEZVOUS, *n.* [Fr. *rendez vous,* render yourselves, repair to a place. This word is anglicized, and may well be pronounced as an English word.] 1. A place appointed for the assembling of troops, or the place where they assemble; or the port or place where ships are ordered to join company.

REPERCUSSION, *n.* 1. The act of driving back; reverberation; as the *repercussion* of sound.
2. In *music,* frequent repetition of the same sound.   *Encyc.*

REPERTORY, *n.* 1. A place in which things are disposed in an orderly manner, so that they can be easily found, as the index of a book, a commonplace book, &c.
2. A treasury; a magazine.

REPINE, *v.i.* To fret one's self; to be discontented; to feel inward discontent which preys on the spirits; with *at* or *against.* It is our duty never to *repine at* the allotments of Providence.

REPRODUCTION, *n.* The act or process of reproducing that which has been destroyed; as the *reproduction* of plants or animals from cuttings or slips. The *reproduction* of several parts of lobsters and crabs is one of the greatest curiosities in natural history.   *Encyc.*

REPUBLIC, *n.* 1. A commonwealth; a state in which the exercise of the sovereign power is lodged in representatives elected by the people. In modern usage, it differs from a democracy or democratic state, in which the people exercise the powers of sovereignty in person. Yet the democracies of Greece are often called *republics*.

REPUTATION, *n.* 1. Good name; the credit, honor or character which is derived from a favorable public opinion or esteem. *Reputation* is a valuable species of property or right, which should never be violated. With the loss of *reputation*, a man and especially a woman, loses most of the enjoyments of life.

REQUISITION, *n.* Demand; application made as of right. Under the old confederation of the American states, congress often made *requisitions* on the states for money to supply the treasury; but they had no power to enforce their *requisitions*, and the states neglected or partially complied with them.

Hamilton.

RESIDE, *v.i.* 1. To dwell permanently or for a length of time; to have a settled abode for a time. The peculiar uses of this word are to be noticed. When the word is applied to the natives of a state, or others who dwell in it as permanent citizens, we use it only with reference to the *part* of a city or country in which a man dwells. We do not say generally, that Englishmen *reside* in England, but a particular citizen *resides* in London or York, or at such a house in such a street, in the Strand, &c.

When the word is applied to strangers or travelers, we do not say, a man *resides* in an inn for a night, but he *resided* in London or Oxford a month or a year; or he may *reside* in a foreign country a great part of his life. A man lodges, stays, remains, abides, for a day or very short time, but *reside* implies a longer time, though not definite.

RESPIRATION, *n.* The act of breathing; the act of inhaling air into the lungs and again exhaling or expelling it, by which animal life is supported. The *respiration* of fishes, [for these cannot live long without air,] appears to be performed by the air contained in the water acting on the gills.

RESTRAIN, *v.t.* To hold back; to check; to hold from action, proceeding or advancing, either by physical or moral force, or by any interposing obstacle. Thus we *restrain* a horse by a bridle; we *restrain* cattle from wandering by fences; we *restrain* water by dams and dikes; we *restrain* men from crimes and trespasses by laws; we *restrain* young people, when we can, by arguments or counsel; we *restrain* men and their passions; we *restrain* the elements; we attempt to *restrain* vice, but not always with success.

RETIRE, *v.i.* 5. To depart or withdraw for safety or for pleasure. Men *retire* from the town in summer for health and pleasure. But in South Carolina, the planters *retire* from their estates to Charleston, or to an isle near the town.

REVOLUTION, *n.* 1. In *physics,* rotation; the circular motion of a body on its axis; a course or motion which brings every point of the surface or periphery of a body back to the place at which it began to move; as the *revolution* of a wheel; the diurnal *revolution* of the earth.

6. In *politics,* a material or entire change in the constitution of government. Thus the *revolution* in England, in 1688, was produced by the abdication of king James II., the establishment of the house of Orange upon the throne, and the restoration of the constitution to its primitive state. So the *revolutions* in Poland, in the United States of America, and in France, consisted in a change of constitution. We shall rejoice to hear that the Greeks have effected a *revolution.*

RHENISH, *a.* Pertaining to the river Rhine, or to Rheims in France; as *Rhenish* wine; as a noun, the wine produced on the hills about Rheims, which is remarkable as a solvent of iron. *Encyc.*

RHINOCEROS, *n.* A genus of quadrupeds of two species, one of which, the *unicorn,* has a single horn growing almost erect from the nose. This animal when full grown, is said to be 12 feet in length. There is another species with two horns, the *bicornis.* They are natives of Asia and Africa. *Encyc.*

RICE, *n.* A plant of the genus Oryza, and its seed. The calyx is a bivalvular uniflorous glume; the corol bivalvular, nearly equal, and adhering to the seed. There is only one species. This plant is cultivated in all warm climates,

---

WEBSTER AND WINE

☞ Webster knew little about wine and cared less. (Johnson, in contrast, had an encyclopedic entry on many different kinds of vine.) The odd fact that RHENISH wine could dissolve iron was probably the only reason Webster decided to define it. He thinks that TOKAY improves "as long as it is kept," gives only perfunctory definitions (which we do not include here) of such familiar wines as sherry, port, Madeira, burgundy, and champagne, and tells us—only for etymological reasons, surely—that claret is "a species of French wine, of a clear pale red color." Wine might indeed TICKLE one's palate, but Webster plucked this phrase from Johnson, where it appeared in a quote from Locke. Webster's experience as a wine-bibber was limited, and his own palate seldom was tickled. ▨

R

and the grain forms a large portion of the food of the inhabitants. In America, it grows chiefly on low moist lands which can be overflowed. It is a light food, and said to be little apt to produce acidity in the stomach. Indeed it seems intended by the wise and benevolent Creator to be the proper food of men in warm climates.

RICH, *a.* 1. Wealthy; opulent; possessing a large portion of land, goods or money, or a larger portion than is common to other men or to men of like rank. A farmer may be *rich* with property which would not make a nobleman *rich.* An annual income of £500 sterling would make a *rich* vicar, but not a *rich* bishop. Men more willingly acknowledge others to be *richer,* than to be wiser than themselves.

RIDICULE, *n.* 1. Contemptuous laughter; laughter with some degree of contempt; derision. It expresses less than *scorn.* Ridicule is aimed at what is not only laughable, but improper, absurd or despicable. Sacred subjects should never be treated with *ridicule.*

    Ridicule is too rough an entertainment for the polished and refined. It is banished from France, and is losing ground in England.   *Kames.*

    2. That species of writing which excites contempt with laughter. It differs from *burlesque,* which may excite laughter without contempt, or it may provoke derision.   *Ibid.*

    Ridicule and *derision* are not exactly the same, as *derision* is applied to persons only, and *ridicule* to persons or things. We *deride* the man, but *ridicule* the man or his performances.

RIDICULOUS, *a.* That may justly excite laughter with contempt; as a *ridiculous* dress; *ridiculous* behavior. A fop and a dandy are *ridiculous* in their dress.

RIFLE, *n.* A gun about the usual length and size of a musket, the inside of whose barrel is *rifled,* that is, grooved, or formed with spiral channels.

RIGHT, *a.* 2. In *morals* and *religion,* just; equitable; accordant to the standard of truth and justice or the will of God. That alone is *right* in the sight of God, which is consonant to his will or law; this being the only perfect standard of truth and justice. In social and political affairs, that is *right* which is consonant to the laws and customs of a country, provided these laws and customs are not repugnant to the laws of God. A man's intentions may be *right,* though his actions may be wrong in consequence of a defect in judgment.

    3. Fit; suitable; proper; becoming. In things indifferent, or which are regulated by no positive law, that is *right* which is best suited to the character, occasion or purpose, or which is fitted to produce some good effect. It is *right* for a rich man to dress himself and his family in expensive clothing, which it would not be *right* for a poor man to purchase. It is *right* for every man to choose his own time for eating or exercise.

Right is a relative term; what may be *right* for one end, may be *wrong* for another.

RINGLEADER, *n.* The leader of any association of men engaged in violation of law or an illegal enterprise, as rioters, mutineers and the like. This name is derived from the practice which men associating to oppose law have sometimes adopted, of signing their names to articles of agreement in a *ring*, that no one of their number might be distinguished as the leader.

RIOT, *n.* 1. In *a general sense*, tumult; uproar; hence technically, in *law*, a riotous assembling of twelve persons or more, and not dispersing upon proclamation.   *Blackstone.*
    The definition of *riot* must depend on the laws. In Connecticut, the assembling of *three* persons or more, to do an unlawful act by violence against the person or property of another, and not dispersing upon proclamation, is declared to be a riot. In Massachusetts and New Hampshire, the number necessary to constitute a riot is twelve.

RIVER, *n.* 1. A large stream of water flowing in a channel on land towards the ocean, a lake or another river. It is larger than a rivulet or brook; but is applied to any stream, from the size of a mill-stream to that of the Danube, Maranon and Mississippi. We give this name to large streams which admit the tide and mingle salt water with fresh, as the *rivers* Hudson, Delaware and St. Lawrence.

ROCK, *v.t.* 1. To move backward and forward, as a body resting on a foundation; as, to *rock* a cradle; to *rock* a chair; to *rock* a mountain. It differs from *shake*, as denoting a slower and more uniform motion, or larger movements. It differs from *swing*, which expresses a vibratory motion of something suspended.

ROGUE, *n.* 1. In *law*, a vagrant; a sturdy beggar; a vagabond. Persons of this character were, by the ancient laws of England, to be punished by whipping and having the ear bored with a hot iron.   *Encyc.   Spenser.*
    2. A knave; a dishonest person; applied now, I believe, exclusively to males. This word comprehends thieves and robbers, but is generally applied to such as cheat and defraud in mutual dealings, or to counterfeiters.

ROMANCE, *n.* 1. A fabulous relation or story of adventures and incidents, designed for the entertainment of readers; a tale of extraordinary adventures, fictitious and often extravagant, usually a tale of love or war, subjects interesting the sensibilities of the heart, or the passions of wonder and curiosity. *Romance* differs from the *novel*, as it treats of great actions and extraordinary adventures; that is, according to the Welsh signification, it vaults or soars beyond the limits of fact and real life, and often of probability.

R

The first *romances* were a monstrous assemblage of histories, in which truth and fiction were blended without probability; a composition of amorous adventures and the extravagant ideas of chivalry. *Encyc.*

ROSICRUCIAN, *n.* [L. *ros*, dew, and *crux*, cross; *dew*, the most powerful dissolvent of gold, according to these fanatics, and *cross*, the emblem of light.] The Rosicrucians were a sect or cabal of hermetical philosophers, or rather fanatics, who sprung up in Germany in the fourteenth century, and made great pretensions to science; and among other things, pretended to be masters of the secret of the philosopher's stone. *Encyc.*

ROTE, *n.* [L. *rota*, a wheel, whence Fr. *routine.*] Properly, a round of words; frequent repetition of words or sounds, without attending to the signification, or to principles and rules; a practice that impresses words in the memory without an effort of the understanding, and without the aid of rules. Thus children learn to speak by *rote;* they often repeat what they hear, till it becomes familiar to them. So we learn to sing by *rote,* as we hear notes repeated, and soon learn to repeat them ourselves.

A *round number,* is a number that ends with a cypher, and may be divided by 10 without a remainder; a complete or full number. It is remarkable that the W. *cant,* a hundred, the L. *centum,* and Sax. *hund,* signify properly a circle, and this use of *round* may have originated in a like idea.

ROUNDROBIN, *n.* A written petition, memorial or remonstrance signed by names in a ring or circle. *Forbes.*

RUDE, *a.* 6. Ignorant; untaught; savage; barbarous; as the *rude* natives of America or of New Holland; the *rude* ancestors of the Greeks.

RUG, *n.* A coarse nappy woolen cloth used for a bed cover, and in modern times particularly, for covering the carpet before a fire-place. This name was formerly given to a coarse kind of frieze used for winter garments, and it may be that the poor in some countries still wear it. But in America, I believe the name is applied only to a bed cover for ordinary beds, and to a covering before a fire-place.

RUMBUD, *n.* A grog blossom; the popular name of a redness occasioned by the detestable practice of excessive drinking. Rumbuds usually appear first on the nose, and gradually extend over the face. *Rush.*

RUMINATE, *v.t.* 1. To chew the cud; to chew again what has been slightly chewed and swallowed. Oxen, sheep, deer, goats, camels, hares and squirrels *ruminate* in fact; other animals, as moles, bees, crickets, beetles, crabs, &c. only appear to *ruminate.* *Peyer. Encyc.*

The only animals endowed with the genuine faculty of rumination, are the *Ruminantia*, or cloven-hoofed quadrupeds, (*Pecora*, Linne;) but the hare, although its stomach is differently organized, is an occasional and partial ruminant.   *Ed. Encyc.*

RUN, *v.i.* 9. To flee for escape. When Gen. Wolfe was dying, an officer standing by him exclaimed, see how they *run*. Who *run?* said the dying hero. The enemy, said the officer. Then I die happy, said the general.

11. To flow in any manner, slowly or rapidly; to move or pass; as a fluid. Rivers *run* to the ocean or to lakes. The Connecticut *runs* on sand, and its water is remarkably pure. The tide *runs* two or three miles an hour. Tears *run* down the cheeks.

38. To pass in an orbit of any figure. The planets *run* their periodical courses. The comets do not *run* lawless through the regions of space.

RUSH, *v.i.* 1. To move or drive forward with impetuosity, violence and tumultuous rapidity; as, armies *rush* to battle; waters *rush* down a precipice; winds *rush* through the forest. We ought never to *rush* into company, much less into a religious assembly.

RUN. James Wolfe (1727–59) died on the Plains of Abraham, near Quebec, along with his adversary, General Montcalm, as New France was falling to the British.

R

S

SABBATH-BREAKING, *n.* A profanation of the sabbath by violating the injunction of the fourth commandment, or the municipal laws of a state which require the observance of that day as holy time. All unnecessary secular labor, visiting, traveling, sports, amusements and the like are considered as *sabbath-breaking.*

SAILOR, *n.* [a more common spelling than *sailer.*] A mariner; a seaman; one who follows the business of navigating ships or other vessels, or one who understands the management of ships in navigation. This word however does not by itself express any particular skill in navigation. It denotes any person who follows the seas, and is chiefly or wholly applied to the common hands.

SALAMANDER, *n.* An animal of the genus Lacerta or Lizard, one of the smaller species of the genus, not being more than six or seven inches in length. It has a short cylindrical tail, four toes on the four feet, and a naked body. The skin is furnished with small excrescences like teats, which are full of holes from which oozes a milky liquor that spreads over the skin, forming a kind of transparent varnish. The eyes are placed in the upper part of the head. The color is dark, with a bluish cast on the belly, intermixed with irregular yellow spots. This animal is oviparous, inhabits cold damp places among trees or hedges, avoiding the heat of the sun. The vulgar story of its being able to endure fire, is a mistake. *Encyc.*

SALMON, *n.* A fish of the genus Salmo, found in all the northern climates of America, Europe and Asia, ascending the rivers for spawning in spring, and penetrating to their head streams. It is a remarkably strong fish, and will

S. It has two uses; one to express a mere hissing, as in *sabbath, sack, sin, this, thus;* the other a vocal hissing, precisely like that of *z,* as in *muse, wise,* pronounced *muze, wize.*

even leap over considerable falls which lie in the way of its progress. It has been known to grow to the weight of 75 pounds; more generally it is from 15 to 25 pounds. It furnishes a delicious dish for the table, and is an article of commerce.

SALOON, *n.* In *architecture*, a lofty spacious hall, vaulted at the top, and usually comprehending two stories, with two ranges of windows. It is a magnificent room in the middle of a building, or at the head of a gallery, &c. It is a state room much used in palaces in Italy for the reception of embassadors and other visitors. *Encyc.*

SALUTARY, *a.* 1. Wholesome; healthful; promoting health. Diet and exercise are *salutary* to men of sedentary habits.
2. Promotive of public safety; contributing to some beneficial purpose. The strict discipline of youth has a *salutary* effect on society.

SANSCRIT, *n.* The ancient language of Hindoostan, from which are formed all the modern languages or dialects of the great peninsula of India. It is the language of the Bramins, and in this are written the ancient books of the country; but it is now obsolete. It is from the same stock as the ancient Persic, Greek and Latin, and all the present languages of Europe.

SARCASM, *n.* A keen reproachful expression; a satirical remark or expression, uttered with some degree of scorn or contempt; a taunt; a gibe. Of this we have an example in the remark of the Jews respecting Christ, on the cross, "He saved others, himself he cannot save."

Sardonian or *sardonic laughter,* a convulsive involuntary laughter, so called from the *herba sardonia,* a species of ranunculus, which is said to produce such convulsive motions in the cheeks and lips as are observed during a fit of laughter. *Encyc.*

SATELLITE, *n.* 1. A secondary planet or moon; a small planet revolving round another. In the solar system, eighteen *satellites* hare been discovered. The earth has *one,* called the moon, Jupiter *four,* Saturn *seven,* and Herschel *six.* *Morse.*

SAUCE, *n.* 1. A mixture or composition to be eaten with food for improving its relish.
2. In New England, culinary vegetables and roots eaten with flesh. This application of the word falls in nearly with the definition.
> Roots, herbs, vine-fruits, and sallad-flowers—they dish up various ways, and find them very delicious *sauce* to their meats, both roasted and boiled, fresh and salt. *Beverly, Hist. Virginia.*

SAUCE. Unsophisticated about food, Webster knows what he likes and likes what he knows. See the note under SITUATION.

Sauce consisting of stewed apples, is a great article in some parts of New England; but cranberries make the most delicious *sauce*.

To serve one the same sauce is to retaliate one injury with another. [*Vulgar.*]

SAVAGE, *n.* A human being in his native state of rudeness; one who is untaught, uncivilized or without cultivation of mind or manners. The *savages* of America, when uncorrupted by the vices of civilized men, are remarkable for their hospitality to strangers, and for their truth, fidelity and gratitude to their friends, but implacably cruel and revengeful towards their enemies. From this last trait of the savage character, the word came to signify,

2. A man of extreme, unfeeling, brutal cruelty; a barbarian.

SAVINGS BANK, *n.* A bank in which the savings or earnings of the poor are deposited and put to interest for their benefit.

SAWYER, *n.* 2. In *America*, a tree which, being undermined by a current of water, and falling into the stream, lies with its branches above water, which are continually raised and depressed by the force of the current, from which circumstance the name is derived. The *sawyers* in the Mississippi render the navigation dangerous, and frequently sink boats which run against them.

SCANDALOUS, *a.* 2. Opprobrious; disgraceful to reputation; that brings shame or infamy; as a *scandalous* crime or vice. How perverted must be the mind that considers seduction or dueling less *scandalous* than larceny!

SCAPAISM, *n.* Among the Persians, a barbarous punishment inflicted on criminals by confining them in a hollow tree till they died.   *Bailey.*

SCARCE, *a.* 1. Not plentiful or abundant; being in small quantity in proportion to the demand. We say, water is *scarce*, wheat, rye, barley is *scarce*, money is *scarce*, when the quantity is not fully adequate to the demand.

2. Being few in number and scattered; rare; uncommon. Good horses are *scarce*.

SCENERY, *n.* The appearance of a place, or of the various objects presented to view; or the various objects themselves as seen together. Thus we may say, the *scenery* of the landscape presented to the view from mount Holyoke, in Hampshire county, Massachusetts, is highly picturesque, and exceeded only by the *scenery* of Boston and its vicinity, as seen from the State house.

Never need an American look beyond his own country for the sublime and beautiful of natural *scenery*.   *Irving.*

S

SCEPTIC, SCEPTICAL, *a.* 2. Doubting or denying the truth of revelation. The *skeptical* system subverts the whole foundation of morals.   *Rob. Hall.*

SCHOOL-HOUSE, *n.* A house appropriated for the use of schools, or for instruction; but applied only to buildings for subordinate schools, not to colleges. In Connecticut and some other states, every town is divided into school-districts, and each district erects its own *school-house* by a tax on the inhabitants.

SCIENCE, *n.* 2. In *philosophy,* a collection of the general principles or leading truths relating to any subject. *Pure science,* as the mathematics, is built on self-evident truths; but the term science is also applied to other subjects founded on generally acknowledged truths, as *metaphysics;* or on experiment and observation, as *chimistry* and *natural philosophy;* or even to an assemblage of the general principles of an art, as the science of *agriculture;* the science of *navigation. Arts* relate to practice, as painting and sculpture.
A principle in *science* is a rule in art.   *Playfair.*

SCOFF, *v.i.* To treat with insolent ridicule, mockery or contumelious language; to manifest contempt by derision; with *at.* To *scoff at* religion and sacred things is evidence of extreme weakness and folly, as well as of wickedness.

SCOLD, *v.i.* To find fault or rail with rude clamor; to brawl; to utter railing or harsh, rude, boisterous rebuke; with *at;* as, to *scold at* a servant. A *scolding* tongue, a *scolding* wife, a *scolding* husband, a *scolding* master, who can endure?

SCORE, *n.* 1. A notch or incision; hence, the number twenty. Our ancestors, before the knowledge of writing, numbered and kept accounts of numbers by cutting notches on a stick or tally, and making one notch the representative of twenty. A simple mark answered the same purpose.

SCOT, SCOTCH, *v.t.* To support, as a wheel, by placing some obstacle to prevent its rolling. Our wagoners and cartmen *scot* the wheels of their wagons and carts, when in ascending a hill they stop to give their team rest, or for other purpose. In Connecticut, I have generally heard this word pronounced *scot,* in Massachusetts, *scotch.*

SCOURGE, *n.* 3. He or that which greatly afflicts, harasses or destroys; particularly, any continued evil or calamity. Attila was called the *scourge* of God, for the miseries he inflicted in his conquests. Slavery is a terrible *scourge.*

SCOUT, *v.t.* To sneer at; to treat with disdain and contempt. [*This word is in good use in America.*]

SCOW, *n*. A large flat bottomed boat; used as a ferry boat, or for loading and unloading vessels. [*A word in good use in New England.*]

SCRAMBLE, *v.i.* 1. To move or climb by seizing objects with the hand, and drawing the body forward; as, to *scramble* up a cliff.

2. To seize or catch eagerly at any thing that is desired; to catch with haste preventive of another; to catch at without ceremony. Man originally was obliged to *scramble* with wild beasts for nuts and acorns.

SCREECH-OWL, *n*. An owl that utters a harsh disagreeable cry at night, no more ominous of evil than the notes of the nightingale.

SCUFFLE, *n*. 1. A contention or trial of strength between two persons, who embrace each other's bodies; a struggle with close embrace, to decide which shall throw the other; in distinction from *wrestling*, which is a trial of strength and dexterity at arm's length. Among our common people, it is not unusual for two persons to commence a contest by wrestling, and at last *close in*, as it is called, and decide the contest by a *scuffle*.

SCUTTLE-BUTT, SCUTTLE-CASK, *n*. A butt or cask having a square piece sawn out of its bilge, and lashed upon deck.   *Mar. Dict.*

SEA-DRAGON, *n*. A marine monster caught in England in 1749, resembling in some degree an alligator, but having two large fins which served for swimming or flying. It had two legs terminating in hoofs, like those of an ass. Its body was covered with impenetrable scales, and it had five rows of teeth.
                                                              Gent. Magazine.

SECOND, *a*. 2. Next in value, power, excellence, dignity or rank; inferior. The silks of China are *second* to none in quality. Lord Chatham was *second* to none in eloquence. Dr. Johnson was *second* to none in intellectual powers, but *second* to many in research and erudition.

SECRETION, *n*. The act of secerning; the act of producing from the blood substances different from the blood itself, or from any of its constituents, as bile, saliva, mucus, urine, etc. This was considered by the older physiologists as merely a separation from the blood of certain substances previously contained in it; the literal meaning of *secretion*. But this opinion is now generally exploded. The organs of secretion are of very various form and structure, but the most general are those called *glands*.   *Ed. Encyc.*

SECURE, *a*. 3. Free from fear or apprehension of danger; not alarmed; not disturbed by fear; confident of safety; hence, careless of the means of defense. Men are often most in danger when they feel most *secure*.

S

SECURE, *v.t.* 2. To make certain; to put beyond hazard. Liberty and fixed laws *secure* to every citizen due protection of person and property. The first duty and the highest interest of men is to *secure* the favor of God by repentance and faith, and thus to *secure* to themselves future felicity.

SEDENTARY, *a.* 1. Accustomed to sit much, or to pass most of the time in a sitting posture; as a *sedentary* man. Students, taylors and women are *sedentary* persons.

SEDUCER, *n.* One that seduces; one that by temptation or arts, entices another to depart from the path of rectitude and duty; pre-eminently, one that by flattery, promises or falsehood, persuades a female to surrender her chastity. The *seducer* of a female is little less criminal than the murderer.

SEIN, *n.* A large net for catching fish. The *seins* used for taking shad in the Connecticut, sometimes sweep nearly the whole breadth of the river.

SELECTMAN, *n.* In *New England,* a town officer chosen annually to manage the concerns of the town, provide for the poor, &c. Their number is usually from three to seven in each town, and these constitute a kind of executive authority.

SELFISHNESS, *n.* The exclusive regard of a person to his own interest or happiness; or that supreme self-love or self-preference, which leads a person in his actions to direct his purposes to the advancement of his own interest, power or happiness, without regarding the interest of others. Selfishness, in its worst or unqualified sense, is the very essence of human depravity, and stands in direct opposition to *benevolence,* which is the essence of the divine character. As God is *love,* so man, in his natural state, is *selfishness.*

SEMINARY, *n.* 5. A place of education; any school, academy, college or university, in which young persons are instructed in the several branches of learning which may qualify them for their future employments. [*This is the only signification of the word in the United States, at least as far as my knowledge extends.*]

SENATE. See CON-
GRESS, where you
need to go to find the
term of a U.S. senator.

SENATE, *n.* 2. In *the United States,* senate denotes the higher branch or house of a legislature. Such is the *senate* of the United States, or upper house of the congress; and in most of the states, the highest and least numerous branch of the legislature, is called the *senate.* In the U. States, the *senate* is an elective body.

Common sense, that power of the mind which, by a kind of instinct, or a short process of reasoning, perceives truth, the relation of things, cause and effect,

&c. and hence enables the possessor to discern what is right, useful, expedient or proper, and adopt the best means to accomplish his purpose. This power seems to be the gift of nature, improved by experience and observation.

Moral sense, a determination of the mind to be pleased with the contemplation of those affections, actions or characters of rational agents, which are called good or virtuous.   *Encyc.*

SEPAWN, SEPON, *n.* A species of food consisting of meal of maiz boiled in water. It is in New York and Pennsylvania what hasty-pudding is in New England.

SERENADE, *n.* Properly, music performed in a clear night; hence, an entertainment of music given in the night by a lover to his mistress under her window. It consists generally of instrumental music, but that of the voice is sometimes added. The songs composed for these occasions are also called *serenades.*   *Encyc.*

SEROON, *n.* 1. A seroon of almonds is the quantity of two hundred pounds; of anise seed, from three to four hundred weight; of Castile soap, from two hundred and a half to three hundred and three quarters.   *Encyc.*

SERVITUDE, *n.* The condition of a slave; the state of involuntary subjection to a master; slavery; bondage. Such is the state of the slaves in America. A large portion of the human race are in *servitude.*

SESAME, SESAMUM, *n.* Oily grain; a genus of annual herbaceous plants, from the seeds of which an oil is expressed. One species of it is cultivated in Carolina, and the blacks use the seeds for food. It is called there *bene.*
                                                    Encyc.   Beloe.

SETTLE, *v.t.* 16. To plant with inhabitants; to colonize. The French first *settled* Canada; the Puritans *settled* New England. Plymouth was *settled* in 1620. Hartford was *settled* in 1636. Wethersfield was the first *settled* town in Connecticut.

SEX, *n.* 1. The distinction between male and female; or that property or character by which an animal is male or female. The male sex is usually characterized by muscular strength, boldness and firmness. The female sex is characterized by softness, sensibility and modesty.

SHABBY, *a.* 3. Mean; paltry; despicable; as a *shabby* fellow; *shabby* treatment.   *Clarendon.*
  [For the idea expressed by *shabby*, there is not a better word in the language.]

SHACK, *n.* In *ancient customs of England,* a liberty of winter pasturage. In Norfolk and Suffolk, the lord of a manor has *shack,* that is, liberty of feeding his sheep at pleasure on his tenants' lands during the six winter months. In Norfolk, *shack* extends to the common for hogs, in all men's grounds, from harvest to seed-time; whence to go *a-shack,* is to feed at large.
Cowel. Encyc.

In New England, *shack* is used in a somewhat similar sense for mast or the food of swine, and for feeding at large or in the forest, [for we have no manors,] and I have heard a shiftless fellow, a vagabond, called a *shack.*

SHADOW, *n.* 1. Shade within defined limits; obscurity or deprivation of light, apparent on a plane and representing the form of the body which intercepts the rays of light; as the *shadow* of a man, of a tree or a tower. The *shadow* of the earth in an eclipse of the moon is proof of its sphericity.

SHAME, *n.* 1. A painful sensation excited by a consciousness of guilt, or of having done something which injures reputation; or by the exposure of that which nature or modesty prompts us to conceal. *Shame* is particularly excited by the disclosure of actions which, in the view of men, are mean and degrading. Hence it is often or always manifested by a downcast look or by blushes, called *confusion of face.*
Shame prevails when reason is defeated.   *Rambler.*

SHAVER, *n.* [Gipsey, *tschabe* or *tschawo,* a boy.] A boy or young man. This word is still in common use in New England. It must be numbered among our original words.

SHEATH, SHEATHE, *v.t.* To sheathe the sword, a figurative phrase, to put an end to war or enmity; to make peace. It corresponds to the Indian phrase, *to bury the hatchet.*

SHEEP, *n.* 1. An animal of the genus Ovis, which is among the most useful species that the Creator has bestowed on man, as its wool constitutes a principal material of warm clothing, and its flesh is a great article of food. The sheep is remarkable for its harmless temper and its timidity. The varieties are numerous.

SHEMITIC, *a.* Pertaining to Shem, the son of Noah. The *Shemitic* languages are the Chaldee, Syriac, Arabic, Hebrew, Samaritan, Ethiopic and Old Phenician.

SHILLY-SHALLY, *n.* [Russ. *shalyu,* to be foolish, to play the fool, to play wanton tricks.] Foolish trifling; irresolution. [*Vulgar.*]
[This word has probably been written *shill-I-shall-I,* from an ignorance of its origin.]

SIGH, *n.* A single deep respiration; a long breath; the inhaling of a larger quantity of air than usual, and the sudden emission of it. This is an effort of nature to dilate the lungs and give vigor to the circulation of the blood, when the action of the heart and arteries is languid from grief, depression of spirits, weakness or want of exercise. Hence *sighs* are indications of grief or debility.

SIGN-POST, *n.* A post on which a sign hangs, or on which papers are placed to give public notice of any thing. By the laws of some of the New England states, a *sign-post* is to be erected near the center of each town.

SILENCE, *v.t.* 5. To restrain from preaching by revoking a license to preach; as, to *silence* a minister of the gospel.   *U. States.*
    The Rev. Thomas Hooker, of Chelmsford in Essex, was *silenced* for nonconformity.   *B. Trumbull.*
    6. To put an end to; to cause to cease.
    The question between agriculture and commerce has received a decision which has *silenced* the rivalships between them.   *Hamilton.*

SILLIMANITE, *n.* A mineral found at Saybrook in Connecticut, so named in honor of Prof. Silliman of Yale College.

SIMILARITY, *n.* Likeness; resemblance as a *similarity* of features. There is a great *similarity* in the features of the Laplanders and Samoiedes, but little *similarity* between the features of Europeans and the woolly haired Africans.

SIMOOM, *n.* A hot suffocating wind, that blows occasionally in Africa and Arabia, generated by the extreme heat of the parched deserts or sandy plains. Its approach is indicated by a redness in the air, and its fatal effects are to be avoided by falling on the face and holding the breath.   *Encyc.*

SING, *v.i.* 2. To utter sweet or melodious sounds, as birds. It is remarkable that the female of no species of birds ever sings.

SIROCCO, *n.* A pernicious wind that blows from the south east in Italy, called the Syrian wind. It is said to resemble the steam from the mouth of an oven.

SIRRAH, *n.* A word of reproach and contempt; used in addressing vile characters. [I know not whence we have this word. The common derivation of it from *sir, ha,* is ridiculous.]

SITUATION, *n.* Position; seat; location in respect to something else. The *situation* of London is more favorable for foreign commerce than that of Paris.

SITUATION. Webster's letters from abroad show how uncomfortable he was in unfamiliar surroundings. "The French," he says "drink wine at breakfast & dinner, & coffee . . . is drank, in the morning, & immediately after dinner. These customs and the cookery are not pleasant to me . . . The butter is all *unsalted,* & in this state, I cannot eat it." And from England he writes that "the Colleges [at Cambridge] are mostly old stone buildings, which look very heavy, cold & gloomy to an American, accustomed to the new public buildings in our country."

The *situation* of a stranger among people of habits differing from his own, cannot be pleasant.

SKUNK, *n.* In America, the popular name of a fetid animal of the weasel kind; the Viverra Mephitis of Linne.

SLAVERY, *n.* Bondage; the state of entire subjection of one person to the will of another.

> *Slavery* is the obligation to labor for the benefit of the master, without the contract or consent of the servant. *Paley.*

Slavery may proceed from crimes, from captivity or from debt. Slavery is also *voluntary* or *involuntary; voluntary,* when a person sells or yields his own person to the absolute command of another; *involuntary,* when he is placed under the absolute power of another without his own consent. Slavery no longer exists in Great Britain, nor in the northern states of America.

SLAVE-TRADE, *n.* The barbarous and wicked business of purchasing men and women, transporting them to a distant country and selling them for slaves.

SLEEP, *n.* That state of an animal in which the voluntary exertion of his mental and corporeal powers is suspended, and he rests unconscious of what passes around him, and not affected by the ordinary impressions of external objects. Sleep is generally attended with a relaxation of the muscles, but the involuntary motions, as respiration and the circulation of the blood, are continued. The mind is often very active in sleep; but its powers not being under the control of reason, its exercises are very irregular. Sleep is the natural rest or repose intended by the Creator to restore the powers of the body and mind, when exhausted or fatigued.

SLEEPER, *n.* 5. In *New England,* a floor timber.

SLEIGH, *n.* A vehicle moved on runners, and greatly used in America for transporting persons or goods on snow or ice. [This word the English write and pronounce *sledge,* and apply it to what we call a *sled.*]

SLIDING-RULE, *n.* A mathematical instrument used to determine measure or quantity without compasses, by sliding the parts one by another.

SLOPSELLER, *n.* One who sells ready made clothes.

SLOTH, *n.* 2. Disinclination to action or labor; sluggishness; laziness; idleness.
> *Sloth,* like rust, consumes faster than labor wears. *Franklin.*

3. An animal, so called from the remarkable slowness of his motions. There are two species of this animal; the ai or three toed sloth, and the unau

SLOTH. Solvers of early American crosswords will recognize the *ai* and the *unau.*

or two toed sloth; both found in South America. It is said that its greatest speed seldom exceeds three yards an hour. It feeds on vegetables and ruminates.   *Dict. Nat. Hist.*

SLUMP, *v.i.* To fall or sink suddenly into water or mud, when walking on a hard surface, as on ice or frozen ground, not strong enough to bear the person. [*This legitimate word is in common and respectable use in New England, and its signification is so appropriate that no other word will supply its place.*]

SMATTERING, *n.* A slight superficial knowledge. [*This is the word commonly used.*]

SMITH, *n.* 1. Literally, the striker, the beater; hence, one who forges with the hammer; one who works in metals; as an iron-*smith;* gold-*smith;* silver-*smith,* &c.

SNARL, *v.t.* 1. To entangle; to complicate; to involve in knots; as, to *snarl* the hair; to *snarl* a skein of thread. [*This word is in universal popular use in New England.*]
   2. To embarrass.

SNICKER, SNIGGER, *v.i.* To laugh slily; or to laugh in one's sleeve. [*It is a word in common use in New England, not easily defined. It signifies to laugh with small audible catches of voice, as when persons attempt to suppress loud laughter.*]

SNOW, *n.* Frozen vapor; watery particles congealed into white crystals in the air, and failing to the earth. When there is no wind, these crystals fall in flakes or unbroken collections, sometimes extremely beautiful.

SODA-WATER, *n.* A very weak solution of soda in water supersaturated with carbonic acid, and constituting a favorite beverage.

SODOMY, *n.* A crime against nature.

SOFA, *n.* An elegant long seat, usually with a stuffed bottom. Sofas are variously made. In the United States, the frame is of mahogany, and the bottom formed of stuffed cloth, with a covering of silk, chintz, calico or hair-cloth. The sofa of the orientals is a kind of alcove raised half a foot above the floor, where visitors of distinction are received. It is also a seat by the side of the room covered with a carpet.

Solar spots, dark spots that appear on the sun's disk, usually visible only by the telescope, but sometimes so large as to be seen by the naked eye. They adhere to the body of the sun; indicate its revolutions on its axis; are very changeable in their figure and dimensions; and vary in size from mere points to spaces 50.000 miles in diameter.

SOLICITOUS, *a.* Careful; anxious; very desirous, as to obtain something. Men are often more *solicitous* to obtain the favor of their king or of the people, than of their Maker.

SONG, *n.* 2. A little poem to be sung, or uttered with musical modulations; a ballad. The *songs* of a country are characteristic of its manners. Every country has its love *songs*, its war *songs*, and its patriotic *songs.*

SOOTHSAYING, *n.* The foretelling of future events by persons without divine aid or authority, and thus distinguished from *prophecy.*

SOUL, *n.* 1. The spiritual, rational and immortal substance in man, which distinguishes him from brutes; that part of man which enables him to think and reason, and which renders him a subject of moral government. The immortality of the *soul* is a fundamental article of the christian system.

> Such is the nature of the human *soul* that it must have a God, an object of supreme affection. *Edwards.*

8. A human being; a person. There was not a *soul* present. In Paris there are more than seven hundred thousand *souls.* London, Westminster, Southwark and the suburbs, are said to contain twelve hundred thousand *souls.*

SOUNDING-BOARD, *n.* A board or structure with a flat surface, suspended over a pulpit to prevent the sound of the preacher's voice from ascending, and thus propagating it farther in a horizontal direction. [*Used in American churches.*]

SOZZLE, *n.* A sluttish woman, or one that spills water or other liquids carelessly. [*New England.*]

SPAN, *n.* 3. A *span of horses,* consists of two of nearly the same color, and otherwise nearly alike, which are usually harnessed side by side. The word signifies properly the same as *yoke,* when applied to horned cattle, from buckling or fastening together. But in America, *span* always implies resemblance in color at least; it being an object of ambition with gentlemen and with teamsters to unite two horses abreast that are alike.

SPANK, *v.t.* To strike with the open hand; to slap. [*A word common in New England.*]

SPATTERDASHES, *n. plu.* Coverings for the legs to keep them clean from water and mud. [Since boots are generally worn, these things and their name are little used.]

SPEECH, *n.* The faculty of uttering articulate sounds or words, as in human beings; the faculty of expressing thoughts by words or articulate sounds. *Speech* was given to man by his Creator for the noblest purposes.

SPELL, *n.* 4. In *New England,* a short time; a little time. [*Not elegant.*] 5. A turn of gratuitous labor, sometimes accompanied with presents. People give their neighbors a *spell.*   *N. England.*

SPELL, *v.i.* To form words with the proper letters, either in reading or writing. He knows not how to *spell.* Our orthography is so irregular that most persons never learn to *spell.*

SPELLING, *n.* The act of naming the letters of a word, or the act of writing or printing words with their proper letters.
2. Orthography; the manner of forming words with letters. Bad *spelling* is disreputable to a gentleman.

SPINNING-JENNY, *n.* An engine or complicated machine for spinning wool or cotton, in the manufacture of cloth.

SPIRAL, *a.* Winding round a cylinder or other round body, or in a circular form, and at the same time rising or advancing forward; winding like a screw. The magnificent column in the Place Vendome, at Paris, is divided by a *spiral* line into compartments. It is formed with *spiral* compartments, on which are engraved figures emblematical of the victories of the French armies. A whirlwind is so named from the *spiral* motion of the air. Water in a tunnel descends in a *spiral* form.

SPIRIT, *n.* 18. A strong, pungent or stimulating liquor, usually obtained by distillation, as rum, brandy, gin, whiskey. In America, *spirit,* used without other words explanatory of its meaning, signifies the liquor distilled from cane-juice, or rum. We say, new *spirit,* or old *spirit,* Jamaica *spirit,* &c.

SPITE, *n.* Hatred; rancor; malice; malignity; malevolence.   *Johnson.*
Spite, however, is not always synonymous with these words. It often denotes a less deliberate and fixed hatred than malice and malignity, and is often a sudden fit of ill will excited by temporary vexation. It is the effect of extreme irritation, and is accompanied with a desire of revenge, or at least a desire to vex the object of ill will.

SPREAD, SPRED, *v.i.* 4. To be propagated from one to another; as, a disease *spreads* into all parts of a city. The yellow fever of American cities has not been found to *spread* in the country.

SPRY, *a.* Having great power of leaping or running; nimble; active; vigorous. [This word is in common use in New England, and is doubtless a contraction of *sprig.*]

SPUR, *n.* 6. In *America,* a mountain that shoots from any other mountain or range of mountains, and extends to some distance in a lateral direction, or at right angles.

SPY, *n.* 1. A person sent into an enemy's camp to inspect their works, ascertain their strength and their intentions, to watch their movements, and secretly communicate intelligence to the proper officer. By the laws of war among all civilized nations, a *spy* is subjected to capital punishment.

SQUAT, *v.i.* 3. In *Massachusetts and some other states of America,* to settle on another's land without pretense of title; a practice very common in the wilderness.

SQUEAK, *n.* A sharp shrill sound suddenly uttered, either of the human voice or of any animal or instrument, such as a child utters in acute pain, or as pigs utter, or as is made by carriage wheels when dry, or by a pipe or reed.

SQUEAL, *v.t.* To cry with a sharp shrill voice. It is used of animals only, and chiefly of swine. It agrees in sense with *squeak,* except that *squeal* denotes a more continued cry than *squeak,* and the latter is not limited to animals. We say, a *squealing* hog or pig, a *squealing* child; but more generally a *squalling* child.

SQUIRE, *v.t.* 2. In *colloquial language,* to attend as a beau or gallant for aid and protection; as, to *squire* a lady to the gardens.

SQUIRREL HUNT, *n.* In *America,* the hunting and shooting of squirrels by a company of men.

STABLE, *n.* A house or shed for beasts to lodge and feed in. In large towns, a stable is usually a building for horses only, or horses and cows, and often connected with a coach house. In the country towns in the northern states of America, a stable is usually an apartment in a barn in which hay and grain are deposited.

STADDLE, *n.* 2. In *New England,* a small tree of any kind, particularly a forest tree. In America, trees are called *staddles* from three or four years old till they are six or eight inches in diameter or more, but in this respect the word is indefinite. This is also the sense in which it is used by Bacon and Tusser.

STAGE, *n.* 7. A place of rest on a journey, or where a relay of horses is taken. When we arrive at the next *stage,* we will take some refreshment. Hence,

8. The distance between two places of rest on a road; as a *stage* of fifteen miles.

9. A single step; degree of advance; degree of progression, either in increase or decrease, in rising or falling, or in any change of state; as the several *stages* of a war; the *stages* of civilization or improvement; *stages* of growth in an animal or plant; *stages* of a disease, of decline or recovery; the several *stages* of human life.

10. [instead of *stage-coach,* or *stage-wagon.*] A coach or other carriage running regularly from one place to another for the conveyance of passengers.

STALL, *n.* 4. A bench, form or frame of shelves in the open air, where any thing is exposed to sale. It is curious to observe the *stalls* of books in the boulevards and other public places in Paris.

STALL, *v.t.* 3. To set; to fix; to plunge into mire so as not to be able to proceed; as, to *stall* horses or a carriage.

[This phrase I have heard in Virginia. In New England, *set* is used in a like sense.]

STANDARD, *n.* 3. That which is established as a rule or model, by the authority of public opinion, or by respectable opinions, or by custom or general consent; as writings which are admitted to be the *standard* of style and taste. Homer's Iliad is the *standard* of heroic poetry. Demosthenes and Cicero are the *standards* of oratory. Of modern eloquence, we have an excellent *standard* in the speeches of lord Chatham. Addison's writings furnish a good *standard* of pure, chaste and elegant English style. It is not an easy thing to erect a *standard* of taste.

STAPLE, *n.* A settled mart or market; an emporium. In England, formerly, the king's *staple* was established in certain ports or towns, and certain goods could not be exported, without being first brought to these ports to be rated and charged with the duty payable to the king or public. The principal commodities on which customs were levied, were *wool, skins* and *lether,* and these were originally the staple commodities. Hence the words *staple commodities,* came in time to signify the principal commodities produced by a country for exportation or use. Thus cotton is the *staple commodity* of South Carolina,

S

Georgia and other southern states of America. Wheat is the *staple* of Pennsylvania and New York.

STAR, *n*. 1. An apparently small luminous body in the heavens, that appears in the night, or when its light is not obscured by clouds or lost in the brighter effulgence of the sun. *Stars* are fixed or planetary. The fixed stars are known by their perpetual twinkling, and by their being always in the same position in relation to each other. The planets do not twinkle, and they revolve about the sun. The stars are worlds, and their immense numbers exhibit the astonishing extent of creation and of divine power.

STARBOARD, *n*. [. . . I know not from what particular construction of a vessel the helm should give name to the right hand side, unless from the tiller's being held by the right hand, or at the right side of the steersman.] The right hand side of a ship or boat, when a spectator stands with his face towards the head, stem or prow.

STAR-SHOOT, *n*. That which is emitted from a star.
> I have seen a good quantity of that jelly, by the vulgar called a *star-shoot,* as
> if it remained upon the extinction of a falling star.   *Bacon.*

[The writer once saw the same kind of substance from a brilliant meteor, at Amherst in Massachusetts. See Journ. of Science for a description of it by Rufus Graves, Esq.]

STATESWOMAN, *n*. A woman who meddles in public affairs; in contempt.
                                                                          Addison.

STATIONER, *n*. A bookseller; one who sells books, paper, quills, inkstands, pencils and other furniture for writing. The business of the bookseller and stationer is usually carried on by the same person.

STATISTICS, *n*. A collection of facts respecting the state of society, the condition of the people in a nation or country, their health, longevity, domestic economy, arts, property and political strength, the state of the country, &c.
                                                                  Sinclair.   Tooke.

STAY, *v.i.* To remain; to continue at a place; to abide for any indefinite time . . . We *staid* at the Hotel Montmorenci.

STEAM-BOAT, STEAM-VESSEL, *n*. A vessel propelled through the water by steam.

STEERING-WHEEL, *n*. The wheel by which the rudder of a ship is turned and the ship steered.

STETHESCOPE, *n.* A tubular instrument for distinguishing diseases of the stomach by sounds.   *Scudamore.*

STILL-LIFE, *n.* 2. Dead animals, or paintings representing the dead.
                                                    Gray.

STILT, *n.* A stilt is a piece of wood with a shoulder, to support the foot in walking. Boys sometimes use *stilts* for raising their feet above the mud in walking, but they are rarely seen.
    Men must not walk upon *stilts.*   *L'Estrange.*

STING, *v.t.* 1. To pierce with the sharp pointed instrument with which certain animals are furnished, such as bees, wasps, scorpions and the like. Bees will seldom *sting* persons, unless they are first provoked.

STINGY, *a.* 1. Extremely close and covetous; meanly avaricious; niggardly; narrow hearted; as a *stingy* churl. [*A word in popular use, but low and not admissible into elegant writing.*]

STOCK, *v.t.* 6. To supply with seed; as, to *stock* land with clover or herds-grass.   *American farmers.*

STOOP, *n.* 4. In *America,* a kind of shed, generally open, but attached to a house; also, an open place for seats at a door.

STORE, *n.* 6. In *the United States,* shops for the sale of goods of any kind, by wholesale or retail, are often called *stores.*

STORM, *n.* 1. A violent wind; a tempest. Thus a *storm of wind,* is correct language, as the proper sense of the word is rushing, violence. It has primarily no reference to a fall of rain or snow. But as a violent wind is often attended with rain or snow, the word *storm* has come to be used, most improperly, for a fall of rain or snow without wind.

STORY, *n.* 1. A verbal narration or recital of a series of facts or incidents. We observe in children a strong passion for hearing *stories.*
    6. A loft; a floor; or a set of rooms on the same floor or level. A story comprehends the distance from one floor to another; as a *story* of nine or ten feet elevation. Hence each floor terminating the space is called a *story;* as a house of one *story,* of two *stories,* of five *stories.* The farm houses in New England have usually two *stories;* the houses in Paris have usually five *stories;* a few have more; those in London four. But in the United States the floor next the ground is the first *story;* in France and England, the first floor or *story,* is the second from the ground.

STOVE, *n.* 2. A small box with an iron pan, used for holding coals to warm the feet. It is a bad practice for young persons to accustom themselves to sit with a warm *stove* under the feet.

STRAND, *n.* The shore or beach of the sea or ocean, or of a large lake, and perhaps of a navigable river. It is never used of the bank of a small river or pond. The Dutch on the Hudson apply it to a landing place; as the *strand* at Kingston.

STRANGER, *n.* A foreigner; one who belongs to another country. Paris and London are visited by strangers from all the countries of Europe.
    2. One of another town, city, state or province in the same country. The Commencements in American colleges are frequented by multitudes of *strangers* from the neighboring towns and states.

STRAY, *n.* Any domestic animal that has left an inclosure or its proper place and company, and wanders at large or is lost. The laws provide that *strays* shall be taken up, impounded and advertised.

STREET, *n.* 1. Properly, a paved way or road; but in usage, any way or road in a city, chiefly a main way, in distinction from a lane or alley.
    2. Among the people of New England, any public highway.

To strike, among workmen in manufactories, in England, is to quit work in a body or by combination, in order to compel their employers to raise their wages.

STRIP, *v.t.* 8. To pull off husks; to husk; as, to *strip* maiz, or the ears of maiz.
                                                                    America.

STRIP, *n.* 2. Waste, *in a legal sense;* destruction of fences, buildings, timber, &c.   *Massachusetts.*

STRIPPINGS, *n.* The last milk drawn from a cow at a milking.
                                                    Grose.   New England.

STUNNING, *ppr.* Overpowering the organs of hearing; confounding with noise.

SUBDUE, *v.t.* 1. To conquer by force or the exertion of superior power, and bring into permanent subjection; to reduce under dominion. Thus Cesar *subdued* the Gauls; Augustus *subdued* Egypt; the English *subdued* Canada. Subduing implies *conquest* or *vanquishing,* but it implies also more permanence of subjection to the conquering power, than either of these words.

SUBJECTION, *n.* 2. The state of being under the power, control and government of another. The safety of life, liberty and property depends on our *subjection* to the laws. The isles of the West Indies are held in *subjection* to the powers of Europe. Our appetites and passions should be in *subjection* to our reason, and our will should be in entire *subjection* to the laws of God.

SUBMISSION, *n.* 4. Obedience; compliance with the commands or laws of a superior. *Submission* of children to their parents is an indispensable duty.

SUBURB, SUBURBS, *n.* A building without the walls of a city, but near them; or more generally, the parts that lie without the walls, but in the vicinity of a city. The word may signify buildings, streets or territory. We say, a house stands in the *suburbs;* a garden is situated in the *suburbs* of London or Paris.

SUBVERT, *v.t.* 1. To overthrow from the foundation; to overturn; to ruin utterly. The northern nations of Europe *subverted* the Roman empire. He is the worst enemy of man, who endeavors to *subvert* the christian religion. The elevation of corrupt men to office will slowly, but surely, *subvert* a republican government.

SUCCEDE, SUCCEED, *v.t.* 1. To follow in order; to take the place which another has left; as, the king's eldest son *succeeds* his father on the throne. John Adams *succeeded* Gen. Washington in the presidency of the United States. Lewis XVIII. of France has lately deceased, and is *succeeded* by his brother Charles X.

SUCCOTASH, *n.* In America, a mixture of green maiz and beans boiled. The dish, as well as the name, is borrowed from the native Indians.

SUFFRAGE, *n.* A vote; a voice given in deciding a controverted question, or in the choice of a man for an office or trust. Nothing can be more grateful to a good man than to be elevated to office by the unbiased *suffrages* of free enlightened citizens.

SUGAR, *n.* A well known substance manufactured chiefly from the sugar cane, *arundo saccharifera;* but in the United States, great quantities of this article are made from the sugar maple, and in France, a few years since, it was extensively manufactured from the beet. The saccharine liquor is concentrated by boiling, which expels the water; lime is added to neutralize the acid that is usually present; the grosser impurities rise to the surface, and are separated in the form of scum; and finally as the liquor cools, the sugar separates from the melasses in grains. The sirup or melasses is drained off, leaving the sugar in the state known in commerce by the name of *raw* or *muscovado* sugar. This is farther purified by means of clay, or more extensively by bullocks' blood, which forming a coagulum, envelops the impurities. Thus clarified, it takes the names of *lump, loaf, refined,* &c. according to the different degrees of purification. Sugar is a proximate element of the vegetable kingdom, and is found in most ripe fruits, and many farinaceous roots. By fermentation, sugar is converted into alcohol, and hence forms the basis of those substances which are used for making intoxicating liquors, as melasses, grapes, apples, malt, &c.

The *ultimate* elements of sugar are oxygen, carbon and hydrogen. Of all vegetable principles, it is considered by Dr. Rush as the most wholesome and nutritious.

SUMPTUARY, *a.* Relating to expense. *Sumptuary* laws or regulations are such as restrain or limit the expenses of citizens in apparel, food, furniture, &c. *Sumptuary* laws are abridgments of liberty, and of very difficult execution. They can be justified only on the ground of extreme necessity.

SUN, *n.* 3. Any thing eminently splendid or luminous; that which is the chief source of light or honor. The natives of America complain that the *sun* of their glory is set.

SUPERFLUITY, *n.* 2. Something that is beyond what is wanted; something rendered unnecessary by its abundance. Among the *superfluities* of life we seldom number the abundance of money.

SUPERIORITY, *n.* Pre-eminence; the quality of being more advanced or higher, greater or more excellent than another in any respect; as *superiority* of age, of rank or dignity, of attainments or excellence. The *superiority* of others in fortune and rank, is more readily acknowledged than *superiority* of understanding.

SUPERNATURAL, *a.* Being beyond or exceeding the powers or laws of nature; miraculous. A *supernatural* event is one which is not produced according to the ordinary or established laws of natural things. Thus if iron has more specific gravity than water, it will sink in that fluid; and the floating of iron on water must he a *supernatural* event. Now no human being can alter a law of nature; the floating of iron on water therefore must be caused by divine power specially exerted to suspend, in this instance, a law of nature. Hence *supernatural* events or miracles can be produced only by the immediate agency of divine power.

SUPERSTITION, *n.* 1. Excessive exactness or rigor in religious opinions or practice; extreme and unnecessary scruples in the observance of religious rites not commanded, or of points of minor importance; excess or extravagance in religion; the doing of things not required by God, or abstaining from things not forbidden; or the belief of what is absurd, or belief without evidence. *Brown.*

SUPPER, *n.* The evening meal. People who dine late, eat no *supper.* The dinner of fashionable people would be the *supper* of rustics.

SUPREME, *a.* 1. Highest in authority; holding the highest place in government or power. In the United States, the congress is *supreme* in regulating commerce and in making war and peace. The parliament of Great Britain is *supreme* in legislation; but the king is *supreme* in the administration of the government. In the universe, God only is the *supreme* ruler and judge. His commands are *supreme,* and binding on all his creatures.

SURPASS, *v.t.* To exceed; to excel; to go beyond in any thing good or bad. Homer *surpasses* modern poets in sublimity. Pope *surpasses* most other poets in smoothness of versification. Achilles *surpassed* the other Greeks in strength and courage. Clodius *surpassed* all men in the profligacy of his life. Perhaps no man ever *surpassed* Washington in genuine patriotism and integrity of life.

SURVIVE, *v.t.* 2. To outlive any thing else; to live beyond any event. Who would wish to *survive* the ruin of his country? Many men *survive* their usefulness or the regular exercise of their reason.

SUSPICION, *n.* The act of suspecting; the imagination of the existence of something without proof, or upon very slight evidence, or upon no evidence at all. *Suspicion* often proceeds from the apprehension of evil; it is the offspring or companion of jealousy.

> *Suspicions* among thoughts, are like bats among birds; they ever fly by twilight.   *Bacon.*

SWAMP, *n.* Spungy land; low ground filled with water; soft wet ground. In *New England,* I believe this word is never applied to marsh, or the boggy land made by the overflowing of salt water, but always to low soft ground in the interior country; wet and spungy land, but not usually covered with water. This is the true meaning of the word. *Swamps* are often mowed. In *England,* the word is explained in books by boggy land, morassy or marshy ground.

SWASH, *n.* 2. Impulse of water flowing with violence. In the southern states of America, *swash* or *swosh* is a name given to a narrow sound or channel of water lying within a sand bank, or between that and the shore. Many such are found on the shores of the Carolinas.

SWEAR, *v.i.* 4. To be profane; to practice profaneness. Certain classes of men are accustomed to *swear.* For men to *swear* is sinful, disreputable and odious; but for females or ladies to *swear,* appears more abominable and scandalous.

SURPASS. Publius Clodius Pulcher (c. 93–52 B.C.) was involved in a famous scandal concerning Julius Caesar's wife, Pompeia. Caesar divorced her, saying that his family should be above suspicion.

S

SWEATING-SICK- ☞
NESS. Webster wrote a
history of pestilential
diseases in 1799. See his
entries on EPIDEMIC,
INFLUENZA, INOCU-
LATE, TASTE, VAC-
CINATE, and YELLOW-
FEVER.

SWEATING-SICKNESS, *n.* A febril epidemic disease which prevailed in some countries of Europe, but particularly in England, in the 15th and 16th centuries. Its first appearance was in the army of the earl of Richmond, afterward Henry VII. on his landing at Milford haven, in 1485. The invasion of the disease was sudden, and usually marked by a local affection producing the sensation of intense heat, afterwards diffusing itself over the whole body, and immediately followed by profuse sweating, which continued through the whole course of the disease or till death, which often happened in a few hours. *Cyc.*

SWIM, *v.i.* 2. To move progressively in water by means of the motion of the hands and feet, or of fins. In Paris, boys are taught to *swim* by instructors appointed for that purpose.

SWINE, *n.* A hog; a quadruped of the genus Sus, which furnishes man with a large portion of his most nourishing food. The fat or lard of this animal enters into various dishes in cookery. The swine is a heavy, stupid animal, and delights to wallow in the mire.

SYCOPHANT, *n.* Originally, an informer against those who stole figs, or exported them contrary to law, &c. Hence in time it came to signify a tale-bearer or informer, in general; hence, a parasite; a mean flatterer; especially a flatterer of princes and great men; hence, a deceiver; an impostor. Its most general use is in the sense of an obsequious flatterer or parasite.

Encyc.   Potter's Antiq.

SYNERGETIC, *a.* Cooperating.   *Dean Tucker.*

T

TAG, *n.* A play in which the person gains who tags, that is, touches another. This was a common sport among boys in Connecticut formerly, and it may be still. The word is inserted here for the sake of the evidence it affords of the affinity of languages, and of the original orthography of the Latin *tango*, to touch, which was *tago*. This vulgar *tag* is the same word; the primitive word retained by the common people. It is used also as a verb, to *tag*.

TALLY, *n.* 1. A piece of wood on which notches or scores are cut, as the marks of number. In purchasing and selling, it is customary for traders to have two sticks, or one stick cleft into two parts, and to mark with a score or notch on each, the number or quantity of goods delivered; the seller keeping one stick, and the purchaser the other. Before the use of writing, this or something like it was the only method of keeping accounts, and *tallies* are received as evidence in courts of justice. In the English exchequer are *tallies* of loans, one part being kept in the exchequer, the other being given to the creditor in lieu of an obligation for money lent to government. *Cyc.*

TARANTULA, *n.* A species of spider, the *Aranea tarantula*, so called, it is said, from Tarentum in Apulia, where this animal is mostly found; a venomous insect, whose bite gives name to a new disease, called *tarantismus*. This is said to be cured by music.

TASKMASTER, *n.* One who imposes a task, or burdens with labor. Sinful propensities and appetites are men's most unrelenting *taskmasters*. They condemn us to unceasing drudgery, and reward us with pain, remorse and poverty. Next to our sinful propensities, fashion is the most oppressive *taskmaster*.

TASTE, *n.* 3. The sense by which we perceive the relish of a thing. This sense appears to reside in the tongue or its papillæ. Men have a great variety of *tastes*. In the influenza of 1790, the *taste*, for some days, was entirely extinguished.

TATTOO, *v.t.* [In the South Sea isles.] To prick the skin, and stain the punctured spots with a black substance, forming lines and figures upon the body.

259

In some isles, the inhabitants *tattoo* the face, in others only the body. The same practice exists among other rude nations.   *Barrow.   Makenzie.*

TAVERNER, TAVERN-KEEPER, *n.* One who keeps a tavern. In the United States, one who is licensed to sell liquors to be drank in his house, and to entertain travelers and lodgers, together with the horses or oxen composing their teams. *Taverners* are by law to be provided with suitable beds for their guests, and with fodder for horses and cattle.   *Laws of Conn.*

TAX, *v.t.* 1. To lay, impose or assess upon citizens a certain sum of money to be paid to the public treasury, or to the treasury of a corporation or company, to defray the expenses of the government or corporation, &c.

> We are more heavily *taxed* by our idleness, pride and folly, than we are *taxed* by government.   *Franklin.*

TAXATION, *n.* A taxing; the act of laying a tax, or of imposing taxes on the subjects of a state by government, or on the members of a corporation or company by the proper authority. *Taxation* is probably the most difficult subject of legislation.

TEA, *n.* 2. A decoction or infusion of tea leaves in boiling water. *Tea* is a refreshing beverage.

TEAM, *n.* 1. Two or more horses, oxen or other beasts harnessed together to the same vehicle for drawing, as to a coach, chariot, wagon, cart, sled, sleigh and the like. It has been a great question whether *teams* of horses or oxen are most advantageously employed in agriculture. In land free from stones and stumps and of easy tillage, it is generally agreed that horses are preferable for *teams*.

TEAM-WORK, *n.* Work done by a team, as distinguished from personal labor.   *New England.*

TEASE, *v.t.* 3. To vex with importunity or impertinence; to harass, annoy, disturb or irritate by petty requests, or by jests and raillery. Parents are often *teased* by their children into unreasonable compliances.

TELEGRAPH. The artist-inventor Samuel F. B. Morse, who painted the portrait of Webster that still graces Merriam-Webster's dictionaries, perfected his own version of the electric telegraph in 1844. ☞

TELEGRAPH, *n.* A machine for communicating intelligence from a distance by various signals or movements previously agreed on; which signals represent letters, words or ideas which can be transmitted from one station to another, as far as the signals can be seen. This machine was invented by the French about the year 1793 or 1794, and is now adopted by other nations.   *Cyc.*

TELESCOPE, *n.* An optical instrument employed in viewing distant objects, as the heavenly bodies. It assists the eye chiefly in two ways; first, by enlarging the visual angle under which a distant object is seen, and thus magnifying that object; and secondly, by collecting and conveying to the eye a larger beam of light than would enter the naked organ, and thus rendering objects distinct and visible which would otherwise be indistinct or invisible. Its essential parts are the *object glass,* which collects the beam of light and forms an image of the object, and the *eye glass,* which is a microscope by which the image is magnified.   *D. Olmsted.*

TEMPERATE, *a.* 2. Moderate in the indulgence of the appetites and passions; as *temperate* in eating and drinking; *temperate* in pleasures; *temperate* in speech.

    Be sober and *temperate,* and you will be healthy.   *Franklin.*

TEMPEST, *n.* 1. An extensive current of wind, rushing with great velocity and violence; a storm of extreme violence. We usually apply the word to a steady wind of long continuance; but we say also of a tornado, it blew a *tempest.* The currents of wind are named, according to their respective degrees of force or rapidity, a *breeze,* a *gale,* a *storm,* a *tempest;* but *gale* is also used as synonymous with *storm,* and *storm* with *tempest. Gust* is usually applied to a sudden blast of short duration. A tempest may or may not be attended with rain, snow or hail.

TEMPT, *v.t.* 1. To incite or solicit to an evil act; to entice to something wrong by presenting arguments that are plausible or convincing, or by the offer of some pleasure or apparent advantage as the inducement.

TERRITORY, *n.* 2. A tract of land belonging to and under the dominion of a prince or state, lying at a distance from the parent country or from the seat of government; as the *territories* of the East India Company; the *territories* of the United States; the *territory* of Michigan; Northwest *territory.* These districts of country, when received into the union and acknowledged to be states, lose the appellation of *territory.*   *Constitution of the U. States.*

TEST, *v.t.* To compare with a standard; to try; to prove the truth or genuineness of any thing by experiment or by some fixed principle or standard; as, to *test* the soundness of a principle; to *test* the validity of an argument.

    Experience is the surest standard by which to *test* the real tendency of the existing constitution.   *Washington's Address.*
    To *test* this position—   *Hamilton, Rep.*
    In order to *test* the correctness of this system—   *Adams' Lect.*

TESTICLE, *n.* The testicles are male organs of generation, consisting of glandular substances, whose office is to secrete the fecundating fluid. *Cyc.*

TEXT-BOOK, *n.* In *universities* and *colleges,* a classic author written with wide spaces between the lines, to give room for the observations or interpretation dictated by the master or regent.   *Cyc.*

2. A book containing the leading principles or most important points of a science or branch of learning, arranged in order for the use of students.

THEFT, *n.* The act of stealing. In *law*, the private, unlawful, felonious taking of another person's goods or movables, with an intent to steal them. To constitute *theft*, the taking must be in private or without the owner's knowledge, and it must be unlawful or felonious, that is, it must be with a design to deprive the owner of his property privately and against his will. Theft differs from *robbery*, as the latter is a violent taking from the person, and of course not private.

THEORY, *n.* 1. Speculation; a doctrine or scheme of things, which terminates in speculation or contemplation, without a view to practice. It is here taken in an unfavorable sense, as implying something visionary.
2. An exposition of the general principles of any science; as the *theory* of music.
3. The science distinguished from the art; as the *theory* and practice of medicine.
4. The philosophical explanation of phenomena, either physical or moral; as Lavoisier's *theory* of combustion; Smith's *theory* of moral sentiments.
Theory is distinguished from *hypothesis* thus; a theory is founded on inferences drawn from principles which have been established on independent evidence; a hypothesis is a proposition assumed to account for certain phenomena, and has no other evidence of its truth, than that it affords a satisfactory explanation of those phenomena.   *D. Olmsted*

THIRDS, *n. plu.* The third part of the estate of a deceased husband, which by law the widow is entitled to enjoy during her life.   *N. England.*

THUMB, THUM, *n.* The short thick finger of the human hand, or the corresponding member of other animals. [The common orthography is corrupt. The real word is *thum.*]

THUNDER-STORM, *n.* A storm accompanied with lightning and thunder. Thunder clouds are often driven by violent winds. In America, the violence of the wind at the commencement, is sometimes equal to that of a hurricane, and at this time the explosions of electricity are the most terrible. This violence of the wind seldom continues longer than a few minutes, and after this subsides, the rain continues, but the peals of thunder are less frequent. These violent showers sometimes continue for hours; more generally, they are of shorter duration.

TICKET, *n.* 3. A piece of paper bearing some number in a lottery, which entitles the owner to receive such prize as may be drawn against that number.

When it draws no prize, it is said to draw a blank, and the holder has nothing to receive.

TICKLE, *v.t.* 2. To please by slight gratification. A glass of wine may *tickle* the palate.

TIGER, *n.* A fierce and rapacious animal of the genus Felis, (*F. tigris;*) one of the largest and most terrible of the genus, inhabiting Africa and Asia. The American tiger is the *Felis onça.* There is also the tiger cat or *Felis capensis.*

TILLAGE, *n.* The operation, practice or art of preparing land for seed, and keeping the ground free from weeds which might impede the growth of crops. Tillage includes manuring, plowing, harrowing and rolling land, or whatever is done to bring it to a proper state to receive the seed, and the operations of plowing, harrowing and hoeing the ground, to destroy weeds and loosen the soil after it is planted; culture; a principal branch of agriculture. *Tillage* of the earth is the principal as it was the first occupation of man, and no employment is more honorable.

TIMBER, *n.* 1. That sort of wood which is proper for buildings or for tools, utensils, furniture, carriages, fences, ships and the like. We apply the word to standing trees which are suitable for the uses above mentioned, as a forest contains excellent *timber;* or to the beams, rafters, scantling, boards, planks, &c. hewed or sawed from such trees. Of all the species of trees useful as *timber,* in our climate, the white oak and the white pine hold the first place in importance.

TIME, *n.* 1. A particular portion or part of duration, whether past, present or future. The *time* was; the *time* has been; the *time* is; the *time* will be.
    Lost *time* is never found again.   *Franklin.*

TIN, *n.* 1. A white metal, with a slight tinge of yellow. It is soft, non-elastic, very malleable, and when a bar of it is bent near the ear, distinguished by a crackling sound called the *cry* of tin. It is used for culinary vessels, being for this purpose usually combined with lead, forming *pewter;* and alloyed with small proportions of antimony, copper and bismuth, is formed into various wares resembling silver, under the names of *block-tin, brittania,* &c. Equal parts of tin and lead compose *soder.* Tin united with copper in different proportions, forms *bronze, bell-metal,* and *speculum-metal.*
                                                                    D. Olmsted.

TIPPLE, *v.i.* To drink spiritous or strong liquors habitually; to indulge in the frequent and improper use of spiritous liquors. When a man begins to *tipple,* let his creditors secure their debts.

TIT, *n.* A small horse, *in contempt;* a woman, *in contempt;* a small bird; a titmouse or tomtit.

TOAD, *n.* A paddoc, an animal of the genus Rana, the *Rana Bufo* of Linne; a small clumsy animal, the body warty, thick and disgusting to the sight, but perfectly harmless, and indeed it is said to be useful in gardens by feeding on noxious worms.

TOBACCO. Webster's etymology is apocryphal.

TOBACCO, *n.* [so named from *Tabaco,* a province of Yucatan, in Spanish America, where it was first found by the Spaniards.] A plant, native of America, of the genus Nicotiana, much used for smoking and chewing and in snuff. As a medicine, it is narcotic. Tobacco has a strong disagreeable smell, and an acrid taste. When first used it sometimes occasions vomiting; but the practice of using it in any form, soon conquers distaste, and forms a relish for it that is strong and almost unconquerable.

TOILET, *n.* 1. A covering or cloth of linen, silk or tapestry, spread over a table in a chamber or dressing room. Hence,
    2. A dressing table.   *Pope.*

TOKAY, *n.* A kind of wine produced at Tokay in Hungary, made of white grapes. It is distinguished from other wines by its aromatic taste. It is not good till it is about three years old, and it continues to improve as long as it is kept.

TOLERABLE, *a.* That may be borne or endured; supportable, either physically or mentally. The cold in Canada is severe, but *tolerable.* The insults and indignities of our enemies are not *tolerable.*

TOLERATION, *n.* The act of tolerating; the allowance of that which is not wholly approved; appropriately, the allowance of religious opinions and modes of worship in a state, when contrary to or different from those of the established church or belief.
    Toleration implies a right in the sovereign to control men in their opinions and worship, or it implies the actual exercise of power in such control. Where no power exists or none is assumed to establish a creed and a mode of worship, there can be no *toleration,* in the strict sense of the word, for one religious denomination has as good a right as another to the free enjoyment of its creed and worship.

TOLL-HOUSE, *n.* A house or shed placed by a road near a toll-gate, or at the end of a toll-bridge, or by a canal, where the man who takes the toll remains.

TO-MORROW, *n.* The day after the present.
    One to-day is worth two *to-morrows.*   *Franklin.*

TONGUE, TUNG, *n.* 5. A language; the whole sum of words used by a particular nation. The English tongue, within two hundred years, will probably be spoken by two or three hundred millions of people in North America.

TOPPING, *a.* 2. Fine; gallant.   *Johnson.*
[*But Johnson's definition is probably incorrect.*]
3. Proud; assuming superiority. [*This is the sense in which the common people of N. England use the word, and I believe the true sense, but it is not elegant.*]

TORNADO, *n.* A violent gust of wind, or a tempest, distinguished by a whirling motion. Tornadoes of this kind happen after extreme heat, and sometimes in the United States, rend up fences and trees, and in a few instances have overthrown houses and torn them to pieces. Tornadoes are usually accompanied with severe thunder, lightning and torrents of rain; but they are of short duration, and narrow in breadth.

TORPEDO, *n.* [L. from *torpeo*, to be numb.] The cramp fish or electric ray, *Raia torpedo.* This fish is usually taken in forty fathoms water, on the coast of France and England, and in the Mediterranean. A touch of this fish occasions a numbness in the limb, accompanied with an indescribable and painful sensation, and is really an electric shock. When dead, the fish loses its power of producing this sensation.   *Cyc.*

TORTURE, *n.* 2. Severe pain inflicted judicially, either as a punishment for a crime, or for the purpose of extorting a confession from an accused person. Torture may be and is inflicted in a variety of ways, as by water or fire, or by the boot or thumbkin. But the most usual mode is by the rack or wheel.
                                                            Paley.   Cyc.

TORY, *n.* [said to be an Irish word, denoting a robber; perhaps from *tor*, a bush, as the Irish banditti lived in the mountains or among trees.] The name given to an adherent to the ancient constitution of England and to the apostolical hierarchy. The tories form a party which are charged with supporting more arbitrary principles in government than the whigs, their opponents.
    In America, during the revolution, those who opposed the war, and favored the claims of Great Britain, were called *tories.*

TOTE, *v.t.* To carry or convey. [*A word used in slaveholding countries; said to have been introduced by the blacks.*]

TOWN-HOUSE, *n.* The house where the public business of the town is transacted by the inhabitants in legal meeting.   *New England.*

TORPEDO. Webster must have known about Robert Fulton's 1805 invention of the weapon. He drew his information about the fish from the three-page entry in Rees's *Cyclopaedia;* had Webster not stopped reading before the final paragraph he would have been reminded of Fulton and his explosive device.

T

TRACK, *n.* 2. A mark or impression left by the foot, either of man or beast. Savages are said to be wonderfully sagacious in finding the *tracks* of men in the forest.

TRADE-WIND, *n.* A wind that favors trade. A trade wind is a wind that blows constantly in the same direction, or a wind that blows for a number of months in one direction, and then changing, blows as long in the opposite direction. These winds in the East Indies are called *monsoons*, which are periodical. On the Atlantic, within the tropics, the trade winds blow constantly from the eastward to the westward.

TRADITION, *n.* 3. That which is handed down from age to age by oral communication. The Jews pay great regard to *tradition* in matters of religion, as do the Romanists. Protestants reject the authority of *tradition* in sacred things, and rely only on the written word. *Traditions* may be good or bad, true or false.

TRAJECTORY, *n.* The orbit of a comet; the path described by a comet in its motion, which Dr. Halley supposes to be elliptical.   *Cyc.*

TRANSIT, *n.* 2. In *astronomy,* the passing of one heavenly body over the disk of another and larger. I witnessed the *transit* of Venus over the sun's disk, June 3, 1769. When a smaller body passes behind a larger, it is said to suffer an *occultation.*

TRANSPORTATION, *n.* The act of carrying or conveying from one place to another, either on beasts or in vehicles, by land or water, or in air. Goods in Asia are *transported* on camels; in Europe and America, either on beasts or on carriages or sleds. But *transportation* by water is the great means of commercial intercourse.

TRAVEL, *v.i.* 1. To walk; to go or march on foot; as, to *travel* from London to Dover, or from New York to Philadelphia. So we say, a man ordinarily *travels* three miles an hour. [This is the proper sense of the word, which implies *toil.*]
2. To journey; to ride to a distant place in the same country; as, a man *travels* for his health; he is *traveling* to Virginia. A man *traveled* from London to Edinburgh in five days.
3. To go to a distant country, or to visit foreign states or kingdoms, either by sea or land. It is customary for men of rank and property to *travel* for improvement. Englishmen *travel* to France and Italy. Some men *travel* for pleasure or curiosity; others *travel* to extend their knowledge of natural history.

TREACHERY, *n.* Violation of allegiance or of faith and confidence. The man who betrays his country in any manner, violates his allegiance, and is guilty of *treachery.* This is treason. The man who violates his faith pledged to his friend, or betrays a trust in which a promise of fidelity is implied, is guilty of *treachery.* The disclosure of a secret committed to one in confidence, is *treachery.* This is perfidy.

TRENCHER, *n.* A wooden plate. *Trenchers* were in use among the common people of New England till the revolution.

TRIBUTARY, *a.* Paying tribute to another, either from compulsion, as an acknowledgment of submission, or to secure protection, or for the purpose of purchasing peace. The republic of Ragusa is *tributary* to the grand seignor. Many of the powers of Europe are *tributary* to the Barbary states.

TRIBUTE, *n.* 1. An annual or stated sum of money or other valuable thing, paid by one prince or nation to another, either as an acknowledgment of submission, or as the price of peace and protection, or by virtue of some treaty. The Romans made all their conquered countries pay *tribute,* as do the Turks at this day; and in some countries the *tribute* is paid in children.   *Cyc.*

TRIUMPH, *n.* 1. Among *the ancient Romans,* a pompous ceremony performed in honor of a victorious general, who was allowed to enter the city crowned, originally with laurel, but in later times with gold, bearing a truncheon in one hand and a branch of laurel in the other, riding in a chariot drawn by two white horses, and followed by the kings, princes and generals whom he had vanquished, loaded with chains and insulted by mimics and buffoons. The triumph was of two kinds, the greater and the less. The lesser triumph was granted for a victory over enemies of less considerable power, and was called an *ovation.*

TROPHY, *n.* 1. Among *the ancients,* a pile of arms taken from a vanquished enemy, raised on the field of battle by the conquerors; also, the representation of such a pile in marble, on medals and the like; or according to others, trophies were trees planted in conspicuous places of the conquered provinces, and hung with the spoils of the enemy, in memory of the victory. Hence,
2. Any thing taken and preserved as a memorial of victory, as arms, flags, standards and the like, taken from an enemy.

TROT, *v.i.* 2. To work or move fast; or to run.
    He that rises late must *trot* all day, and will scarcely overtake his business at night.   *Franklin.*

TRUCK, *n.* 3. A small wheel; hence *trucks,* a low carriage for carrying goods, stone, &c. Indeed this kind of carriage is often called a *truck,* in the singular.

TRUCK, *v.i.* To exchange commodities; to barter. Our traders *truck* with the Indians, giving them whiskey and trinkets for skins. [*Truck* is now vulgar.]

TRIBUTARY. Ragusa is the modern Dubrovnik. It was an independent city-state from the fourteenth to the nineteenth century, the only Dalmatian town free of Venice. It retained most of its independence even when it came under Ottoman protection in 1481. Its governing rules included "it is better that a republic be governed by laws than by men."

T

TRUMPET, *n.* 1. A wind instrument of music, used chiefly in war and military exercises. It is very useful also at sea, in speaking with ships. There is a speaking trumpet, and a hearing trumpet. They both consist of long tubular bodies, nearly in the form of a parabolic conoid, with wide mouths.

TURBAN. Almost ☞ word for word from *Cyc.,* which adds: "The grand signor's turban is as big as a bushel, and is so exceedingly respected by the Turks that they dare scarce touch it."

TURBAN, *n.* A head dress worn by the orientals, consisting of a cap, and a sash of fine linen or taffeta artfully wound round it in plaits. The cap is red or green, roundish on the top, and quilted with cotton. The sash of the Turks is white linen; that of the Persians is red woolen.   *Cyc.*

TURKEY, TURKY, *n.* [As this fowl was not brought from Turkey, it would be more correct to write the name *turky.*] A large fowl, the Meleagris gallopavo, a distinct genus. It is a native of America, and its flesh furnishes most delicious food. Wild turkies abound in the forests of America, and domestic turkies are bred in other countries, as well as in America.

TURNPIKE, *n.* Strictly, a frame consisting of two bars crossing each other at right angles, and turning on a post or pin, to hinder the passage of beasts, but admitting a person to pass between the arms.
2. A gate set across a road to stop travelers and carriages till toll is paid for keeping the road in repair. 3. A turnpike road.

TUTOR, *n.* 3. In *universities* and *colleges,* an officer or member of some hall, who has the charge of instructing the students in the sciences and other branches of learning. In *the American colleges,* tutors are graduates selected by the governors or trustees, for the instruction of undergraduates of the three first years. They are usually officers of the institution, who have a share, with the president and professors, in the government of the students.

U

UMBREL, UMBRELLA, *n.* A shade, skreen or guard, carried in the hand for sheltering the person from the rays of the sun, or from rain or snow. It is formed of silk, cotton or other cloth extended on strips of elastic whalebone, inserted in or fastened to a rod or stick. [See *Parasol.*]

UMPIRE, *n.* 2. A person to whose sole decision a controversy or question between parties is referred. Thus the emperor of Russia was constituted *umpire* between Great Britain and the United States, to decide the controversy respecting the slaves carried from the states by the British troops.

UNCIVILIZED, *a.* Not reclaimed from savage life; as the *uncivilized* inhabitants of Canada or New Zealand.

UNCONSTITUTIONAL, a. Not agreeable to the constitution; not authorized by the constitution; contrary to the principles of the constitution. It is not *unconstitutional* for the king of Great Britain to declare war without the consent of parliament; but for the president of the United States to declare war, without an act of congress authorizing it, would be *unconstitutional.*

UNDER, *prep.* 11. In a state of liability or obligation. No man shall trespass but *under* the pains and penalties of the law. Attend to the conditions *under* which you enter upon your office. We are *under* the necessity of obeying the

---

U. Some modern writers make a distinction between the sound of *u*, when it follows *r*, as in *rude, truth*, and its sound when it follows other letters, as in *mute, duke;* making the former sound equivalent to *oo; rood, trooth;* and the latter a diphthong equivalent to *eu* or *yu*. This is a mischievous innovation, and not authorized by any general usage either in England or the United States.

laws. Nuns are *under* vows of chastity. We all lie *under* the curse of the law, until redeemed by Christ.

UNDERTAKING, *n.* Any business, work or project which a person engages in, or attempts to perform; an enterprise. The canal, or the making of the canal, from the Hudson to lake Erie, a distance of almost four hundred miles, was the greatest *undertaking* of the kind in modern times. The attempt to find a navigable passage to the Pacific round North America, is a hazardous *undertaking*, and probably useless to navigation.

UNDULATION, *n.* A waving motion or vibration; as the *undulations* of a fluid, of water or air; the *undulations* of sound. The *undulations* of a fluid are propagated in concentric circles.
    3. In music, a rattling or jarring of sounds, as when discordant notes are sounded together. It is called also *beat.*   *Cyc.*

UNICORN. John-
son wondered whether
it is "real or fabulous."

UNICORN, *n.* 1. An animal with one horn; the monoceros. This name is often applied to the rhinoceros.
    2. The *sea unicorn* is a fish of the whale kind, called narwal, remarkable for a horn growing out at his nose.   *Cyc.*

UNIVERSITY, *n.* An assemblage of colleges established in any place, with professors for instructing students in the sciences and other branches of learning, and where degrees are conferred. A university is properly a universal school, in which are taught all branches of learning, or the four faculties of theology, medicine, law, and the sciences and arts.   *Cyc.*

UNLEARN, *v.t.* To forget or lose what has been learned. It is most important to us all to *unlearn* the errors of our early education.

UNLOCATED, *a.* In *America,* unlocated lands are such new or wild lands as have not been surveyed, appropriated or designated by marks, limits or boundaries, to some individual, company or corporation.

UNPARALLELED, *a.* Having no parallel or equal; unequaled; unmatched.
         Addison.
    The *unparalleled* perseverance of the armies of the U. States, under every suffering and discouragement, was little short of a miracle.   *Washington.*

UNRULY, *a.* Disregarding restraint; licentious; disposed to violate laws; turbulent; ungovernable; as an *unruly* youth.
    2. Accustomed to break over fences and escape from inclosures; apt to break or leap fences; as an *unruly* ox.

UNSEASONABLE, *a.* Not agreeable to the time of the year; as an *unseasonable* frost. The frosts of 1816, in June, July and August, in New England, were considered *unseasonable,* as they were unusual.

URANIUM, *n.* A metal discovered in 1789 by Klaproth, in the mineral called pechblend. It is occasionally found native in uran-ocher and uran-mica; but more generally it is obtained from pechblend, in which it exists with iron, copper, lead, and sometimes with arsenic, cobalt and zink. *Henry.*

V

VACATION, *n.* 3. The intermission of the regular studies and exercises of a college or other seminary, when the students have a recess.

VACCINATION, *n.* The act, art or practice of inoculating persons with the cow-pox.

VACUUM, *n.* Space empty or devoid of all matter or body. Whether there is such a thing as an absolute *vacuum* in nature, is a question which has been much controverted. The Peripatetics assert that nature abhors a vacuum.
Torricellian vacuum, the vacuum produced by filling a tube with mercury, and allowing it to descend till it is counterbalanced by the weight of the atmosphere, as in the barometer invented by Torricelli.

VAGABOND, *n.* A vagrant; one who wanders from town to town or place to place, having no certain dwelling, or not abiding in it. By the laws of England and of the United States, *vagabonds* are liable to be taken up and punished.

VAIL, *n.* 2. A piece of thin cloth or silk stuff, used by females to hide their faces. In some eastern countries, certain classes of females never appear abroad without *vails*.

VALLEY, *n.* 2. A low extended plain, usually alluvial, penetrated or washed by a river. The valley of the Connecticut is remarkable for its fertility and beauty.

VAMPIRE, *n.* In *mythology*, an imaginary demon, which was fabled to suck the blood of persons during the night.
2. In *zoology*, a species of large bat, the *Vespertilio vampyrus* of Linne, called also the ternate bat. It inhabits Guinea, Madagascar, the E. India Isles, New Holland and New Caledonia. These animals fly in flocks, darkening the air by their numbers. It is said that this bat will insinuate his tongue into the vein of an animal imperceptibly, and suck his blood while asleep. This name is also given by Buffon to a species of large bat in South America, the *V. spectrum* of Linne.   *Cyc.*

273

VANITY, *n.* 7. Inflation of mind upon slight grounds; empty pride, inspired by an overweening conceit of one's personal attainments or decorations. Fops cannot be cured of their *vanity.*

VAPOR, *n.* 6. *Vapors,* a disease of nervous debility, in which a variety of strange images float in the brain, or appear as if visible. Hence hypochondriacal affections and spleen are called *vapors.*

VASE, *n.* 2. An ancient vessel dug out of the ground or from rubbish, and kept as a curiosity.

VATICAN, *n.* In Rome, the celebrated church of St. Peter; and also, a magnificent palace of the pope; situated at the foot of one of the seven hills on which Rome was built. Hence the phrase, the *thunders of the Vatican,* meaning the anathemas or denunciations of the pope.

VEHICLE, *n.* 1. That in which any thing is or may be carried; any kind of carriage moving on land, either on wheels or runners. This word comprehends coaches, chariots, gigs, sulkies, wagons, carts of every kind, sleighs and sleds. These are all *vehicles.* But the word is more generally applied to wheel carriages, and rarely I believe to water craft.
2. That which is used as the instrument of conveyance. Language is the *vehicle* which conveys ideas to others. Letters are *vehicles* of communication.
A simple style forms the best *vehicle* of thought to a popular assembly.
Wirt.

VENERATE, *v.t.* To regard with respect and reverence; to reverence; to revere. We *venerate* an old faithful magistrate; we *venerate* parents and elders; we *venerate* men consecrated to sacred offices. We *venerate* old age or gray hairs. We *venerate,* or ought to *venerate,* the gospel and its precepts.

VENGEANCE, *n.* The infliction of pain on another, in return for an injury or offense. Such infliction, when it proceeds from malice or mere resentment, and is not necessary for the purposes of justice, is revenge, and a most hainous crime. When such infliction proceeds from a mere love of justice, and the necessity of punishing offenders for the support of the laws, it is *vengeance,* and is warrantable and just. In this case, vengeance is a just retribution, recompense or punishment. In this latter sense the word is used in Scripture, and frequently applied to the punishments inflicted by God on sinners.

VENISON, *n.* The flesh of beasts of game, or of such wild animals as are taken in the chase. It is however, in the United States, applied exclusively to the flesh of the deer or cervine genus of animals.

VERNACULAR, *a.* [L. *vernaculus,* born in one's house, from *verna,* a servant.] 1. Native; belonging to the country of one's birth. English is our *vernacular* language. The *vernacular* idiom is seldom perfectly acquired by foreigners.

VERSIFICATION, *n.* The act, art or practice of composing poetic verse. Versification is the result of art, labor and rule, rather than of invention or the fire of genius. It consists in adjusting the long and short syllables, and forming feet into harmonious measure. *Cyc.*

VESTIBULE, *n.* 3. An apartment in large buildings, which presents itself into a hall or suit of rooms or offices. An area in which a magnificent staircase is carried up is sometimes called a *vestibule.*

VETO, *n.* A forbidding; prohibition; or the right of forbidding; applied to the right of a king or other magistrate or officer to withhold his assent to the enactment of a law, or the passing of a decree. Thus the king of Great Britain has a veto upon every act of parliament; he sometimes prevents the passing of a law by his *veto.*

VIBRATION, *n.* 2. In *mechanics,* a regular reciprocal motion of a body suspended; a motion consisting of continual reciprocations or returns; as of the pendulum of a chronometer. This is frequently called *oscillation.* The number of *vibrations* in a given time depends on the length of the vibrating body; a pendulum three feet long, makes only ten *vibrations* while one of nine inches makes twenty. The *vibrations* of a pendulum are somewhat slower at or near the equator than in remote latitudes. The *vibrations* of a pendulum are isochronal in the same climate. *Cyc.*
3. In *physics,* alternate or reciprocal motion; as the *vibrations* of the nervous fluid, by which sensation has been supposed to be produced, by impressions of external objects propagated thus to the brain. *Cyc.*
4. In *music,* the motion of a chord, or the undulation of any body, by which sound is produced. The acuteness, elevation and gravity of sound, depend on the length of the chord and its tension.

VICE, *n.* 1. Properly, a spot or defect; a fault; a blemish; as the *vices* of a political constitution. *Madison.*
2. In *ethics,* any voluntary action or course of conduct which deviates from the rules of moral rectitude, or from the plain rules of propriety; any moral unfitness of conduct, either from defect of duty, or from the transgression of known principles of rectitude. *Vice* differs from *crime,* in being less enormous. We never call murder or robbery a *vice;* but every act of intemperance, all falsehood, duplicity, deception, lewdness and the like, is a *vice.* The excessive indulgence of passions and appetites which in themselves are

innocent, is a *vice*. The smoking of tobacco and the taking of snuff, may in certain cases be innocent and even useful, but these practices may be carried to such an excess as to become *vices*. This word is also used to denote a habit of transgressing; as a life of *vice*. *Vice* is rarely a solitary invader; it usually brings with it a frightful train of followers.

VICEGERENT, *n.* A lieutenant; a vicar; an officer who is deputed by a superior or by proper authority to exercise the powers of another. Kings are sometimes called God's *vicegerents*. It is to be wished they would always deserve the appellation.

VICTUALS, *n.* [. . . This word is now never used in the singular.] Food for human beings, prepared for eating; that which supports human life; provisions; meat; sustenance. We never apply this word to that on which beasts or birds feed, and we apply it chiefly to food for men when cooked or prepared for the table. We do not now give this name to flesh, corn or flour, in a crude state; but we say, the *victuals* are well cooked or dressed, and in great abundance. We say, a man eats his *victuals* with a good relish.

Such phrases as to buy *victuals* for the army or navy, to lay in *victuals* for the winter, &c. are now obsolete. We say, to buy *provisions;* yet we use the verb, to *victual* an army or ship.

VIEW, *v.t.* 1. To survey; to examine with the eye; to look on with attention, or for the purpose of examining; to inspect; to explore. *View* differs from *look, see,* and *behold,* in expressing more particular or continued attention to the thing which is the object of sight. We ascended mount Holyoke, and *viewed* the charming landscape below. We *viewed* with delight the rich valleys of the Connecticut about the town of Northampton.

VIGILANCE, *n.* 2. Watchfulness; circumspection; attention of the mind in discovering and guarding against danger, or providing for safety. *Vigilance* is a virtue of prime importance in a general. The *vigilance* of the dog is no less remarkable than his fidelity.

VIOLIN, *n.* A musical instrument with four strings, played with a bow; a fiddle; one of the most perfect and most powerful instruments that has been invented.   *Cyc.*

VIS-A-VIS, *n.* A carriage in which two persons sit face to face.

VISCERA, *n.* The bowels or intestines; the contents of the abdomen and thorax. In its most general sense, tbe organs contained in any cavity of the body, particularly in the three venters, the head, thorax and abdomen.
                                                                            Cyc.   Parr.

VISIT, *v.i.* To keep up the interchange of civilities and salutations; to practice going to see others. We ought not to *visit* for pleasure or ceremony on the Sabbath.

VISIT, *n.* 2. The act of going to see; as a *visit* to Saratoga or to Niagara.

VITIATE, *v.t.* 1. To injure the substance or qualities of a thing, so as to impair or spoil its use and value. Thus we say, luxury *vitiates* the humors of the body; evil examples *vitiate* the morals of youth; language is *vitiated* by foreign idioms.

VOCABULARY, *n.* A list or collection of the words of a language, arranged in alphabetical order and explained; a dictionary or lexicon. We often use *vocabulary* in a sense somewhat different from that of *dictionary,* restricting the signification to the list of words; as when we say, the *vocabulary* of Johnson is more full or extensive than that of Entick. We rarely use the word as synonymous with *dictionary,* but in the other countries the corresponding word is so used, and this may be so used in English.

VOLCANO, *n.* In *geology,* an opening in the surface of the earth or in a mountain, from which smoke, flames, stones, lava or other substances are ejected. Such are seen in Etna and Vesuvius in Sicily and Italy, and Hecla in Iceland. It is vulgarly called a *burning mountain.* Herschel has discovered a *volcano* in the moon.

VOLTAISM, *n.* [from *Volta,* an Italian.] That branch of electrical science which has its source in the chimical action between metals and different liquids. It is more properly called *galvanism,* from Galvani, who first proved or brought into notice its remarkable influence on animals.

VOLUME, *n.* [Fr. from L. *volumen,* a roll; *volvo,* to roll. To make *u* long, in this word, is palpably wrong.] 1. Primarily a roll, as the ancients wrote on long strips of bark, parchment or other material, which they formed into rolls or folds. Of such volumes, Ptolemy's library in Alexandria contained 3 or 700,000.

5. A book; a collection of sheets of paper, usually printed or written paper, folded and bound, or covered. A book consisting of sheets once folded, is called a folio, or a folio *volume;* of sheets twice folded, a quarto; and thus according to the number of leaves in a sheet, it is called an octavo, or a duodecimo. The Scriptures or sacred writings, bound in a single *volume,* are called the Bible. The number of *volumes* in the Royal Library, in Rue de Richlieu, at Paris, is variously estimated. It is probable it may amount to 400,000.

An odd *volume* of a set of books, bears not the value of its proportion to the set. *Franklin.*

VOCABULARY. John Entick (c. 1703–73) came out with *The New Spelling Dictionary* in 1765. A fifth edition was published in 1812.

V

VOLUNTARY. ☞ The "method of writing voluntaries," impossible to imagine from this definition, is described clearly in *Cyc*.

VOLUNTARY, *n.* 2. In *music*, a piece played by a musician extemporarily, according to his fancy. In the Philosophical Transactions, we have a method of writing *voluntaries*, as fast as the musician plays the notes. This is by a cylinder turning under the keys of the organ. *Cyc.*

VOMIT, *v.i.* To eject the contents of the stomach by the mouth. Some persons vomit with ease, as do cats and dogs. But horses do not vomit. *Cyc.*

VORTEX, *n.* 3. In *the Cartesian system*, the circular motion originally impressed on the particles of matter, carrying them around their own axes, and around a common center. By means of these *vortices*, Descartes attempted to account for the formation of the universe.

VOTE, *v.i.* To express or signify the mind, will or preference, in electing men to office, or in passing laws, regulations and the like, or in deciding on any proposition in which one has an interest with others. In elections, men are bound to vote for the best men to fill offices, according to their best knowledge and belief.

To *vote* for a duelist, is to assist in the prostration of justice, and indirectly to encourage the crime. *L. Beecher.*

VOYAGE, *n.* A passing by sea or water from one place, port or country to another, especially a passing or journey by water to a distant place or country. Captain L. made more than a hundred *voyages* to the West Indies. A *voyage* over lake Superior is like a voyage to Bermuda.

W

WAGES, *n.* Hire; reward; that which is paid or stipulated for services, but chiefly for services by manual labor, or for military and naval services. We speak of servant's *wages,* a laborer's *wages,* or soldier's *wages;* but we never apply the word to the rewards given to men in office, which are called *fees* or *salary.* The word is however sometimes applied to the compensation given to representatives in the legislature.   [*U. States.*]

WAGON, *n.* [. . . The old orthography, *waggon,* seems to be falling into disuse]. 1. A vehicle moved on four wheels, and usually drawn by horses; used for the transportation of heavy commodities. In America, light wagons are used for the conveyance of families, and for carrying light commodities to market, particularly a very light kind drawn by one horse.

WAGON, *v.i.* To practice the transportation of goods in a wagon. The man *wagons* between Philadelphia and Pittsburg.

WAISTCOAT, *n.* A short coat or garment for men, extending no lower than the hips, and covering the waist; a vest. This under garment is now generally called in America a *vest.*

WAITS, *n.* 2. Nocturnal musicians who attended great men.   *Cyc.*

WALK, *v.i.* [Sax. *wealcan,* to roll or revolve; *wealcere,* a fuller, whence the name *Walker;* D. *walken,* to work a hat; G. *walken,* to full, to felt hats. . . . The primary sense is simply to move or press, but appropriately to roll, to press

---

W. The name, *double u,* being given to it from its form or constitution, and not from its sound, ought not to be retained. Every letter should be named from its sound, especially the vowels. [cf. Webster's entry for DIGAMMA].

279

by rolling, as in hatting, and this is the origin of *walker*, for the practice of felting hats must have preceded that of fulling cloth in mills. Our ancestors appropriated the verb to moving on the feet, and the word is peculiarly expressive of that rolling or wagging motion which marks the walk of clownish people.] 1. To move slowly on the feet; to step slowly along; to advance by steps moderately repeated; as animals. Walking in men differs from running only in the rapidity and length of the steps; but in quadrupeds, the motion or order of the feet is sometimes changed.

WALKING-STAFF, WALKING-STICK, *n.* A staff or stick carried in the hand for support or amusement in walking.

WALLOP, *v.i.* To boil with a continued bubbling or heaving and rolling of the liquor, with noise.

WALNUT, *n.* A tree and its fruit, of the genus Juglans. The black walnut, so called, grows in America, and is indigenous in the southern and middle states, as far north as the river Hudson. That is said to be the limit of its indigenous growth, but when transplanted, it grows well in the eastern states. In America there are several species of hickory nut, called by this name.

WALTZ, *n.* A modern dance and tune, the measure of whose music is triple; three quavers in a bar.   *Busby.*

WAMPUM, *n.* Shells or strings of shells, used by the American Indians as money or a medium of commerce. These strings of shells when united, form a broad belt, which is worn as an ornament or girdle. It is sometimes called wampumpeague, and wompeague, or wampampeague, of which *wampum* seems to be a contraction.   *Winthrop.   Gookin.*

WANTON. The ☞ allusion to "wanton boys" killing flies is Shakespearean, and quoted by Johnson. Webster does not acknowledge this.

WANTON, *a.* 1. Wandering or roving in gayety or sport; sportive; frolicksome; darting aside, or one way and the other. *Wanton* boys kill flies for sport.

WAPPE, *n.* A species of cur, said to be so called from his voice. His only use is to alarm the family by barking when any person approaches the house.   *Cyc.*

WAR, *n.* 1. A contest between nations or states, carried on by force, either for defense, or for revenging insults and redressing wrongs, for the extension of commerce or acquisition of territory, or for obtaining and establishing the superiority and dominion of one over the other. These objects are accomplished by the slaughter or capture of troops, and the capture and destruction of ships, towns and property. Among rude nations, war is often waged and carried on for plunder. As war is the contest of nations or states, it always implies that such contest is authorized by the monarch or the sovereign power of the nation. When war is commenced by attacking a nation in peace, it is called an *offensive* war, and such attack is *aggressive*. When war is undertaken to repel invasion or the attacks of an enemy, it is called *defensive*, and a defensive war is considered as justifiable. Very few of the wars that have desolated nations and deluged the earth with blood, have been justifiable. Happy would it be for mankind, if the prevalence of christian principles might ultimately extinguish the spirit of war, and if the ambition to be great, might yield to the ambition of being good.

Preparation for *war* is sometimes the best security for peace.—*Anon.*

Holy war, a crusade; a war undertaken to deliver the Holy Land, or Judea, from infidels. These *holy wars* were carried on by most unholy means.

WARBLER, *n.* 2. The common name of a genus of small birds (*Sylvia,*) comprising most of the small woodland songsters of Europe and N. America. They feed on insects and are very lively and active. The blue-bird is a species of the genus.   *Ed. Encyc.   Wilson.*

WARP, *v.i.* 3. To fly with a bending or waving motion; to turn and wave, like a flock of birds or insects. The following use of *warp* is inimitably beautiful.
As when the potent rod
Of Amram's son, in Egypt's evil day,
Wav'd round the coast, up called a pitchy cloud
Of locusts, *warping* on the eastern wind—   *Milton.*

WARP. Webster is rarely smitten by a poet's language. He appears never to have been overwhelmed by music or by art.

WARRANT, *v.t.* 1. To authorize; to give authority or power to do or forbear any thing, by which the person authorized is secured or saved harmless from any loss or damage by the act. A commission *warrants* an officer to seize an enemy. We are not *warranted* to resist legitimate government, except in extreme cases.

WASTE, *v.t.* 3. To expend without necessity or use; to destroy wantonly or luxuriously; to squander; to cause to be lost through wantonness or negligence. Careless people *waste* their fuel, their food or their property. Children *waste* their inheritance.

WATER, *n.* A fluid, the most abundant and most necessary for living beings of any in nature, except air. Water when pure, is colorless, destitute of taste and smell, ponderous, transparent, and in a very small degree compressible. It is reposited in the earth in inexhaustible quantities, where it is preserved fresh and cool, and from which it issues in springs, which form streams and rivers. But the great reservoirs of water on the globe are the ocean, seas and lakes, which cover more than three fifths of its surface, and from which it is raised by evaporation, and uniting with the air in the state of vapor, is wafted over the earth, ready to be precipitated in the form of rain, snow or hail.

W

Water by the abstraction or loss of heat, becomes solid, or in other words, is converted into ice or snow; and by heat it is converted into steam, an elastic vapor, one of the most powerful agents in nature. Modern chimical experiments prove that water is a compound substance, consisting of a combination of oxygen and hydrogen gases, or rather the bases or ponderable matter of those gases; or about two volumes or measures of hydrogen gas and one of oxygen gas. The proportion of the ingredients in weight, is nearly 85 parts of oxygen to 15 of hydrogen.   *Lavoisier.   Vauquelin.   Fourcroy.*

Milky way, in *astronomy,* the galaxy; a broad luminous belt or space in the heavens, supposed to be occasioned by the blended light of an immense number of stars. By means of a telescope of uncommon magnifying powers, Dr. Herschel has been able to ascertain this fact, by distinguishing the stars.

WEIGHT, *n.* 1. The quantity of a body, ascertained by the balance; in a philosophical sense, that quality of bodies by which they tend towards the center of the earth in a line perpendicular to its surface. In short, weight is gravity, and the weight of a particular body is the amount of its gravity, or of the force with which it tends to the center. The weight of a body is in direct proportion to its quantity of matter.   *Newton.*
2. A mass of iron, lead, brass or other metal, to be used for ascertaining the weight of other bodies; as a *weight* of an ounce, a pound, a quarter of a hundred, &c. The *weights* of nations are different, except those of England and the United States, which are the same.

WENCH, *n.* 2. A young woman of ill fame.   *Prior.*
3. In *America,* a black or colored female servant; a negress.

WEST, *n.* 2. A country situated in the region towards the sun-setting, with respect to another. Thus in the United States, the inhabitants of the Atlantic states speak of the inhabitants of Ohio, Kentucky or Missouri, and call them people of the *west;* and formerly, the empire of Rome was called the empire of the *West,* in opposition to the empire of the *East,* the seat of which was Constantinople.

WHARF, *n.* A perpendicular bank or mound of timber or stone and earth, raised on the shore of a harbor, or extending some distance into the water, for the convenience of lading and unlading ships and other vessels. This name is also given to the wider part of a canal, where boats lie while loading and unloading. The two longest *wharfs* in New England are at Boston and at New Haven. The latter is much the longest, extending into the harbor about three quarters of a mile.

WHEN. Webster had hoped to meet Lafayette as he left France for America, but could only catch a glimpse of him.   ☞

WHEN, *adv.* 1. At the time. We were present *when* Gen. La Fayette embarked at Havre for New York.

WHIG, *n.* [origin uncertain.] One of a political party which had its origin in England in the seventeenth century, in the reign of Charles I. or II., when great contests existed respecting the royal prerogatives and the rights of the people. Those who supported the king in his high claims, were called *tories*, and the advocates of popular rights were called *whigs*. During the revolution in the United States, the friends and supporters of the war and the principles of the revolution, were called *whigs*, and those who opposed them, were called *tories* and *royalists*.

    Where then, when *tories* scarce get clear,
    Shall *whigs* and congresses appear?   *M'Fingal.*

WHIPPOWIL, *n.* The popular name of an American bird, so called from its note, or the sounds of its voice. [Not *whip-poor-will.*]

WHIRLIGIG, *n.* A toy which children spin or whirl round.   *Johnson.*
    2. In *military antiquities,* an instrument for punishing petty offenders, as sutlers, brawling women, &c.; a kind of wooden cage turning on a pivot, in which the offender was whirled round with great velocity.   *Cyc.*

WHIRLING-TABLE, *n.* A machine contrived to exhibit and demonstrate the principal laws of gravitation, and of the planetary motions in curvilinear orbits.   *Cyc.*

WHISPER. v.i. 1. To speak with a low hissing or sibilant voice. It is ill manners to *whisper* in company.

WHIST, *n.* A game at cards, so called because it requires silence or close attention. It is not in America pronounced *whisk.*

WHITTLE, *v.t.* To pare or cut the surface of a thing with a small knife. Some persons have a habit of *whittling,* and are rarely seen without a penknife in their hands for that purpose. [*This is, I believe, the only use of this word in New England.*]

WHOOP, *n.* 2. A shout of war; a particular cry of troops when they rush to the attack. The Indians of America are remarkable for their war *whoop.*

WIGWAM, *n.* An Indian cabin or hut, so called in America. It is sometimes written *weekwam.*

WILDERNESS, *n.* A desert; a tract of land or region uncultivated and uninhabited by human beings, whether a forest or a wide barren plain. In the United States, it is applied only to a forest. In Scripture, it is applied frequently to the deserts of Arabia. The Israelites wandered in the *wilderness* forty years.

WILL, *n.* 1. That faculty of the mind by which we determine either to do or forbear an action; the faculty which is exercised in deciding, among two or more objects, which we shall embrace or pursue. The will is directed or influenced by the judgment. The understanding or reason compares different objects, which operate as motives; the judgment determines which is preferable, and the *will* decides which to pursue. In other words, we *reason* with respect to the value or importance of things; we then *judge* which is to be preferred; and we *will* to take the most valuable. These are but different operations of the mind, soul, or intellectual part of man. Great disputes have existed respecting the freedom of the *will.*

Will is often quite a different thing from *desire.*

A power over a man's subsistence, amounts to a power over his *will.*

Federalist, Hamilton.

WINDOW, *n.* 1. An opening in the wall of a building for the admission of light, and of air when necessary. This opening has a frame on the sides, in which are set movable sashes, containing panes of glass. In the U. States, the sashes are made to rise and fall, for the admission or exclusion of air. In France, *windows* are shut with frames or sashes that open and shut vertically, like the leaves of a folding door.

WISDOM, *n.* 1. The right use or exercise of knowledge; the choice of laudable ends, and of the best means to accomplish them. This is wisdom in *act, effect,* or *practice.* If wisdom is to be considered as a *faculty* of the mind, it is the faculty of discerning or judging what is most just, proper and useful, and if it is to be considered as an *acquirement,* it is the knowledge and use of what is best, most just, most proper, most conducive to prosperity or happiness. Wisdom in the first sense, or *practical wisdom,* is nearly synonymous with *discretion.* It differs somewhat from *prudence,* in this respect; *prudence* is the exercise of sound judgment in avoiding evils; *wisdom* is the exercise of sound judgment either in avoiding evils or attempting good. *Prudence* then is a species, of which *wisdom* is the genus.

WIT, *n.* 8. *Wits,* in the plural, soundness of mind; intellect not disoriented; sound mind. No man in his *wits* would venture on such an expedition. Have you lost your *wits?* Is he out of his *wits?*

WITCH, *n.* A woman who by compact with the devil, practices sorcery or enchantment.

WITNESS, *v.t.* To see or know by personal presence. I *witnessed* the ceremonies in New York, with which the ratification of the constitution was celebrated, in 1788.

WOMAN, *n. plu.* [. . . The plural as written, seems to be *womb-men.* But we pronounce it *wimen,* and so it ought to be written, for it is from the Saxon *wif-man,* wife-man.] 1. The female of the human race, grown to adult years.

> *Women* are soft, mild, pitiful, and flexible.   *Shak.*

> We see every day *women* perish with infamy, by having been too willing to set their beauty to show.   *Rambler.*

> I have observed among all nations that the *women* ornament themselves more than the men; that wherever found, they are the same kind, civil, obliging, humane, tender beings, inclined to be gay and cheerful, timorous and modest.
>   *Ledyard.*

WOUND, *n.* A breach of the skin and flesh of an animal, or of the bark and wood of a tree, or of the bark and substance of other plants, caused by violence or external force. The self-healing power of living beings, animal or vegetable, by which the parts separated in *wounds,* tend to unite and become sound, is a remarkable proof of divine benevolence and wisdom.

WRECK, *v.t.* 1. To strand; to drive against the shore, or dash against rocks, and break or destroy. The ship Diamond of New York, was *wrecked* on a rock in Cardigan Bay, on the coast of Wales.

WROUGHT, *pret.* and *pp.* of *work.* 1. Worked; formed by work or labor; as *wrought* iron.

Y

YAHOO, *n.* A word used by Chesterfield, I suppose for a savage, or a person resembling a savage.

YANKEE, *n.* A corrupt pronunciation of the word *English* by the native Indians of America.   *Heckewelder.*

YARD, *n.* 1. A measure of three feet or thirty six inches. It is just seven ninths of the Paris ell.

2. An inclosure; usually, a small inclosed place in front of or around a house or barn. The yard in front of a house is called a *court*, and sometimes a *court-yard.* In the United States, a small yard is fenced round a barn for confining cattle, and called *barn-yard* or *cow-yard.*

YELK, *n.* The yellow part of an egg; the vitellus. It is sometimes written and pronounced *yolk*, but *yelk* is the proper word. *Yolk* is a corruption.

YELL, *v.i.* To cry out with a hideous noise; to cry or scream as with agony or horror. Savages *yell* most frightfully when they are rushing to the first onset of battle.

YELLOW-FEVER, *n.* A malignant disease of warm climates, which often suffuses the skin with a yellowish color.

YEOMANRY, *n.* The collective body of yeomen or freeholders. Thus the common people in America, are called the *yeomanry.*

YOUNGER, *a.* Not so old as another. A person of ninety years old is *younger* than one of a hundred, though certainly not a *young* man, nor in the first part of life.

YANKEE. John G. E. Heckewelder (1743–1823) was a pioneer Moravian Church missionary to Indians in the Ohio region. He was probably only guessing about the origin of *Yankee.* Most modern dictionaries, including the eleventh edition of *Merriam-Webster's Collegiate,* say that its origin is unknown or indeterminate, but in any case more likely to be Dutch than Indian.

Y

287

Z

ZEBRA, *n.* An animal of the genus Equus, beautifully marked with stripes; a native of Africa.

ZERO, *n.* Cipher; nothing. The point of a thermometer from which it is graduated. Zero, in the thermometers of Celsius and Reaumur, is at the point at which water congeals. The zero of Fahrenheit's thermometer is fixed at the point at which the mercury stands when immersed in a mixture of snow and common salt. In Wedgewood's pyrometer, the zero corresponds with 1077° on Fahrenheit's scale.

ZOOLOGY, *n.* A treatise on animals, or the science of animals; that branch of natural history which respects the forms, classification, history and habits of animals, particularly of brutes or irrational animals.

ZUFFOLO, *n.* A little flute or flageolet, especially that which is used to teach birds.   *Busby.*

Z

ACKNOWLEDGMENTS

The compiler's task was greatly facilitated by the staff members of the libraries of the University of Virginia, especially those of the Scholars' Lab.

ABOUT THE AUTHORS

Arthur Schulman is a retired cognitive psychologist and veteran crossword-puzzle constructor whose puzzles have appeared in the *New York Times* for many years.

Jill Lepore is the David Woods Kemper '41 Professor of American History at Harvard University and a regular contributor to *The New Yorker*. Her books include *A Is for American* and *Blindspot*, a novel written jointly with Jane Kamensky.

Printed in the United States
By Bookmasters